The New Electronic Guitarist

To access online media visit:
www.halleonard.com/mylibrary
Enter code:

4644-8661-3379-0246

The New Electronic Guitarist

New Technologies and Techniques for the Modern Guitar Player

MARTY CUTLER

Hal Leonard Books
An Imprint of Hal Leonard LLC

Published in 2017 by Hal Leonard Books
An Imprint of Hal Leonard LLC
7777 West Bluemound Road
Milwaukee, WI 53213

Trade Book Division Editorial Offices
33 Plymouth St., Montclair, NJ 07042

Unless otherwise noted, all illustrations are either from the author's collection or in the public domain.

Printed in the United States of America

Book design by Kristina Rolander

Library of Congress Cataloging-in-Publication Data is available upon request.

ISBN: 978-1-4950-4745-9

www.halleonardbooks.com

This book is dedicated to Edith Cutler, whose deep love for music was instilled in me at an early age; music continues to sustain us both. For Cinnie Cole, my muse, my wife, my life partner and organizer, whose life is music to me. This book is also dedicated to the memory of heroes, friends, and musical co-conspirators Ikutaro Kakehashi of Roland Corporation, Allan Holdsworth, Marty Laster, Richard Shulberg, and Eric Udel.

CONTENTS

FOREWORD

My early musical journey was eclectic. I started out banging on my mother's pots and pans, and my parents finally got the hint and bought me a conga drum, and then a drum set. But that wasn't enough. I was fascinated with other instruments that I was blessed to have around me: an upright piano, an old but still functional vibraphone that my Dad used to play professionally, and a cheap $40 acoustic nylon string guitar that my sister had long abandoned in the corner of the living room, gathering dust. After having dabbled on all of these instruments for a few years and not ever really mastering any of them to any large degree, I found myself drawn to the guitar, and started to painstakingly strum out a few chords from an instructional book that was lying in the case.

Fast forward to roughly six months later, and good fortune came to me by way of my dad bringing home an old beat up Gibson SG—albeit with a broken truss rod, which I found out later—my first electric guitar. Having no guitar amp, I figured out a way to wire it up to the family stereo system and was indoctrinated into the world of amplification, not knowing a thing about low vs. high impedance, etc. Several blown fuses later (my bassist friend insisted on plugging in as well), I got a used amp from Sears Roebuck and started to collect all kinds of guitar pedals, officially launching my life of guitar gadgetry.

At some point in my late high school years (circa 1980–1981), I hooked up with some college-age musicians in the Boston area who had some of the most unusual musical gear that I had yet come across. Besides the keyboard player's precious Mellotron, there was a Roland GR-300—the first guitar synthesizer I had ever encountered. I remember the first time I put it in my hands. Already impressed just by the Roland guitar itself, I was blown away by the experience of being able to create new sonic landscapes from an instrument that I had already invested a few solid years to learn. It was a strange experience at first to hear these sounds emanating from a guitar, and although I wasn't too enamored with most of the sounds it came with, I could see its future promise as a potent instrument.

It wasn't until years later, after moving to New York and starting to play and tour professionally (and paying off huge student loans), that I finally got my first guitar synthesizer, a Roland GR-50, which was a one-space, rackmount MIDI controller and sound module. I quickly installed the GK-1 pickup system onto my Strat, plugged in the 13-pin cable, and probably didn't leave the house or sleep much for the next several days! The sounds were very up to date and offered a wide variety of control and expression parameters. It was also around the time I started to get into some early sequencers, notably the sleek Alesis MMT-8 standalone MIDI sequencer—which was a joy to use when it didn't crash, causing me to lose everything—and then to more trusty platforms like the Atari personal computer, and eventually to the world of Macintosh.

Things have changed quite dramatically since my first encounter with that guitar synth. Guitarists now have direct access from their instrument to MIDI, computers, sequencers, virtual instruments, signal processing gear, and physical guitar-and-amp modeling software and hardware, putting guitarists, technologically speaking, on par with any keyboardist and even beyond, given the unique expressive abilities of our six-string friend. This access has enabled me personally to realize and express some of my childhood multi-instrumentalist dreams mentioned earlier, and has helped me become a more intuitive and expressive composer, arranger, and producer.

Not just a fascinating trip down memory lane through the history and development of modern electric guitar, this book explores in depth the cutting-edge, up-to-date technology of today, and inspires and encourages the reader's mind to explore the creative sonic potential yet to be realized in this relatively new digital age of guitar. Marty helps you to navigate through the sometimes bewildering choices of today's effects processors, guitar processing software, guitar and amp modeling choices, DAWs, and plug-ins by clearly illustrating what they do and how they do it—and in a way that a more or less "non-instruction manual" person like myself can understand. Particularly enlightening to me is the chapter on guitar and amp modeling, and how it actually works, which was always somewhat of a mystery given my beginnings in the world of trigger-based MIDI devices.

And remember, after all, as Marty writes, this is all in service to ". . . ultimately produce sounds we call music—in our case, we are doing this with guitars, the instrument of Nigel Tufnel"!

Enjoy/Create/Inspire/Love

—DAVID GILMORE

ACKNOWLEDGMENTS

This book reflects years of learning and help from so many that a complete and accurate accounting is virtually impossible, but I'll give it a go anyway. Huge thanks to the alumni and denizens of Splash Studios: Daniel DiPaola, Robby Kilgore, Mary Kessler, Rob Schwimmer, Jonathon Peretz, Jimi Tunnell, and Michael Wooten. Thanks also to Bob Ward, my MIDI guitar mentor; Gene Perla, who started me off on a teaching career; my gurus and friends at Korg USA: Jack Hotop, James Sajeva, and Jerry Kovarsky; my editorial confreres past and present at *Electronic Musician* and *Mix* magazines: Steve Oppenheimer (who also aided and abetted me in his role at Presonus), Gino Robair, Geary Yelton, Barry Cleveland, Michael Levine, Sarah Jones, George Petersen, and Matt Gallagher; my old friends at *Keyboard* magazine: Ernie Rideout, Mark Vail, and Jim Aikin; and the folks I worked with at Seer Systems: Stanley Jungleib, Dave Smith, and David Roach.

This book would be incomplete without the folks who helped me with products and information: Chris DiMaria at Fishman, Clint Ward at Line 6, Starr Ackerman at IK Multimedia, Rebecca Eaddy of Roland Corporation, Jonathan Miller at Miller Music and Media, Matt Picone at Fractal Audio Systems, Keith McMillen at Keith McMillen Instruments, Peter Giles at Giles Communications, Chasey Elion of YouRock Guitars, Thomas Wendt at Integrative Concepts, Harvey Starr at Starr Labs, Paul De Benedictis and Eric Persing at Spectrasonics, Laure Ledien at UVI, Dave Fraser and Neil Goldberg at Heavyocity, Brian Zarlenga at Output, Joe Trupiano at Sample Logic, Jason Davies at Eleven Dimensions Media, Ole Kristensen at Jam Origin, Antoni Ozynski at PSP Audioware, Peter Linsener at LinPlug, Johannes Kraemer and Constantin Köhncke of Native Instruments, Sara Griggs at Avid, Eric Thibeault at Applied Acoustics, Lacey Haines at Apple, Jim Cooper at Mark of the Unicorn, Michelle Moog-Koussa at the Bob Moog Foundation, and Cole Goughary at Ableton.

Special thanks to Susan Lauscher, for legal advice and for wisdom beyond the call of duty, to Martina McConnon of Music MarCom, who put me in touch with the ever-patient John Cerullo and Lindsay Wagner at Hal Leonard, and to Kevin Lohman at Apple, without whose help this would have been a manuscript written in crayon on napkins.

Thank you all for your immeasurable help and friendship.

INTRODUCTION
Guitar Meets Computer

What's a computer doing in my guitar rig? What's a guitar rig doing in my computer?

It's surprising that a number of guitarists, both electric and acoustic, often regard the digital side of music technology as something relatively alien to their experience, even as they tune their instruments with a digital clip-on tuner, power up the automated mixer, and stomp on their digital delay pedal. Of course, there are many degrees of immersion in the technology; most of the aforementioned examples don't require a very deep understanding of the engine under the hood to use them. What's interesting to me (and probably to you, seeing as how you're holding this book in your hand) is that the underlying principles of all these entry-level digital gadgets have direct links to more advanced applications, and that once those principles become clearer, the more complex stuff becomes less complicated, far less intimidating, and a great deal more intriguing. My goal here is not to swamp the prospective electronic guitarist with equations or lots of hexadecimal number-crunching. It's easy enough to get the mainstream concepts and get to work.

The same core principles that enable clip-on tuners, for instance, are found in digital reverb, digital delay, and sampling, as well as recording with your computer, your iPad, and even your smartphone. My current mobile phone—an iPhone 5—is already four years old as I write this, and yet it's faster and more powerful than the last top-of-the-line Power Mac laptop. My smartphone and iPad are brimming with guitar-processor software, a bunch of great-sounding synthesizers, a complete multitrack recording program or two with built-in software synthesizers, and even an app that converts a normal guitar to a MIDI controller to play those synthesizers.

Of course, personal computers have come a long way since the Power Mac, but my point is to illustrate how widespread the landscape is for digital music, and guitarists have plenty of terrain to explore. Computers, tablets, iPads, and smartphones have taken the stage, enhancing and even replacing stomp boxes and entire guitar rigs. On occasion, my laptop becomes the nerve center for live performance, with synthesizers, samplers, loopers, and drum machines all "inside the box," and my guitar playing through an elaborate rig of reverbs, chorus, compressors, and more—all emanating from the computer.

For those who are willing to dig a little deeper, the digital-guitar connection opens doors to a truly mind-boggling wealth of new tone colors, rhythms, compositional and learning tools, collaboration, and so much more. It's the intention of this book to lay out the scope of current and emerging digital technology, which can enhance the guitarist's creativity in so many ways. New software and hardware arrives every day, making it difficult for this book to remain on the bleeding edge of electronic guitar technology, but the guiding principles and applications remain relatively consistent, and those will, I hope, provide an overview and a depth of understanding that will allow musicians to keep up with all the changes that are sure to come.

The profusion of available products and applications makes it impossible to cover every device on every platform; to make things manageable, I have let my personal biases guide me in choosing which products will be representative for any given application. Where a feature of another product might stand out from the rest, I include that too, but my guiding principle is that most of the technology works in the same way, and in most cases, the difference simply lies in the manufacturer's nomenclature or its location in a menu. That said, no book can tell you whether you prefer Windows over Mac OS or Korg products over those from Roland any more than a book can tell you whether to choose a Les Paul over a Strat. You will find more than enough here to guide you toward the tools that suit your workflow best. The proof is still in the playing.

For some, it might not be necessary to read this book from cover to cover. Although I've tried to make the layout of knowledge a logical path from one thing to the next, you are welcome to skim and use the bits that interest you. Either way, this book will provide a clear foundation for understanding existing digital technologies and some insight into their use even as we adapt to future developments. For instance, sampling, initially best known for its faithful playback of drums and acoustic instruments in general, is now capable of slicing, dicing, and bending sound into fantastic soundscapes. MIDI itself is over 30 years old as I write this, and its usefulness has expanded way beyond its initial intentions.

There has never been a better time to enter the world of electronic guitars, and it's my hope that this book will serve as a portal to that world for you.

The New Electronic Guitarist

CHAPTER 1

Guitars, Sound, and Synthesis

What is sound? How do guitars produce sound? Guitar synthesizers: from voltage control to digital guitars.

What Is Sound?

An understanding of how sound happens is essential to guitar-tone production, whether it's a solo acoustic guitar or an elaborate onstage rack crammed with processors and computers. There's no better foundation for understanding sound in the digital world than to start in the analog world, where it originates.

Sound is caused by the disturbance and displacement of air molecules. If you think of a pebble tossed into a pond of still water, you can easily conceptualize sound waves. The pebble displaces the water, and more water moves in to fill in the displaced water, even as waves radiate outward. This is similar to the way air molecules respond to physical impulses: perhaps the vibration of a plucked string, a note on a piano or trumpet, or a stick on a snare drum's head. That last example provides a simple illustration of the process: The stick hits and creates a slight, temporary concavity in the drum head, and air molecules rush in to fill the space. When the head snaps back, the molecules are forced outward, and the process repeats itself. Molecules moving together is *compression*, and

A pebble displaces the water molecules in the pond, causing water molecules to fill in the gap created by the pebble. (Photograph by Roger McLassus/Wikimedia Commons)

as they move outward—*rarefaction*. Our eardrums respond similarly to the compression and rarefaction of air molecules.

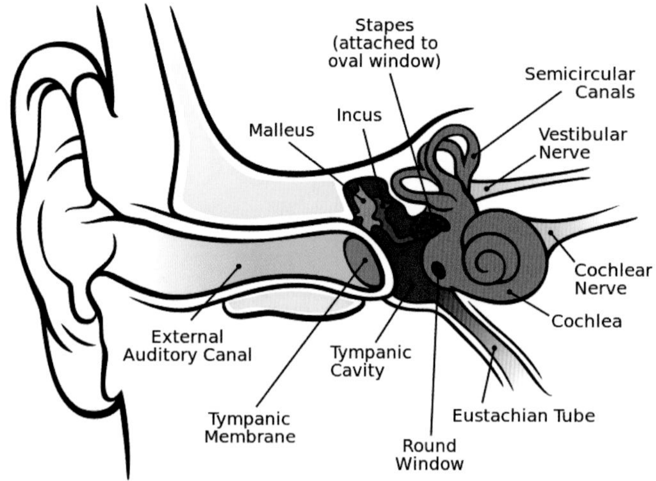

Anatomy of the human ear. Air molecules strike the tympanic membrane (ear drum), initially forming a concavity, which fills with air molecules, which are then forced outward as the membrane vibrates outward. The response of the ear drum to the vibrations is passed along through the malleus, incus, and stapes, small bones in the tympanic cavity. The bones conduct vibrations into the cochlea, which conducts the vibrations to the nervous system.

Pitch, Timbre, and Loudness

If a guitar feeds back in the forest and there is no one to hear it, does it still make a sound?

There is no sound until our perceptions come into play. The motion of the air molecules comes into contact with our hearing apparatus: our ears, in combination with our nervous system and brain. In other words, sound is our perception of that motion of air molecules. The number of cycles of compression and rarefaction per second is referred to as *frequency*. If you've ever used a tuning fork or other guitar tuner, it usually references A440—that is, 440 cycles per second—and it represents the sound of your guitar's first string played on the fifth fret. When it's in tune, your guitar's fifth string sounds at 110 cycles per second, and the third string on the second fret is 220. You might notice a pattern here; each octave represents a doubling or halving of frequency.

We measure frequency in Hertz (Hz), named after the German physicist Heinrich Hertz. The ear perceives the number of cycles as pitch. More cycles per second, and we hear a higher pitch; fewer, and the pitch is lower. In other words, pitch is the human ear's perception of the frequency of sound waves. The range of human hearing is said to be between 20Hz and 20kHz (that's 20,000Hz), although that's a pretty optimistic assessment; as we age, our ability to hear the higher frequencies diminishes, and if you've abused your ears over a period of time, you're probably lucky if you can hear up to 10kHz.

Timbre!

Sound is, of course, more complex than a simple pebble-in-a-pond analogy can convey. Assuming we have sounds of the same pitch and loudness, how do we tell them apart? What distinguishes an A440 on a guitar from an A440 on a trumpet, crash cymbal, or banjo? For that matter, how do our ears tell us we are listening to a cheap-sounding guitar rather than a high-ticket instrument? What causes some sounds to be muted and warm while others are bright and edgy?

Here's a simple thought experiment: Pick up your guitar, and with your fingers (rather than a pick), play a variety of chords, ranging from simple, open chords to complex and dissonant ones. Now play those same chords, emphasizing some of the notes over others, paying attention to how the qualities of the chord change. In this same way, sounds can be thought of as chords composed of individual, pure waves at different frequencies, and variations in the balance of frequencies create variations in timbre. The purest wave is the sine wave, which possesses only a fundamental frequency; as a result, sine waves are pure but bland-sounding waveforms, with no additional frequencies. They rarely occur naturally; the closest approximation you can create acoustically is with a tuning fork. Jean-Baptiste Joseph Fourier was a French mathematician who posited that wave functions were the sum of simple sine waves. For our purposes, this means that complex sounds can be thought of as chords of sine waves vibrating at different frequencies.

When we pluck a guitar string, it vibrates, as does the guitar's bridge, body, neck, tuners, and other parts. These multiple compressions and rarefactions interact, sometimes interfering with or reinforcing each other, at multiple frequencies. Combine that with other factors in the environment, such as the density of the vibrating medium or the length of the vibrating object, and you create a number of compression and rarefaction cycles at different frequencies, adding to the sonic complexity. On a guitar, different materials in the body, the bridge, the strings, and even the neck, can create major changes in the tonal qualities of the instrument. We perceive these complexities as timbre: individual, simple sine waves forming a composite tone.

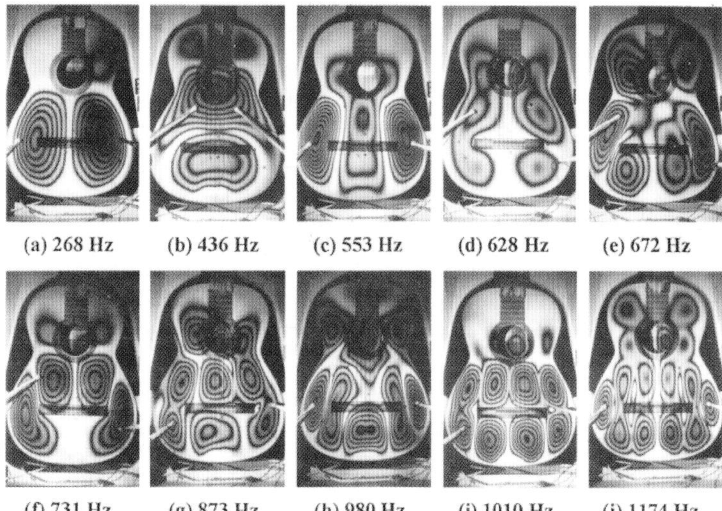

An interferogram illustrating how a plucked guitar string sets off a series of complex, interacting vibrations. Different frequencies create different areas and patterns of vibration; that is largely responsible for the diverse tonal properties from instrument to instrument. (Photograph courtesy of Bernard Richardson)

Our ears derive a sound's pitch from its loudest frequency, called the *fundamental*, and the presence of additional, higher frequencies above the fundamental determine our sense of timbre. *Overtones* are frequencies that occur in addition to the fundamental. Harmonic content has immediate practical applications, as well as musical uses. For example, harmonic content lets us distinguish between vowels in human speech.

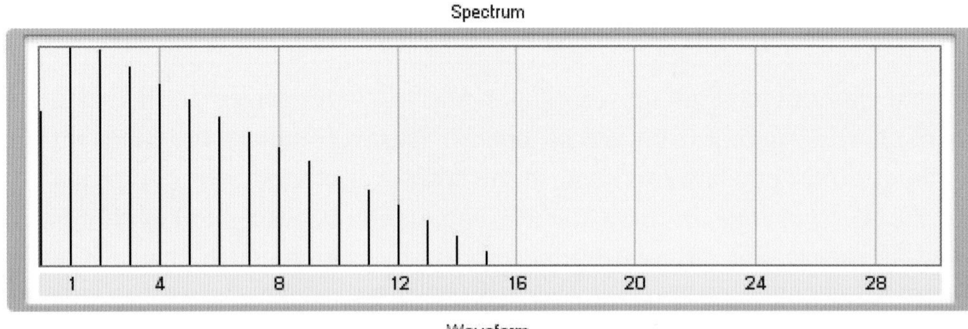

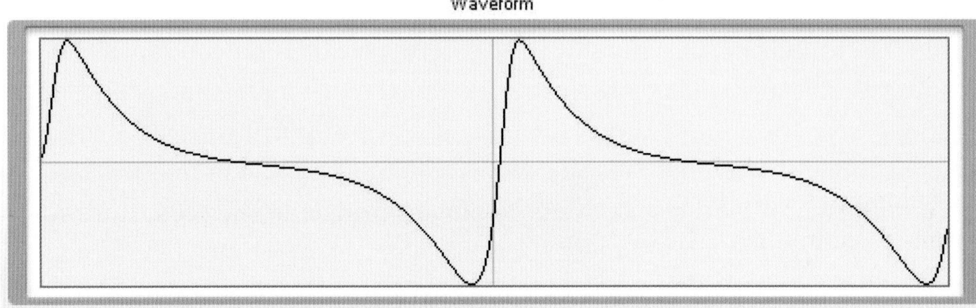

A simple waveform displayed in Native Instruments FM8 synthesizer. Frequencies run from low on the left to higher frequencies on the right. Amplitude is traced vertically, and in this example, the fundamental is the first (and tallest) frequency.

A Disturbance in the Force

The greater the initial force applied to a string, the greater the height of each cycle above and below a mid-point axis—and the greater the amplitude. To use the analogy of a pebble in a pond, replace dropping the pebble with hurling the pebble forcefully; the waves will get taller, although they're not likely to radiate at a higher frequency. We measure this height as amplitude—sound pressure levels (SPL) expressed in decibels, or dB SPL, which the human ear interprets as loudness. Sound-pressure levels can be felt physically in addition to perceiving loudness.

Rupturing eardrum	**150dB**
Military jet taking off (from about 50 ft)	**140 dB**
Threshold of Pain	**120dB**
Motorcycle (25 ft away)	**96dB**
Garbage disposal, dishwasher	**80dB**
Passenger car (65 mph at 25 ft)	**77dB**
Conversation in restaurant	**60dB**
Whisper	**20dB**
Quiet Breathing	**10dB**
Threshold of hearing	**0dB**

A table of the sound-pressure levels (SPL) in different environments. The minimum perceptible increase in SPL the ear can detect is 3dB SPL.

If you've ever gone to a club where the sound is excessively loud, you may have felt your chest pounding from the pressure of loud sound waves in addition to experiencing an uncomfortable listening experience. Because high sound-pressure levels can damage your hearing, we need to be mindful of how loud sounds may be in our environment. Amplitude and loudness aren't the same thing; in fact, lower-frequency sounds are less readily perceived (that is, they sound softer) than higher-frequency sounds played at an equal amplitude. If your home stereo system has a loudness switch, it doesn't really make anything louder; it simply reduces mid-range frequencies to allow lower frequencies to "speak."

Few sounds are static; loudness, pitch, and timbre usually change. These changes are often referred to as an *envelope*, and it is most frequently used to illustrate a sound wave's changes in amplitude over time. You will probably hear the term ADSR, meaning Attack, Decay, Sustain, and Release, in conjunction with envelopes; it's a term often used with synthesis techniques. The abbreviation is an oversimplification when it's applied to naturally occurring sounds, as real-world, nonsynthesized sounds are almost always more complex than a simple four-stage ADSR life cycle. The concept of envelopes plays an important role in understanding synthesis and is equally important for guitarists who need to come to grips with adapting their guitar technique to playing synths. For now, keep these sonic basics in mind as we go; we'll revisit and elaborate on them in later sections.

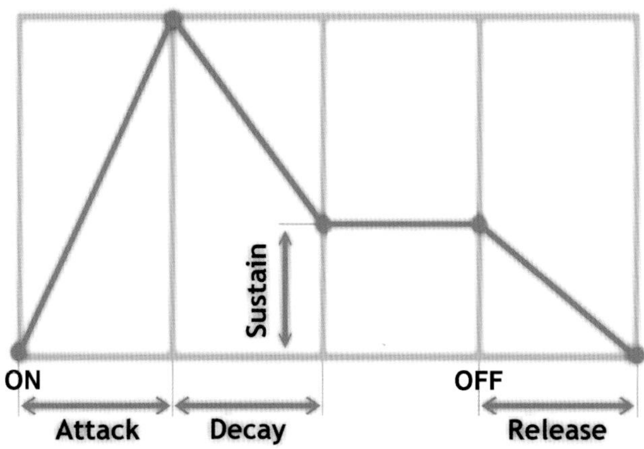

Contrast the simple attack, decay, sustain, and release envelope with the real-world envelope of a crash cymbal.

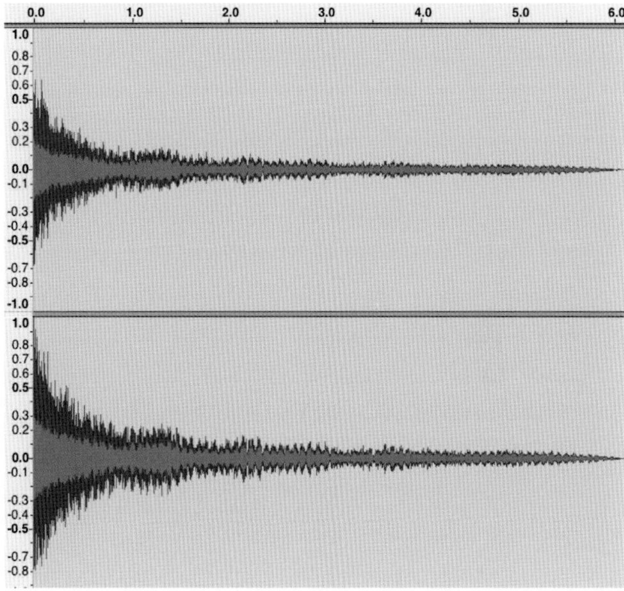

The Body Electric

So far, I've discussed acoustic properties, but what happens with guitars and amps? In almost everything this book covers, there is a conversion process, a transfer of energy taking place. In the case of the guitar, the plucked string vibrates over a pickup, which produces a current based on the vibration's frequency. On the amplifier end of the cable, this current moves the amp's speaker cones to vibrate at the same frequencies, moving air, and producing sound. Typical MIDI guitar systems rely on pickups at the start of the signal chain but convert the signal into digital data that triggers synthesizer notes. This is somewhat of an oversimplification, but it should serve our purposes for now.

Start Here

It's only natural that guitarists gravitated toward expanding the instrument's sonic palette. It's easy enough to establish a trail from at least the '70s, but the guitarist's deviant sonic tendencies started well before the late '60s, when distorted guitars came into prominence. A casual search of the internet will yield musicians as varied as Link Wray, Marty Robbins (with Grady Martin's blatantly fuzzed-out, distorted guitar solo), Pat Hare (who played guitar for Howlin Wolf), and Paul Burlison (who worked with rockabilly star Johnny Burnette). Numerous anecdotes and unsubstantiated tales of mutilated speaker cones in the service of growling fuzz abound.

No matter when the exploration of altered guitar tones started, within the concept of busted speaker cones, overdriven amps, and other sonic delights, we can find pieces of the groundwork for guitar synthesis and signal processing: clipping and hex fuzz. *Hex*, of course, refers to six, the number of strings on a guitar. Hex pickups have six discrete poles divided into six discrete channels. Hex pickups are commonly referred to as *divided pickups*. Because each string's signal is isolated, there is no interference among signals, and the resulting waveform is more consistent for each string. As it turns out, the independence of each string's output is vital to the success of MIDI guitars, as we'll discover later.

Clipping is caused by an overdriven audio signal whose increased gain peaks distort and lop off the higher frequencies. The resulting waveform more closely resembles a square wave, which characteristically sounds hollow and very unlike a clean guitar signal. Additionally, the overdriven instrument possesses greater sustain—which has long been the holy grail for electric guitarists.

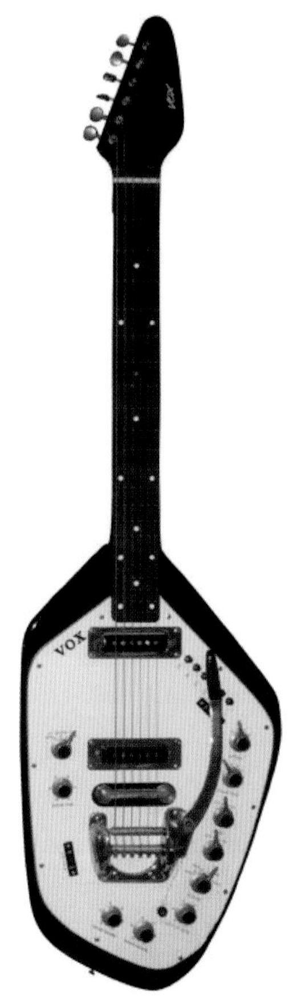

Predating guitar synthesis and MIDI, Vox released the model 251 Guitar Organ, which laid the groundwork for fret-switching technology on later instruments. (Photograph courtesy of Guitar Player)

In the mid-'60s, Vox implanted the guts of its popular Continental Organ into a somewhat abstract-looking guitar body to create the Vox 251 Guitar Organ. It had a few impressive innovations that survive to this day in some very sophisticated guitar controllers, notably fret switching—using six segmented (one for each string) columns of frets that switched notes on and off when the strings made contact with them. The technology allowed playing with just the fretting hand, or two-handed tapping, foreshadowing Eddie Van Halen by nearly two decades. An array of knobs studded the playing surface, allowing overall tuning of the organ as well as knobs that served as drawbars. Of course, you could also play organ sounds by strumming and picking, and you could blend organ and guitar tones. There are a few demos of the Guitar Organ online, along with the Musiconics Guitorgan, which used a similar mode of fret-switching operation

The ARP Avatar Guitar Synthesizer was a much-ballyhooed and largely unsuccessful guitar synthesizer, based on the sound-generating engine of the ARP Odyssey. (Photograph courtesy of Guitar Player)

on a more conventional ES-335 type body. Both instruments had ancillary cables, pedals, and a separate mixer unit. These did not last long in the marketplace, perhaps because of the additional paraphernalia required. Because of the wiring of each string to its own circuitry, these hybrids of organ and guitar were polyphonic, that is, capable of playing multiple notes simultaneously. It's debatable whether to consider these as early guitar synthesizers, but they certainly led the way to more interesting developments, such as the Synthaxe and the Starr guitar controllers.

Early guitar synths would couple basic synth tones with clipped signals directly from the guitar and pass them through the synthesizer's processors. The clipped guitar tones were polyphonic. Arguably the first actual guitar synthesizer was developed by Walter Sear, recording engineer, studio owner, and collaborator with Doctor Robert Moog. The device used a digital system to interpret the guitarist's intentions and send control voltages to an analog synthesizer. Its $15,000 price tag put it out of circulation quickly.

This pitch-to-voltage technology had its drawbacks. For one thing, standard pitch-to-voltage conversion didn't allow for polyphony, which meant that guitarists had to be especially precise; the conversion process did not tolerate accidentally brushed strings or unwanted harmonics. Playing guitar synthesizer effectively required modified techniques, including using the picking hand to mute all but the intended note: not a bad thing to learn, but overall, this was not the rock 'n' roll way.

One of the more notorious pitch-to-voltage instruments was the ARP Avatar, a coupling of an ARP Odyssey module with guitar. The ARP Avatar's ability to cleanly and accurately interpret a guitarist's musical nuance and articulation was finicky, and the instrument was expensive (around $3,000). Many blame ARP's venture into guitar synthesis—research and development and manufacturing costs and all—as a major reason for the company's demise. If there was any positive outcome to the ARP Avatar, it was that the synthesizer unit could be repurposed as an expander module for the Odyssey, and that it was arguably the first guitar-synthesis system that didn't require a proprietary electric guitar. You can hear Jimmy Page press the Avatar into service with his solo on the Led Zeppelin track "Fool in the Rain." Despite Page's prodigious guitar facility, you can still hear the synth fighting back.

Similar guitar synths included the 360 Systems Spectre and the Hear Zetaphon, which never quite made an incursion into mass marketing. Another novel approach was the LGS Touch 6000 Guitar Synthesizer from Oncor Sound. This offered a built-in synth and onboard controls and programming, and it used fret switching. Unlike the guitar organs, the Oncor used strings of equal gauge that triggered sound on the guitar body and raised switches on the fingerboard that gave the illusion of strings. From personal experience with playing similar devices, this takes some getting used to, but it opened a gateway for a number of innovative guitar-like controllers.

The GR-500 was Roland's first guitar synthesizer and the first guitar synth capable of polyphony by way of wave-shaping applied to the actual guitar signal. (Photograph courtesy of Roland Corporation)

Enter Roland Corporation and the GR-500 system. The most notable aspects of this instrument were that it was expandable, meaning you could send control voltages to any compatible synth; it had a wave-shaping section for each string, making it polyphonic for some sounds, which you could sustain infinitely. But the unit's resulting sounds were crude and cheesy, and much the same could be said for its monophonic, voltage-controlled synth section. Roland sold a proprietary guitar, which was required to play the unit. Both guitar and synth connected with a 24-pin cable, which became standard over several iterations of Roland and other guitar synths. Gaining control over the GR-500 required navigating a complex jungle of knobs and switches that might confound a seasoned synthesizer programmer. For all its ambitious features, the GR-500 wasn't welcomed into the arms of the guitar community.

Undaunted, Roland went back to the drawing board and came up with the GR-300 and turned some heads. The 300 tracked more fluidly and—more importantly—was equipped with six voltage-controlled oscillators, one for each string. Finally, here was a guitar synth with a truly polyphonic analog synthesizer! In addition, the GR-300 retained the hex-fuzz feature, which could also run through the voltage-controlled filter and add a bit of extra beef to the tones. The user interface of the synth was significantly simplified, and although the pickup and cable system was still proprietary, Roland offered a choice of several different guitars that came with the synth controls already mounted.

Although the sounds were mostly brash and raw, the filter went a long way toward taming the synth, and so the GR-300 found its way into many studio recordings. A good example is the braying, trumpet-like lead sound heard on so many of Pat Metheny's projects. Interestingly enough, that became a standardized sound that found its way onto many artist's projects, becoming a signature sound that is still replicated on a number of synthesizers today.

There were many more precursors to modern guitar synthesis, but perhaps the most significant leap into the future was Roland's GR-700 system, which sported a new and unusual five-pin jack at the rear of the synthesizer unit. The epic saga of the guitar synthesizer will continue in Chapter 3, but first, it will be helpful for you to know just what MIDI is, and fortunately, that is sufficiently covered in the next chapter.

CHAPTER 2

What's a MIDI?

Before MIDI. MIDI protocol for guitarists: Channel vs. System messages. MIDI modes as they apply to guitar.

With the constant flow of new computers, gadgets, and guitars, it's hard to believe that anything has escaped change; that's especially true of the digital world in which this season's must-have gizmo or operating system is part of next season's scrap heap. All the same, MIDI—while still remaining at version 1.0 and now over 30 years old—keeps rocking while adding new capabilities extending well beyond music. MIDI's seemingly evergreen status is a result of its tremendously pliable architecture, allowing it to be used for everything from simple musical applications to animating lighting and special effects at theme parks. MIDI guitar is one of the great examples of the MIDI specification's adaptability, and MIDI guitar is only one of many streams of the digital world that intersect with guitar.

Before MIDI

The limitations of earlier electronic musical systems make it clear why MIDI was developed. Before any sort of digital systems, voltage control was the most common control system for synthesizers. Synthesizers were modular; sounds were generated by voltage-controlled oscillators (VCOs), which determined the initial tone and base frequency of the synthesized sound. You could further modify the tone, frequency, and loudness of the synthesizer by routing voltage to various modular components that could, in turn, cause the oscillators to respond to increased or decreased voltages. For instance, a pre-MIDI synthesizer could increase or decrease its voltage to determine pitch. Play notes from low to high, the voltage increases and the pitch rises; play successively lower notes, and you decrease the voltage, lowering the pitch (although some keyboardists, notably Joe Zawinul, would invert the voltage across the keyboard for interesting performance techniques).

Dr. Bob Moog and Keith Emerson standing in front of Keith's Moog modular synthesizer. (Photograph by Mark Hockman, used with permission of the Bob Moog Foundation)

Voltage control seems like a fairly simple arrangement—until you attempt to combine synthesizer systems from different manufacturers. In fact, there were multiple issues in building à la carte systems derived from different manufacturers. For starters, some manufacturers instituted a different voltage-per-octave scheme. Cables that were required to connect one system were often incompatible with other systems. As a guitarist, you're probably quite used to plugging a Les Paul into a Fender amp with custom speakers for a little tonal variety, or layering tracks with different guitars. Switching to a different synthesizer from the same keyboard would seem like an advantage that synths had over guitars, but in fact, this necessitated additional keyboards. If you've seen old footage of keyboard players with arms outstretched, playing two keyboards, you now know that this was not necessarily done simply for dramatic effect. We take layering sounds from a single keyboard for granted now, but this was not easily done before MIDI.

Quite often, manufacturers would develop an entire system around their synthesizers to include drum machines, sequencers, and other time-based devices. In order to keep everything in step with the music, the devices had to lock to a common pulse. The clock driving most analog systems produced bursts of on-and-off pulses at consistent intervals, with a specific number of *clocks* defining the duration of a quarter note. The shorter the time between bursts, the quicker the tempo. Longer intervals produced slower tempos. Here again, there was no standard interval; some systems relied on 24 clocks per quarter note, while others divided their clocks by a different resolution.

The elements that shaped the synthesizer's tones and expressive capabilities were connected or patched together by cables that routed the voltage to the various modules. The cost of the average modular synthesizer system was well beyond the reach of the struggling musician. Each sound required its own settings, and this was accomplished by manually rerouting and adjusting settings on the fly. At the time, many high-profile performers whose set lists required a quick change from one sound to another would have multiple instruments with the cables and controls taped to prevent accidental alteration, simply to change from (for instance) a lead synth to a slow, droning, sweeping tone. Today, most of our sound's settings are stored in memory, but in a salute to the old ways, we call them *patches*.

The Minimoog Model D was the first hard-wired analog synth. (Photograph provided by the Bob Moog Foundation)

One intermediate response to the need for a quick-change synthesizer was to create an instrument whose keyboard and tone-generating apparatus was self-contained; instead of necessitating patch cords to connect one module to the other, the components were hard-wired, and knobs and sliders helped shape the sounds, rather than nests of wires joining components together. Dr. Robert Moog's Model-D Minimoog was the first to incorporate this type of setup. The result was a comparatively easy-to-program instrument in a single chassis, which reduced weight, parts, and cost considerably, although the ability to add custom modules had virtually disappeared.

Up until the early '70s, synthesizers were mostly monophonic, and at best duophonic; that is, they could generate only two voices at a time. That was fine for those soaring, gliding lead sounds, but not very useful for sophisticated chords, or even triads. The first solution was an obvious if not practical one: build multiple synthesizers into a unit to take up the slack. The PolyMoog followed that design, at the expense of sophisticated controls. The same year the PolyMoog was introduced, Yamaha brought the GX1 to market. Yamaha's new synth stored settings, allowing musicians to recall a sound instantly and without the need to reroute cables; this in itself was revolutionary, but it wasn't very user friendly. It required a separate control panel for each sound and small screwdrivers and tools just to tweak the sounds! It wasn't until Sequential Circuits released the Prophet 5—an analog synthesizer with digital circuitry—that synthesizer presets could be stored and recalled with the push of a button. Furthermore, the instrument allowed musicians to play as many as five simultaneous notes.

With the incursion of digital data into the synthesizer world, manufacturers began developing ways for multiple synthesizers to communicate. In Japan, Roland had developed the Digital Control Bus (DCB), which found its way into two synthesizers—the Juno 60 and the Jupiter 6—as well as the JSQ-60 and MSQ-700, two devices that could record and play back MIDI notes (see Chapter 8, "What Is a Sequencer?"). Apart from sending note information digitally, DCB was good for little else and was not implemented beyond the aforementioned synths and devices. MIDI, as we'll soon see, had a much larger role to play in the world of music technology.

Along Came MIDI

MIDI was waiting in the wings as early as 1981, when, by way of a paper presented at the Audio Engineering Society (AES), Dave Smith (Sequential Circuits) proposed a system called the Universal Synthesizer Interface. The system basically called for an industry-wide standard for connecting synthesizers and computers, which by this time were becoming commonplace in the home. Smith and Ikutaro Kakehashi (Roland Corporation) collaboratively devised and expanded on Smith's proposal, and finally, in 1983, eyes widened when a Sequential Circuits Prophet 600 was connected by a single cable to a Roland JP6, and one instrument remotely triggered the other. This marked the debut of MIDI at the January convention of the National Association of Music Manufacturers (NAMM).

MIDI went way beyond the basic note-on and -off and synchronization capabilities of its predecessors, and with its newfound capabilities came solutions to the problems plaguing synthesists for so long. MIDI standardized pitch. Having 128 notes—each described by a number—meant that (for instance) Note Number 60 defined middle C, and when transmitted to another instrument, it could at least be expected to play a C (one element of some debate was whether *middle C* was Note Number 60 or 72).

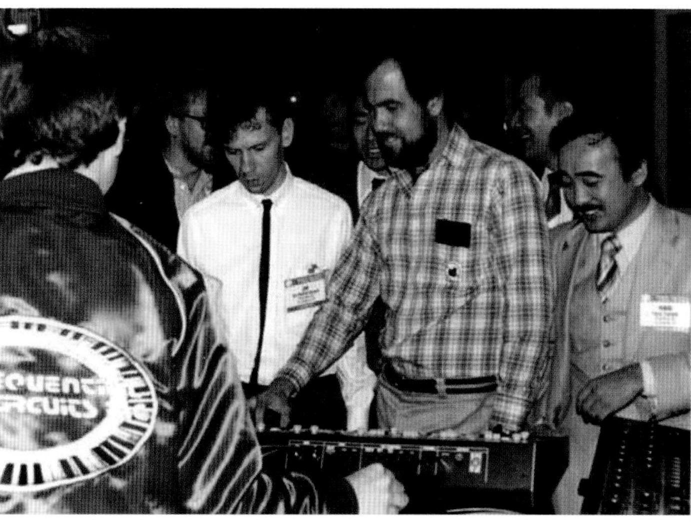

The first demonstration of MIDI at the NAMM Convention in 1983. (Photograph used with permission of Dave Smith)

MIDI devised a standard clock pulse for driving drum machines, sequencers, and synchronization to tape: 24 pulses per quarter note (PPQN). This standard also helped give birth to virtual tracking, the ability to record live instruments to tape while synchronized synthesizers and drum machines accompanied the recording. That was no small boon to musicians whose recorders featured modest track counts. Once the live tracks were recorded, they could be bounced to free up track space for the synths.

Another benefit of standardized pitches between manufacturers was that redundant keyboards were no longer needed. Rack-mounted synthesizer modules, complete synthesizers minus keyboards, thrived—certainly great news for roadies and guitarists who wanted to play synthesizer. An ancillary economic benefit of this development was that synths without keyboards were considerably less expensive to manufacture, and consequently, they cost far less to sell. With MIDI, keyboardists (and guitarists) could develop elaborate, complex performance systems that provide a widescreen musical backdrop to a solo performer or flesh out a live band and make it sound larger than life.

Most importantly, MIDI defined an entire set of standards for how this information would be transmitted, received, and interpreted, including the type of cables and the routing required to direct the digital information from source to destination. Although MIDI was originally defined as a musical language, it has been repurposed for many aspects of stage performance, including lighting and equipment automation.

How MIDI Works

MIDI is an acronym for *Musical Instrument Digital Interface*. A good overall definition for MIDI is that it is a digital language that enables compatible devices to exchange and interact with digital information. I know that sounds somewhat nondescript (and a bit dull), but bear with me. The most important concept to grasp is that MIDI is not sound. Think of a player piano: The perforated roll of paper that is spooled inside the piano makes no sound, but without it, the player piano is a blank slate, making no sound until the perforations trigger notes. MIDI is somewhat like that paper spool of instructions that switches notes on and off on the player piano, albeit with capabilities providing for greater expression and flexibility.

As the spool turns, the perforations catch pins on a barrel, which causes the hammers to strike strings.

At the top level, MIDI divides into two main branches: Channel and System messages. Generally speaking, System messages are more global in nature, governing messages that are sent throughout an entire MIDI layout, whereas Channel messages are designed to be more device-specific, containing instructions from some individual source in a MIDI system that are sent over a MIDI channel to a device that is "listening" on that channel.

MIDI Signal Flow

When you press a key on a MIDI keyboard, several events occur, starting with a trio of 8-bit messages signaling that you just played a note on a specific MIDI channel, what MIDI Note Number was played, and how forcefully you played that note (Velocity). Between the time you press and release that key, any number of messages can ensue—for example, increasing or decreasing pressure on the keyboard can send a continuous flow of messages commonly referred to as Aftertouch (there's lots more to be said about Aftertouch and similar messages, but for now, just know that this exists). Finally, when you release a key, yet another trio of bytes signify the Note Off event on that MIDI channel, its Note Number, and how quickly the note was released. Not all synthesizers transmit or respond to all these messages; Note Off Velocity and Aftertouch are more expensive to implement in keyboards; nonetheless, Note Off data is sent with a neutral value if it isn't implemented.

In general, MIDI messages consist of at least two bytes. The first is called a Status byte, and it signals the transmission of an event. That is followed by Data bytes, which indicate the value of the message. For instance, a MIDI Volume message will indicate that it is being sent, while the ensuing byte will specify a volume from 0 to 128. Broken down that way, MIDI sounds a bit like a cluttered and convoluted way of getting the music out, but at 31,250 bits per second, MIDI is fast enough to send these messages out with no perceptible delay, and that's probably a lot faster than you can play. The other bit of good news is that you don't need to understand these messages at a granular level to play synthesizers with your guitar.

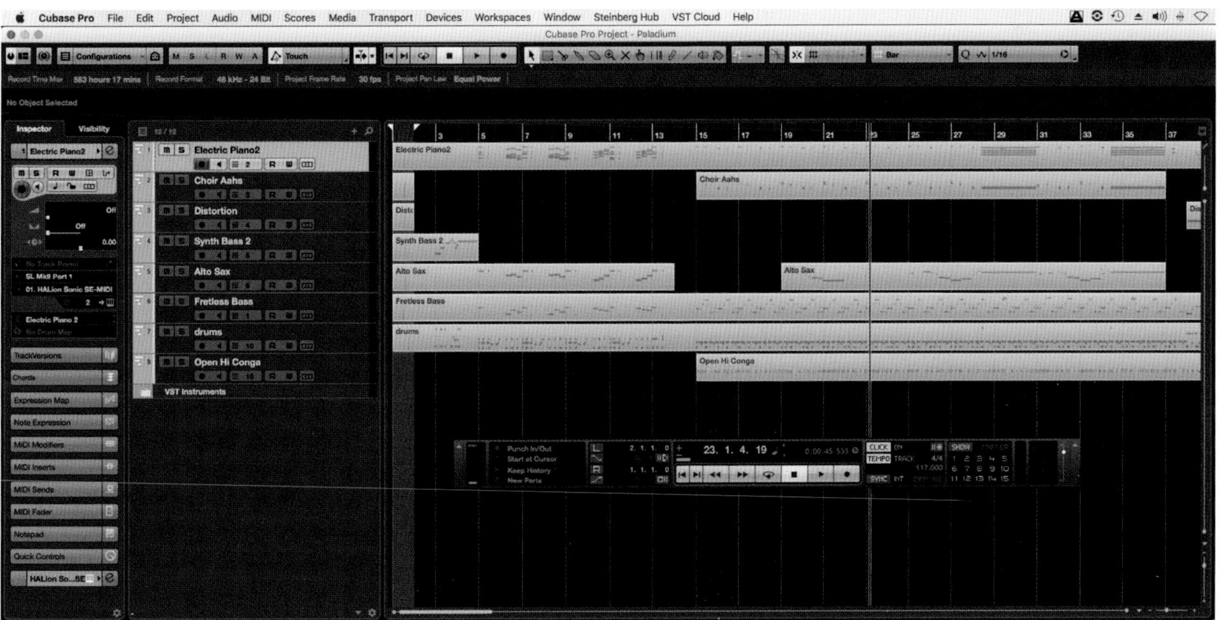

A MIDI arrangement in a sequencer. Tracks route MIDI data to discrete MIDI channels with patches assigned to each track in order for the arrangement to play properly.

The original MIDI specification called for 16 MIDI channels. Loosely put, you can think of Channel messages in terms of an orchestra or band members; the Channel messages tell the individual instruments what to play: notes to the piano, vibrato to the strings, whether to play a kick or snare on drums—in short, something akin to charts or scores for individual musicians. These are Channel messages, and they are important: You probably don't want the piano player to work from the guitarist's charts, or vice versa. You'd want to use vibrato or bend notes on a lead guitar part, but an entire band following suit might get ugly. In this way, synthesizers and other tone generators, such as drum machines, respond to channel-based MIDI messages, ignoring incoming messages from other channels. For example, you could be directing your MIDI guitar to play a horn section on a sampler on MIDI channel 3, and afterward, switch your guitar to trigger a drum machine on MIDI Channel 10. Alternately, by assigning each string to transmit over its own MIDI channel, you could have a different instrument assigned to each string—a sampled acoustic bass on the two lowest strings with a piano sound on the top four strings, or practically any combination you can conceive of. That ability—as we will soon learn—is key to making MIDI guitars perform like real guitars.

Control Changes

Staying with the orchestra-and-channel analogy, you would want the instruments at your command to do more than just run through the notes. To that end, Channel Voice and Control Change (CC) messages offer commands such as Program Change and Bank Select; Pan Position; MIDI Volume; Expression; Modulation; and Pitch Bend. These are MIDI messages that choose a synthesizer patch, adjust each sound's location in the stereo field, transmit overall loudness, or indicate whether notes are bent, along with other performance instructions.

Some CCs simply engage a general-purpose command, which can be interpreted by a synthesizer (for instance) to perform different functions; for example, Control Change number 1 (AKA Modulation) is often used to create a vibrato effect, but it can create almost any change in your synthesizer depending on how you program the synth to respond. That response could include sweeping filter effects, crossfading from one sound to another, or increasing or altering reverb to change the perceived distance from the sound. The way you program your synthesizer to respond to this message is the determining factor. MIDI Volume (CC7) offers 128 possible volume levels, whereas CC11, Expression, is typically used to control volume within the constraints of CC7. Pan Position is CC10, and this message is used for placing a sound in the stereo field. For an overview of the Control Change messages, please see Appendix A.

The Bends

Pitch Bend is one of the most important features for guitarists, and it requires extra information in order to work convincingly. Translating note bending from an electric or acoustic guitar into MIDI data is considerably more involved than it is with a keyboard controller. In fact, with any remote controller, such as another MIDI keyboard or desktop controller gadget, it is important to match the range of Pitch Bend you are sending with the range the target sound source is capable of receiving; if you plan to bend notes as high as an octave above or below pitch, your guitar controller's bend range needs to be set for an octave, and your target synthesizer needs to match that range in order to respond in kind. For more about Pitch Bend, see Chapter 5.

The MIDI specification has 16 channels, but it would prove to be extremely limiting if the ceiling for orchestrations were restricted to a maximum of 16 instruments. These days, many devices offer multiple MIDI ports, each port supporting a bank of 16 MIDI channels, and software instruments can often support more than 16 channels to multiple banks, allowing for huge orchestrations.

You're in My System

System Messages are global in nature. There are, for instance, messages that govern tempos and time signatures for playback of your recording gear or a sequencer, synchronization between clock-driven devices (such as a drum machine or an external recorder), setup of synthesizer programming and other devices, and much more. To complete the orchestra analogy, System Messages are akin to the conductor, the musical director, or the people who set up instruments and maintain the backline.

One good example of System Messages is System Real-Time, a group of messages that detail synchronization, tempo, transport, and general "housekeeping" commands. If you have ever owned a drum machine, you will probably be familiar with buttons labeled Start, Stop, and Continue. The first two commands need little explanation, being instructions for the drum machine to start or stop playing. Once you start arranging your drum beats in song form, as opposed to simply looping a single pattern, you will need the Continue button to pick up a song from where you left off. Imagine arranging 70-some-odd bars of drumming; if you hit Start, the song will always start from the beginning rather than that pattern in bar 64 you just edited. In complete sequenced arrangements, on more sophisticated devices, the Continue message works hand in hand with a message called Song Position Pointer to resume playing where you last stopped playback, from the nearest 16th note; that's a much handier arrangement when you are synchronized to an external recording system and need to punch in at some later point in the song.

It doesn't happen very often these days, but if your system of synthesizers gets stuck notes or doesn't update other settings, such as Pitch Bend or Volume levels, System Reset is another global message that restores all your devices to their state at startup. You might have one recalcitrant instrument in your system, but rather than hunt down one bad actor in a complex setup, this message is akin to a "nuclear option" for your MIDI system.

Probably the most expansive System message is System Exclusive, due to its open-ended nature. Most often, System Exclusive deals with synthesizer program data, but it has been stretched to deal with many other areas, including MIDI Time Code, which is widely used to synchronize computer-based synthesizer compositions to motion-picture events as well as in recording projects that require extensive overdubbing of live players in real time.

As a MIDI guitarist, System Exclusive (also called SysEx) is also useful as a means for editing, storing, saving, retrieving, and sharing synthesizer patches. Software editor-librarians can handle all these tasks with ease, and they are covered in Chapter 5. System Exclusive enables a cottage industry of professional sound designers who frequently offer fresh takes on a synthesizer's factory sounds. In fact, the internet is loaded with user groups and forums rife with patches for almost any MIDI-capable synthesizer you might own.

It's important (and interesting) to understand a little about the way System Exclusive operates. Not all synthesizers are equal; one might offer built-in effects and two filters, while another offers no effects and no filters at all. Because of this, patches from one type of synth are meaningless to another type. In order to work properly, System Exclusive must take into account every MIDI device that is capable of being programmed. To that end, a complete System Exclusive file has no specific size.

Typically, MIDI device manufacturers (for example, Korg, Roland, and Yamaha) register their latest and greatest with the MIDI Manufacturer's Association, which in turn grants each device a manufacturer's ID number as well as a unique ID number for each new device.

After an initial message to receive or transmit any System Exclusive message, the two ID messages follow, then just about everything else in the message is dependent on what you need to transmit or receive. Do you want to load an entire bank of sounds, or just a single patch? Do you want to dump the entire memory of your synth to the computer or just update your synthesizer with a minor parameter change? System Exclusive takes all these situations into account, and considerably more.

It might seem contradictory that a system-wide message is used to address a single device on a MIDI system, but the message can target any specific MIDI-capable device and ignore all others in a system. That capability is especially useful in MIDI systems whose size and complexity would make the matching of MIDI channels impractical.

Guitars and MIDI

Unlike guitar, keyboards are perfectly suited to the basic, on-and-off, switch-like nature of MIDI commands, and they are generally tailored to a linear progression from one pitch to the next using either equal temperament or another tuning system, with little variation, whereas guitar technique routinely plays the notes between the exact pitches: vibrato, upward and downward slides, and bends. Generally speaking, those techniques don't come native to keyboards—at least, not until the advent of the synthesizer, which can use a variety of modulation tricks to accomplish similar effects. Still, there are limitations to the ways in which a keyboard can emulate guitars.

In particular, keyboards are not the best medium for articulations such as independently bent notes, hammer-ons, slides, and many other tricks of the trade that guitarists take for granted. Although MIDI synthesizers can mimic guitar behavior in a number of ways (pitch bend is the most obvious example), there's a catch: Try holding down a chord and bending *some* of the notes. Unlike on a guitar, all the keyboard's notes will bend by the same amount; bending some of the notes in a chord—for example, bending one pitch up a half-step while another bends by a whole step, or bending notes in opposite directions—is impossible. MIDI flags Pitch Bend messages as Channel messages, so any bent notes will affect all notes on that synthesizer's MIDI channel. At this point, you might wonder: "How then, does a guitar playing a synthesizer accomplish independent bent notes?"

MIDI à la Mode

At this point, we need to understand the four MIDI modes. These determine how your synth will respond to incoming MIDI notes, and they are built from two basic performance states: Omni On or Off, and Mono or Poly. With Omni On, your synthesizer will respond to all incoming notes and other data. Omni On is not an effective setting for your synthesizer when it is used as a sound source for a sequence with multiple MIDI parts, because everything that is received, regardless of what MIDI message or MIDI channel, will be played with a single patch, and that would be the equivalent of making one instrument in an orchestra attempt to play the entire score, which would sound pretty unmusical.

With Omni Off, your synth becomes channel-specific: All MIDI data issuing from your guitar is routed to a single MIDI channel, presumably to a single sound, be it a string section, a brass ensemble, or a piano sound. Omni On is mostly a holdover from the days when musicians wished to simply layer sounds from different synthesizers without the bother of matching MIDI channels on both synths. Omni On is also useful for diagnosing whether a synthesizer's MIDI and audio connections are working without having to determine its MIDI channel.

Poly or Mono?

Most modern synthesizers are, by default, polyphonic, meaning that you can play more than one note at a time. Omni Off, Poly is ideally suited to sequencing, when you want to create orchestrations one synthesizer at a time and with no restrictions on each part's polyphony.

Mono refers to a synthesizer setting that limits the instrument to play no more than one note at a time. There are a number of reasons why a synth would be set to Mono: You can create gliding effects and trills by holding a note down and playing another with the first note still pressed; no matter how long you hold a note, playing the next note will instantly cut off the previous note—and that is of major significance to achieving guitar-like performance. Time for another experiment: Play a series of notes on any single guitar string. Notice that no matter how quickly you move to the next note, the previous note cuts off. As guitarists, that's easy to take for granted, but polyphonic MIDI synthesizers can play related notes without clipping the previous note, and can even play multiple instances of the same note unless they are specifically programmed to only play one note at a time; that gives the guitarist a more guitar-like control over the synth.

Most synthesizers these days are multitimbral; that means that the synth can play more than one sound—or timbre—at a time. How that instrument arranges those sounds is up to you. Common approaches (depending on the sophistication of the synth) include layers, splits (in which different sounds occupy different ranges of the keyboard, such as a piano and bass split), velocity splits (in which another sound emerges when keys are struck with greater force), or combinations of these. But for our immediate purposes, it is important that the synth can be set up to play monophonically on each of six MIDI channels (one for each string). That means the synth will be set up to respond in Omni Off, Mono. Because each string triggers a Mono patch on its own MIDI channel, there is no smearing of notes from

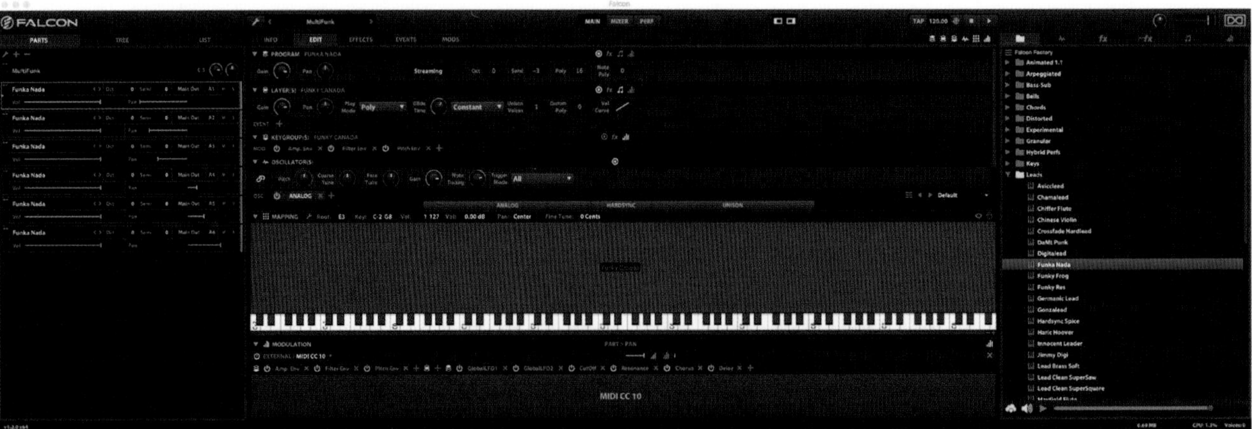

UVI Falcon is a deeply programmable instrument, yet it's extremely easy to set up for MIDI guitar. The Multi setup is displayed in the left-hand panel, an edit page in the center displays some of the patch-editing capabilities, and the right-hand panel is the patch browser. Simply drag a patch from the browser to the Multi window, and they are automatically assigned consecutive MIDI channels.

one to the next, and glitching or false triggering is minimized. Of course, Pitch Bend ranges must match in the guitar as well as the synth, and that means you must make sure that each of the six MIDI channels in your synthesizer is set to receive the same range of Pitch Bend. The bend range on your guitar is usually a single setting, whether it's transmitting on a single MIDI channel or six.

If this all seems like a lot of bother, you just haven't experienced the exhilaration of playing synthesizers from your guitar. Once you have committed these ideas to practice and memory, it will all become second nature. For detailed examples of setting up select guitar and synthesizer systems, please see Chapter 8.

CHAPTER 3

Guitar Meets MIDI

A brief history of MIDI guitar.

It's helpful to draw a distinction between guitar synthesizer and MIDI guitar: Guitar synthesis is usually meant to describe a proprietary system in which a guitar, either directly or by way of control voltages, plays a dedicated synthesizer. The distinction is important to the understanding of how to use your guitar with any MIDI-equipped synthesizer—and those are by far the majority of synths these days.

MIDI guitar sends audio to an analog-to-digital conversion system (frequently called a *guitar-to-MIDI converter*) that translates the guitar impulses into streams of MIDI data, usually (but not always) to trigger synthesizers. To confuse the issue, some modern MIDI guitars have direct access to synthesizers built into a rack or floor unit, but they still require MIDI to address gear outside of the built-in system.

Converting to MIDI

With MIDI, it's important to grasp that the guitar is a controller, and what you take for granted in a normal guitar performance requires a conversion process so that it is understood by the synthesizer—and synthesizers often have their own rules for producing sound. Guitars have one way of generating sound, synthesizers have a completely different mechanism, and MIDI makes them work together.

In order to convert a guitar to MIDI, the signal from each string needs to be isolated. Without that isolation, the converter would not be able to identify the individual notes. That is an analog-to-digital process commonly called *pitch-to-MIDI*. To that end, and taking a cue from Roland, most guitars use some form of divided pickup, essentially six discrete magnetic or piezoelectric pickups, one for each of the guitar's strings. The pickup converts each string's vibrations into

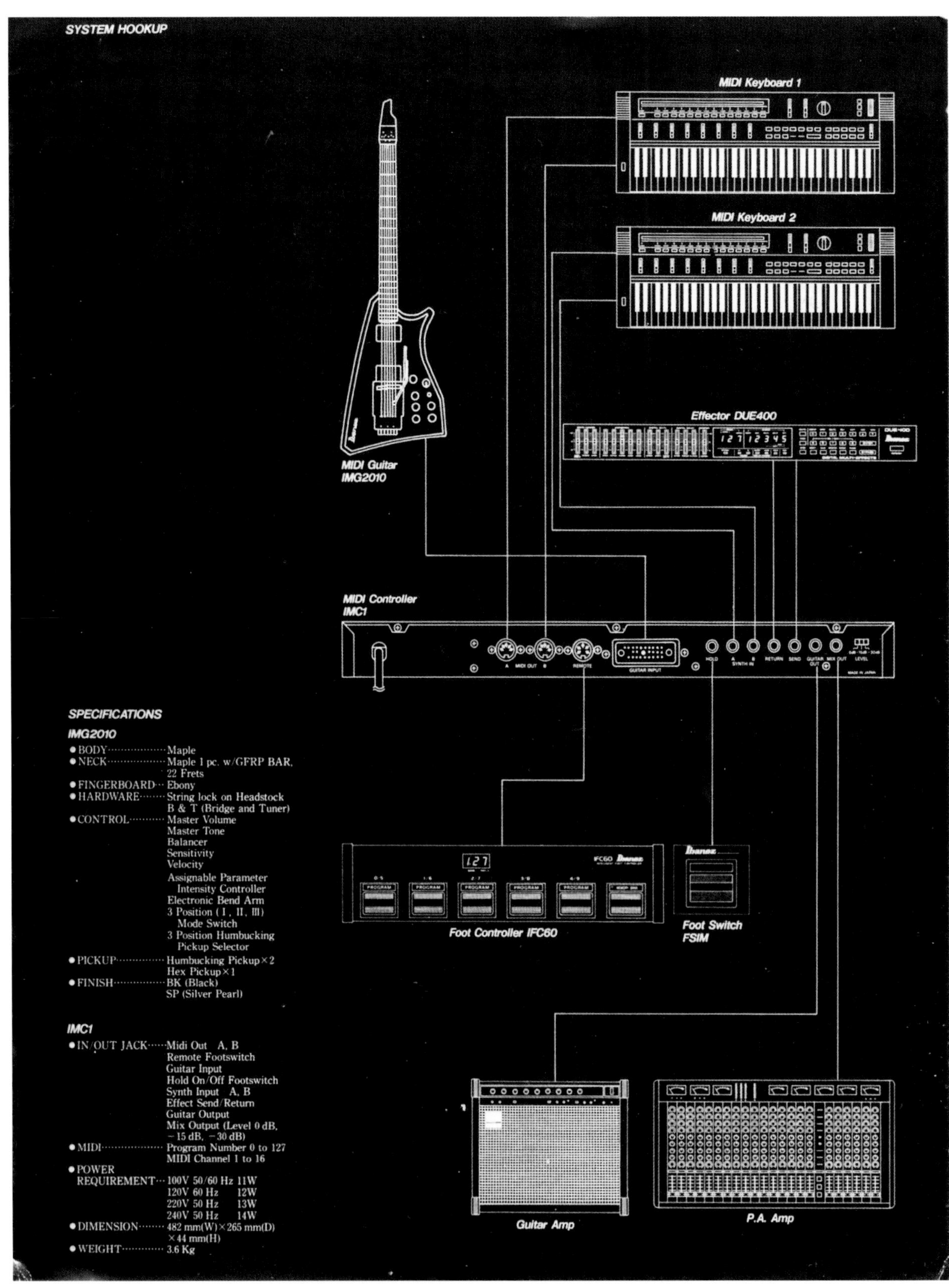

This depicts the signal flow from divided pickup to MIDI converter, to synths and processors, and finally, to amp. (Photograph courtesy of Ibanez Guitars)

electronic signals, and an analog-to-digital converter reads the frequency and dynamics of each signal and turns it into digital information—in this case, MIDI Note Numbers and MIDI Velocity. The fact that the guitar is using a divided pickup makes it a relatively simple task for the converter to route the MIDI data to a specific MIDI channel, or over several channels at once.

Why Wait?

Tracking on a nicely set-up, well-tuned MIDI guitar was a new and exciting experience for guitarists in the '80s, and the technology was widely adopted. It was still not without its problems, though; all MIDI guitars of the time suffered from a bit of lag time between picking a string and the ensuing synthesizer response. In fairness, that was partially due to a lack of understanding about how synthesizers produce sound, but there were also real issues with the conversion process.

First, picking a string is not a pristine affair; the onset of the signal produces a bit of noise, which needed to be filtered out in the conversion process. Filtering prevented the string noise from being interpreted as MIDI data and sent out to the synthesizer, creating glitches. The other phenomenon is that an excited string cycles in and out of tune and takes a few milliseconds before it settles into a stable pitch. For that reason, the conversion process required a couple of cycles of the string's waveform before it could analyze the pitch properly. To make matters more complicated, the slower-cycling waveforms of lower-pitched strings caused the converter to take longer to sort out the proper frequency—which created a perceptible increase in delay when playing the guitar's lower strings.

First out of the Gate

The aforementioned issues made MIDI guitar an awkward and frustrating experience at times. Still, prominent guitarists, such as Pat Metheny, John Abercrombie, and John McLaughlin, made it work, and largely due to the persistence of Roland and other companies, the art and science of guitar synthesis has survived and evolved. Modern-day MIDI guitar systems have essentially solved these problems, and with a bit of attentive setup, synthesis via guitar is a tactile, expressive experience.

Roland's first MIDI guitar was a package released in 1984 and featuring the G-707, an impressively strange-looking, angular guitar—so angular, in fact, that it acquired the nickname "The Dalek's Handbag" and "Cubist Flymo" (Flymo is a sort of unholy congress between a hovercraft and lawnmower, an already surreal concept). The guitar connected to a floor-unit synth and MIDI converter, the GR-700. The pair connected by way of Roland's standard bulky—and often fragile—24-pin cable. The synth was essentially the guts of a JX-3P, which provided

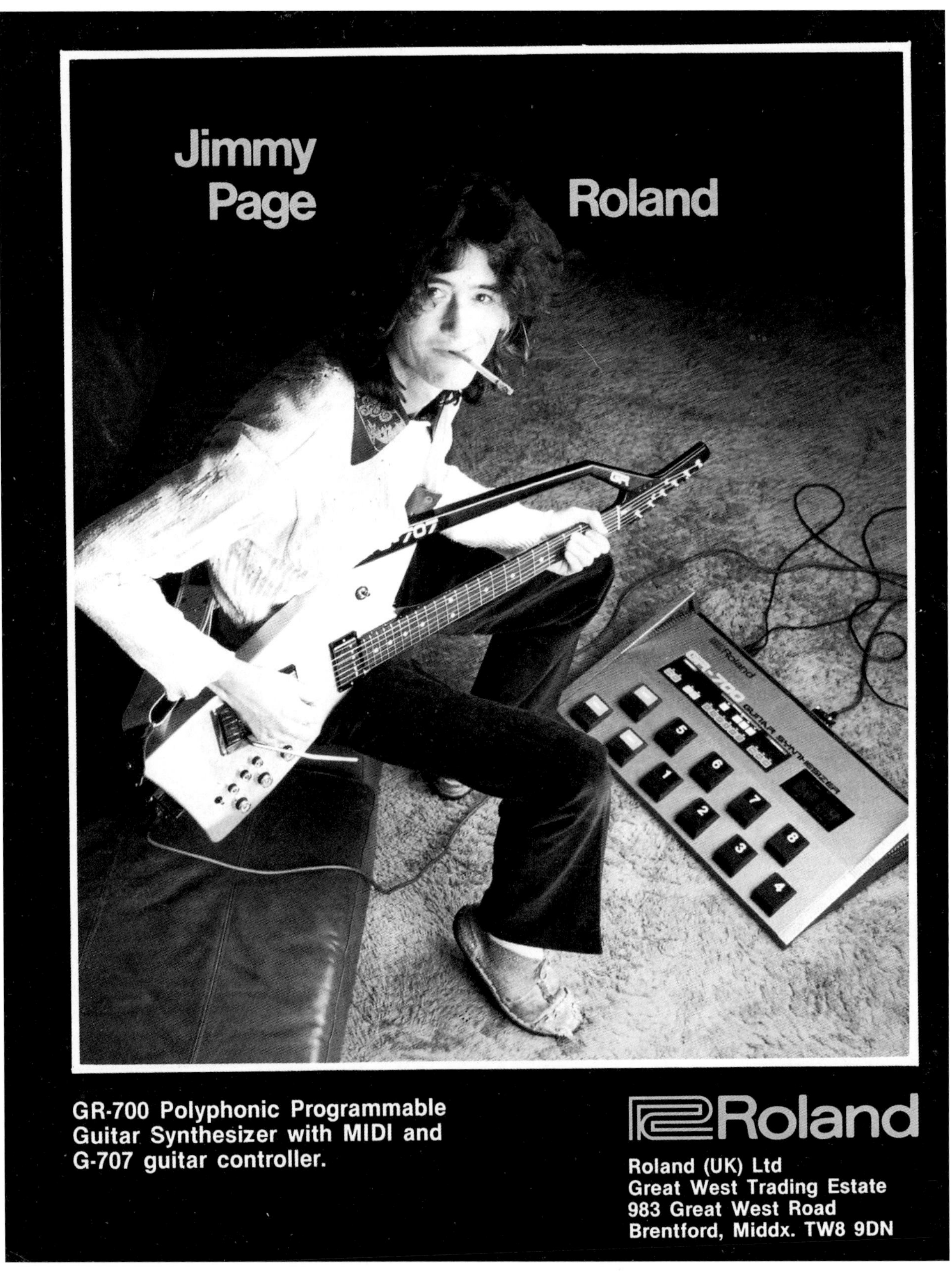

Guitarist Jimmy Page with the Roland GR-707/700 system, the world's first MIDI guitar. The body exemplified Roland's concept of futuristic design. (Photograph courtesy of Roland Corporation)

DESIGNS FOR A NEW WORLD
At Ibanez we feel there is no perfect guitar, as there is no perfect guitar player. The instrument is only what the musician makes of it. We also feel guitar players haven't been given the opportunity to use available technology to expand their musical direction. Ibanez is trying to unlock the future of guitar by broadening the artists musical perspectives and open the doors of technology to guitarists. We want guitar players to enjoy the limitless sound possibilities keyboard players have been enjoying for over ten years.
Current guitar synthesizers are limited by their sound and memory availability. That is why Ibanez chose the MIDI (musical instrument digital interface) data interface for their control system. This enables the user to make his instrument the controller for any external sound source operating on MIDI information. Finally guitar players can control computers, keyboards, sequencers and drum machines with their own playing technique. With the MIDI Guitar System, Ibanez hopes to be helping guitar players realize their potential..........AND USE IT!
Ibanez

From an Ibanez brochure. The Ibanez MIDI guitar system bundled a great-sounding, futuristic-looking guitar with a single-rackspace MIDI converter and a sophisticated MIDI implementation. (Photograph courtesy of Ibanez Guitars)

two digitally controlled oscillators with a voltage-controlled filter, providing the synth with a fat, analog-sounding tone. What distinguished the unit from earlier guitar synthesizers was the presence of a jack on the rear of the floor unit for MIDI output, meaning that you could control any connected, MIDI-equipped synthesizer. As a reliable conduit from guitar to synthesizer, its implementation was primitive, with no provision to bend notes on connected synthesizers (although the built-in sounds responded to note bends). Any connected synthesizer would need to be set to receive on MIDI Channel One—as the GR was capable of transmitting only on that MIDI channel.

The guitar looked intriguing because of the large "stabilizer bar," whose purpose was to mute spurious vibrations and prevent misfired notes. The guitar was awkward and often difficult to play, partially because of the looming presence of the stabilizer bar, but also as a result of a fat, Louisville Slugger of a neck. Fortunately, Roland's then-standard 24-pin connector interfaced with other, more playable guitars that Roland had designed for the purpose, and soon afterward, other manufacturers adopted the 24-pin connector as a standard for interfacing guitars with their MIDI converters and joined in on the MIDI guitar fray.

My very first MIDI guitar was a bright silver Ibanez IMG2010 system, which offered a graphite-reinforced neck, a more elegant option to the GR-700's intrusive stabilizer bar. The guitar used the same 24-pin cable as the Roland units, making it backward-compatible with the GR-700 as well as the earlier Roland forebears. Ibanez also improved on the GR's internal electronics with more robust connections. The Ibanez had no accompanying synthesizer unit, relying instead on the MC-1, its single Rackspace MIDI converter, to access the MIDI-equipped synth of your choice. Accordingly, the unit's MIDI implementation was far superior to the GR-700. For starters, you could set the system to transmit on a single MIDI channel of your choice or send MIDI on a channel-per-string basis. It had assignable knobs to send MIDI data plus an

From a Synthaxe brochure. It's not a guitar, but it's a MIDI controller for guitarists. The Synthaxe was one of the first guitar-like controllers.

assignable MIDI whammy bar. You could assign it to its equivalent guitar function—wide Pitch Bend swoops—or to practically any other MIDI function you need. One of my favorites was to assign Aftertouch to sweep filters on some sounds. Naturally, you could store these settings as patches.

Not too long after Ibanez released its system, many companies, including Charvel, Kamen, and IVL, followed suit with somewhat similar instruments and a few variations on the theme, including built-in basic sequencers, alternate-note conversion schemes (such as Photon's optical fret scanning, which measured the distance from the sensor to the finger's position on the fretboard), and other innovations.

Soon after, enterprising manufacturers attempted to bypass the guitar's persistent, finicky issues with MIDI by designing guitar-like MIDI controllers which eschewed the traditional string-and-pickup arrangement in favor of fret wiring, buttons, pads, and string-like triggers in an attempt to impart a guitar-like feel to an instrument that was no longer a guitar. These were not widely accepted by the guitar community, although some units, such as the Synthaxe, were adopted by guitar luminaries, such as Alan Holdsworth and Lee Ritenour. The Synthaxe tracked easily, without any translational quibbling, and had a ton of MIDI-controlled expressiveness accessible right under the fingertips. One of the biggest barriers to mainstream acceptance of these types of controllers was their expense. The Synthaxe initially sold for around $13,000, and understandably so: Production was limited, and they were made from aerospace- and military-grade hardware. Purportedly, there were fewer than 100 Synthaxes still in existence. Many guitarists have moved on from the technology, although you can still see Roy "Futureman" Wooten of Bela Fleck and the Flecktones play MIDI drums on a repurposed Synthaxe.

Careful with That Axe

These controllers, as accurate as they might have been, proved alien to the average guitar player. Guitarists understandably didn't feel at home with anything but their own guitars, and once again, Roland got the message and took another major step forward with the GM-70 . This time around, Roland offered no proprietary guitar; instead, they bundled a divided pickup that fit under the strings of your guitar with a single-rackspace conversion unit that hosted a powerful CPU for faster, more accurate tracking along with a brilliant and deep MIDI implementation. You could adapt the pickup to almost any guitar—even acoustic instruments, whose live acoustic resonance could create tracking issues for lesser converters.

With 128 patches, the GM-70 was loaded. Every patch had four branches, a sort of sub-patch designed to address the burgeoning number of effects and synthesizers that needed a discrete MIDI control stream. The branches could be assigned individual MIDI channels and addressed simultaneously—consequently, you could control reverb or a multi-effects unit on one branch while playing synthesizer solos on another. Each branch could have its own Pitch Bend settings to address different synths with different capabilities. You could scale the MIDI Velocity output on any branch—a boon, as not all synths responded equally to playing dynamics. On selecting

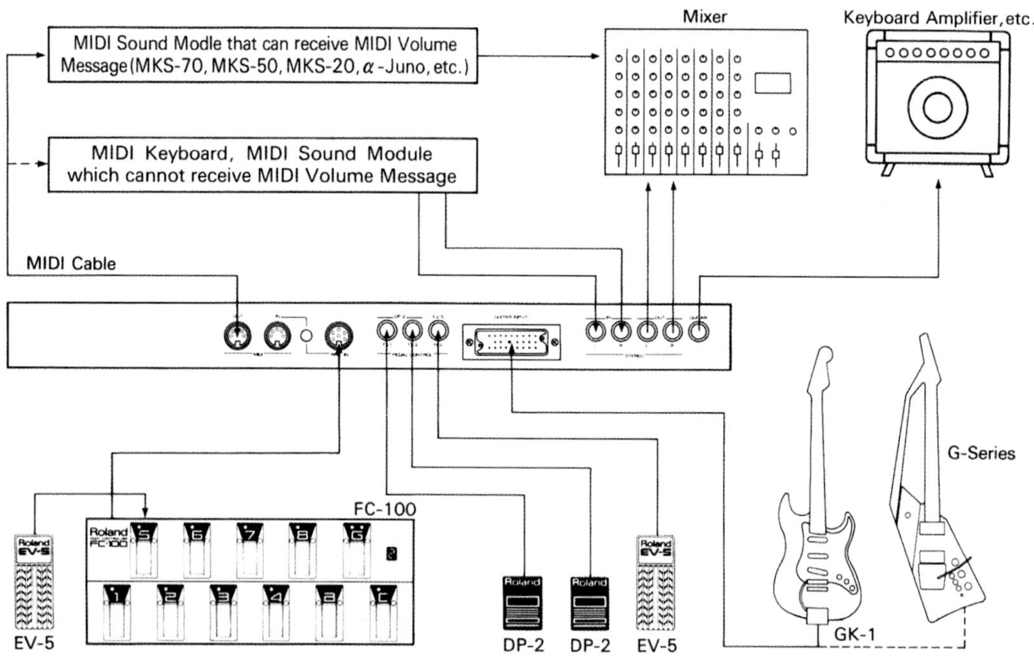

A diagram from the Roland GM-70 user manual demonstrates its flexibility; it was the first MIDI converter that could be used with any guitar. It had a brilliant MIDI implementation and faster, more accurate tracking. (Photograph courtesy of Roland Corporation)

a patch, you could even transmit initial MIDI Volume settings to synths on any branch, thereby balancing relative levels for each patch. Clearly, Roland had done its homework.

By now, you may be sensing my bias toward Roland MIDI guitar systems, and you'd be correct; it should also be obvious by now that Roland has tirelessly supported electronic guitar, and guitar synthesis in particular. There has been a profusion of guitar synthesizers on the market—many more than I can include in this book—but with few exceptions, Roland has led while other companies have followed.

As wonderful as the GM-70 was, much of its feature set went over the heads of many who simply wanted to play synthesizer from a guitar, and not too long afterward, Roland released the GR-50, a rackmount MIDI guitar converter with a built-in Roland D-110 synthesizer. The synth used one of Roland's newer sound-design technologies, which combined short samples of sounds, including pick noise, violin-bow attacks, flute chiffs, and more, providing a touch of realism (or surrealism) when grafted onto a more conventional synthesizer engine. The MIDI routing was greatly simplified in the interest of plug-and-play, but the unit introduced several new features. The built-in synth was multitimbral, offering two independent synthesizer parts and a drum part that could receive MIDI signals from an external source, for instance, a keyboard or a computer. You could record the MIDI data into a software sequencing program and play it back with your GR-50's built-in synth.

Perhaps more significant was the GR-50's departure from the bulky and awkward 24-pin cable to a 13-pin format that was lighter, easy to maintain, and considerably less expensive to manufacture. This cable format eventually became standard among other manufacturers, and you could argue that its widespread adoption spurred the growth of MIDI guitar in the marketplace. Roland went on to release new MIDI guitars, many with improved sounds and marginally better tracking, but nothing very new or revolutionary for quite some time. Other companies manufactured MIDI guitars of note, including Korg, whose Z3 system included a very nice-sounding, built-in synth, whose tone generator was patterned after Yamaha's popular line of FM synthesizers, covered in Chapter 4. Other significant instruments were Casio's MG 500 and MG 510 MIDI guitars; these offered two body designs: One was a black, Stratocaster-type body, and the other exemplified a more futuristic design, to put it charitably. Whatever their appearance, the coolest aspect of these guitars was that all the MIDI conversion took place in the guitar—just run a MIDI cable out of the guitar and into the synth of your choice, and you were good to go. They tracked pretty darn well, too. A later model, the PG380, upped the ante even further with a really nice built-in FM synth. This became a popular MIDI guitar, but because it used FM synthesis, its days were numbered when Yamaha, who held a patent, sued Casio over the use of FM and put them out of the synthesizer market for a long time.

Axon

As fast as MIDI guitar tracking was then, the lower notes still could not quite keep up with the higher pitches. The Blue Chip Axon guitar converters were the next leap forward, introducing a conversion process that could reliably extract the pitch from the attack transient of the plucked string. First, it meant that the difference in frequency between low notes and high didn't make much difference in the conversion, and because it shaved off a couple of cycles of analysis, conversion from pitch to MIDI was faster. It might not seem like much, but even the slightest perceivable delay can fatigue the best players, and the consistency of response between high and low notes was a godsend.

Blue Chip produced several desktop-sized Axon units, some with a built-in synthesizer, and the Axon AX100 rackmount unit. In addition to a built-in, multitimbral synthesizer, the AX100

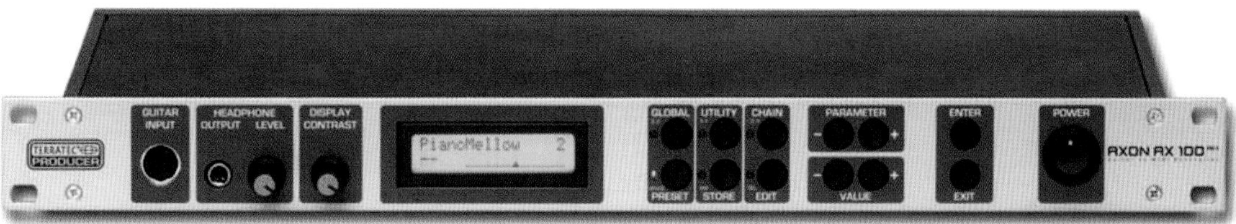

The Axon AX100 tracked like a dream and could turn gestures, such as pick position, into MIDI data.

had a monophonic mic input, so you could sing or play saxophone into it, trigger the internal synthesizer, and send MIDI notes. I never had much success with the input, but then again, I was never much of a singer.

Axon was ultimately purchased by a German company, Terratec, and they introduced the AX100 MKII, which used a different synthesizer and replaced the mic input with a headphone jack. Besides tracking absolutely beautifully, the unit's MIDI implementation was rich. You could increase or decrease the MIDI message of your choice based on your picking-hand distance between bridge and neck—great for sweeping filters for real-time timbre changes. Likewise, you could set up zones across the fingerboard addressing different sounds for each, or you could send patch changes by note. The detail of fine tuning the Axon's response to your picking style was thoughtful and effective.

Terratec also released the AX50 USB, an equally proficient MIDI guitar converter with MIDI via USB as well as Standard MIDI Input and Output (I/O). The unit was functionally as deep as the AX100 but had no front-panel programming, relying instead on a software editor. Unfortunately, Mac OS X 10.7 rendered the editor inoperable, along with the AX50 USB connection. As far as I know, it still works with Windows. Although the Axon is no longer in production, the brilliance of its pitch-detection scheme survives in an improved, wireless state in the Fishman Triple-Play system, and we'll cover that and other contemporary MIDI guitar systems in the section about guitar controllers.

CHAPTER 4

What Is a Synthesizer?

Understanding how synths work. Common types of synthesis.

Q: How can you tell if a synthesist is ringing your doorbell?
A: It doesn't sound like a real doorbell.

We've all heard that synthesizers can imitate any instrument or sound we can hear. While that is a compelling thought, it's not really true; if it were true, why would we need so many of them? Practically anyone who has spent time with synthesizers will tell you synths occupy their own sonic space, and while emulating other instruments is an art and science unto itself, imitation is usually beside the point of synthesis. Each type of synthesizer has its own strengths and limitations, and at this point, there's an exciting menagerie of instruments that can lead guitarists into undiscovered territories. For all that, synthesizers rely on so many of the same acoustic behaviors and principles that we are used to as natural byproducts of sound; they just go about re-creating them in a different way. It's always useful to refer to acoustic behavior in the shaping of synth sounds as a human reference point. There are tons of new synthesizers with new approaches to sound design, and intriguing new technologies to pull it off. I could easily devote a book to the subject, but this is still a book about digital applications for guitar, so I'll focus on just a few popular synthesis types, with the thought that understanding the principles that synths use to create and animate sound is crucial to making MIDI guitar work for you.

Subtractive Synthesis

Often used interchangeably with *analog synthesis* (though they're not the same), *subtractive synthesis* derives its name from the generation of harmonically rich waveforms whose tone is shaped by filters. I've always liked the comparisons with sculpture, whose final product is the result of removal of materials rather than combining them. Analog synthesis is the result of a voltage-generated waveform and a voltage-controlled wave signal path. Its main engine is usually subtractive, but again, its filters and other modifiers are shaped by voltage.

Subtractive synthesis is easily the most common synthesis technique, often showing up at the core of digital synths of all stripes, including wavetable, sampling, and sample playback, and even as an adjunct to some additive synthesizers I've seen. Many of the sound-shaping elements of subtractive synthesis recur often in other synthesizer types, which is why I give it the lion's share of coverage.

Subtractive Synthesis in a Nutshell

The three main components of subtractive synthesis are the *oscillator*, the *filter*, and the *amplifier*. The oscillator generates the waveform and sets its frequency, the filter shapes the raw waveform's harmonic content, and the amplifier determines the waveform's amplitude. The waveform is literally the shape of the amplitude of its component frequencies, which determine the timbre of the sound. Analog subtractive synthesis provides a fairly limited selection of periodic waveforms: sine, triangle, saw, square, pulse (similar to square), and noise. *Periodic* means that it repeats its values at regular intervals.

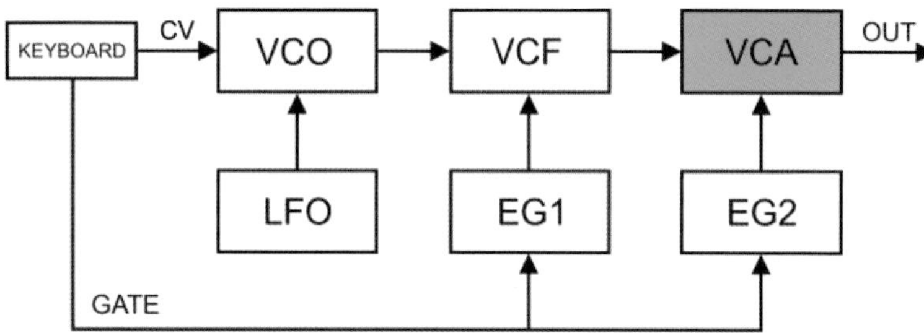

A simplified diagram illustrating the typical signal flow of subtractive synthesis.

Your Basic Waveform

A sine wave is the purest waveform, consisting of only the fundamental frequency. Bland and not very interesting by itself, it is the building block of more complex sounds. The triangle wave is only slightly more complex, consisting of the fundamental frequency and odd harmonics of successively weaker amplitude. Generally, triangle waves sound similar, if only a bit brighter and hollower, than the sine wave because the decrease in amplitude of the harmonics occurs at an exponential rate, rather than in the linear fashion of other waveforms. Among other things, sine and triangle waves are good starting points for flute-like sounds. Sine waves are also great

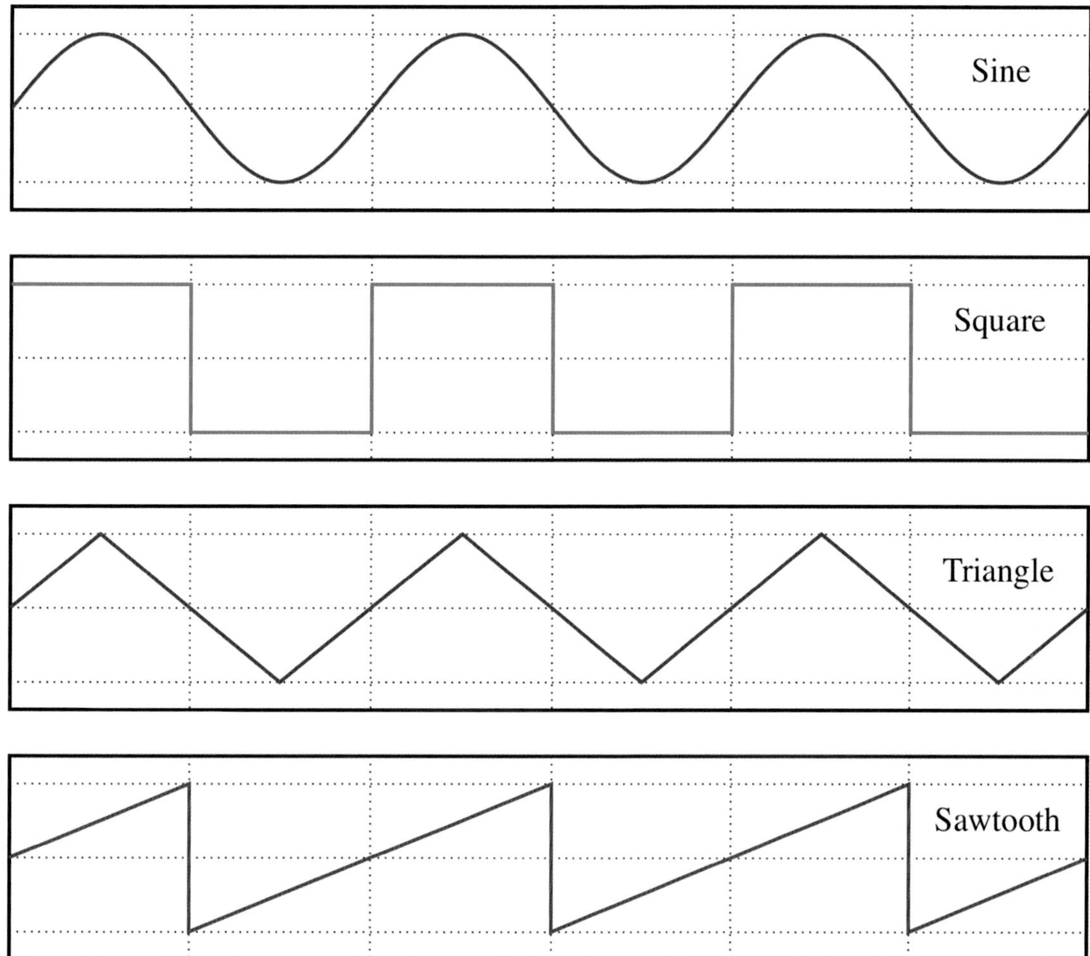

Here's a sampled banjo waveform reproduced in Camel Audio's Cameleon CA5000 additive synthesizer, with the fundamenta Analog oscillators typically generate a few periodic waveforms. It is up to filters and other modifiers to alter the harmonic content of the waveform.

when tuned to lower frequencies to add extra bottom to bass and other sounds because they can reinforce the low end without extra harmonic content to muddy the sound.

Saw (or *sawtooth*) *waves* consist of the fundamental and all harmonics at successive, linear, decreasing amplitude. If we plotted out its harmonic content, the wave takes on the shape of a saw tooth, which is where the name comes from. The rich harmonic content of the saw wave gives it a bright, buzzy tone, and its versatility extends to brass-ensemble sounds, trumpets, bass, pads, strings, and a lot more.

Square waves comprise the fundamental frequency and all odd-numbered harmonics in a linear, decreasing amplitude. Like the saw wave, it also sounds bright and buzzy, but with a characteristically hollow tone reminiscent of the clarinet. In fact, square waves are the logical choice when designing clarinet-type sounds. The pulse wave, also called a rectangular wave, is similar to the square wave but with the ability to expand or contract the on-and-off cycle, or *pulse width*, of the waveform—which changes its harmonic content. At a 50 percent pulse width, the waveform is a square wave, but as the percentage goes above or below 50 percent, its sound gets thinner and reedier. From a sonic standpoint, it's impossible to distinguish between sounds that are equally positive or negative from that median value—for example, 75 percent versus 25 percent.

Finally, many synthesizers generate noise of various types. *White noise* generates all frequencies at equal amplitude. *Pink noise* has equal amplitude per octave and is more useful than white noise for analyzing a room for equalization purposes. Noise waveforms have their uses in synthesizer sound effects, such as wind or sweeping, nonmusical dance sounds, but they can also be shaped into drum sounds and provide breathy "chiff" artifacts for flute sounds.

Filters

The raw waveform passes through the filter, which can be one of many types. For now, let's stick with the most common one, the *low-pass filter*. As its name hints, lower frequencies are allowed to pass to the next stage unaltered, but the higher frequencies are cut off. So far, I've described nothing more than a tone control, and synthesis would sound pretty boring if all you could do was cut off the high end. For starters, low-pass filters are usually accompanied by resonance controls, which boost the frequencies around the filter's cutoff settings. Most natural sounds have resonant frequencies that give them a unique sonic imprint. The human voice is a great example; resonance is largely why we can distinguish one person's voice from another's. The cavity of the mouth, the shape of the head and vocal tract, and the position of the tongue and lips emphasize or de-emphasize tonal qualities of the voice and impart a unique timbral signature. If you have ever sped up or slowed down a recording of your voice, you might have noticed that the resulting change in speed alters the pitch and produces an unnatural quality that you wouldn't get by modulating the pitch of your

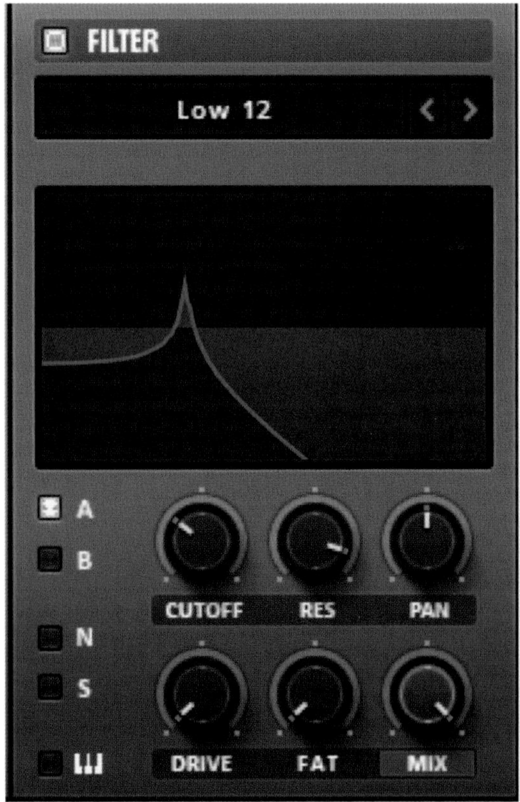

Adding resonance to a low-pass filter emphasizes frequencies at the filter's cutoff point.

voice, whose natural, resonant frequencies do not change with pitch. To get a feel for how filters and resonance work with the human voice, slowly (very slowly) pronounce the vowels: A-E-I-O-U. Repeat them at different volumes and, especially, different pitches, remaining cognizant of how the changing shape in your head affects the sound, and observe that some aspects of the tone you produce remain constant. Internalizing this concept has been very useful to me when creating synthesizer sounds.

Amplifier

The last stage before passing synthesizer sounds to the output (or its built-in effects chain) is the synth's built-in amp section. Usually, all a garden-variety amp does is set the level of the oscillator's output. Most modern synths have two oscillators or more, which would necessitate a mixer of sorts to manage the sounds in some way. Where that mixer occurs in the signal flow depends on the synthesizer's design. In some cases, synths share a common filter, or the oscillators are used in ways other than a simple combination of tones—possibly using one waveform to modulate the sound of the other. In a synth, modulation is where things get interesting.

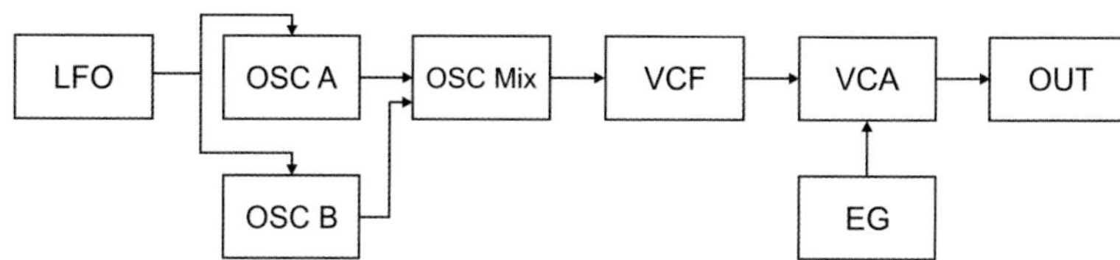

Synthesizers with more than a single oscillator can use mixers in different ways. Here, the mixer simply balances the level between two independent oscillators.

Time for another experiment: Pluck an unamplified guitar's strings and let each note ring out until it fades from existence. Pick successively higher-pitched notes and observe two aspects of the sound. First, the sound eventually dies out. Second, as you play higher on the fingerboard, the sound dies out more quickly. Try it on a piano; notes at the bottom end of the keyboard last far longer than the highest notes. We take this behavior for granted, if we think about it at all, but synthesizer sounds don't do this naturally; they need assistance to emulate that behavior.

The Envelope, Please

When you pluck a string or play a piano, the sound instantly reaches its top volume. It might bloom temporarily, fade to a slightly lower level, and sustain for a time before it dies out. A tuba behaves slightly differently; because the player needs to build up a column of air to produce sound, it takes more time to reach its loudest level. Theoretically, a healthy, nonsmoking tuba player could hold a consistent volume before changing notes or stopping to gather breath for the next note.

Envelope is a term we use to describe a sound's amplitude stages over time, and an envelope is often casually called an ADSR—Attack, Decay, Sustain, and Release. As discussed in Chapter 1, the envelopes of many acoustic sounds are considerably more complex, and many modern synths can deploy many more stages. Synths use a device called an Envelope Generator, or EG, to modulate the oscillator's amplitude over time.

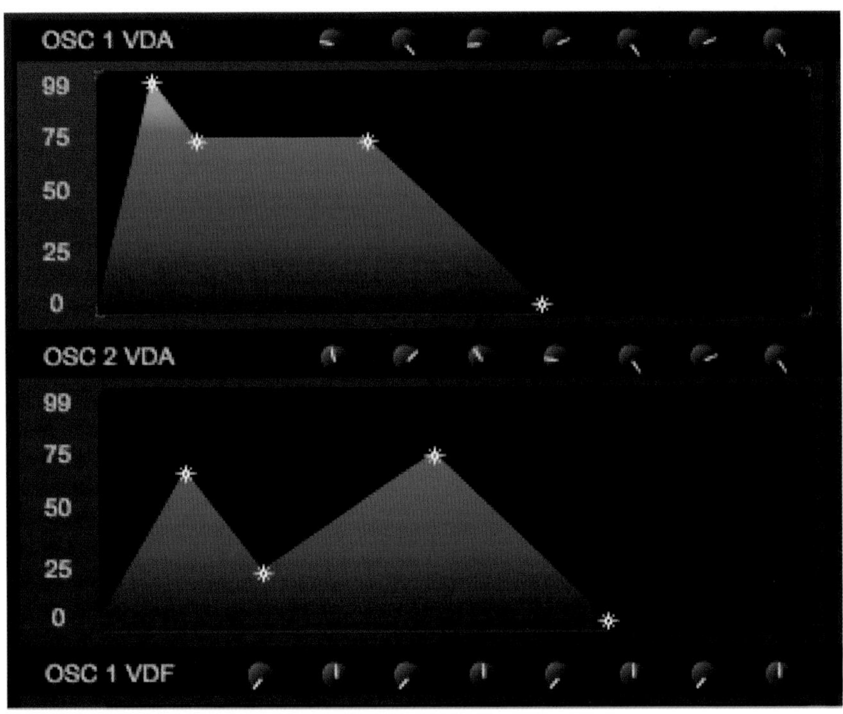

Contrast the standard ADSR envelope with the Envelope Generator from a Korg M1 synthesizer, which has an extra level and an extra rate.

A simple ADSR comprises three rates and one level. Attack is the time it takes to reach maximum amplitude. Decay is the time for a sound to reach a held amplitude level, or sustain, after the attack, and release is the time it takes for a sound to fade to silence, predicated on the release of a key or the ceasing of whatever energy is creating a note. On an organ, the release is instantaneous. In fact, organ notes are typically only attack, sustain, and release. On a guitar, notes can ring on after they are plucked or strummed. It is the job of the EG to mimic that behavior. One of the cool aspects of synths, especially for guitarists, is that some sounds, such as pads, can be made to sustain indefinitely.

If you listen to a sustained acoustic guitar or piano note, you'll notice that the tone changes over time, too. Sounds start off bright and full of overtones, and as the sound loses energy, some of the higher frequencies fade away, leaving a pure, fundamental tone, until it dies out. In order to make this happen on a synth, we can add an EG that controls the filter over time. In this case, the filter will control the contours of the oscillator's timbre in accordance with the rates and levels of the EG.

Key Follow and Velocity

So far, we can change the way a sound behaves over time with respect to amplitude and timbre, but that doesn't account for the rate at which this behavior slows down or speeds up in relation to pitch. We need some element to make lower notes last longer and higher ones die more quickly. And so far there's no mechanism to account for sounds getting brighter at higher pitches. Enter Key Follow, which adjusts the life cycle of an envelope by note value. In conventional use, Key Follow applied to an envelope can make its rates slower or faster based on playing lower or higher notes. Applied to a filter, it can open up on higher pitches and make the tone brighter. The cool thing about synthesizers is that they have the potential to depart from a feature's intended use. Envelopes can be inverted, and Key Follow can be reversed. The late Joe Zawinul, cofounder of Weather Report, used Key Follow to invert the pitch of his synth, creating some fascinating and unusual solos.

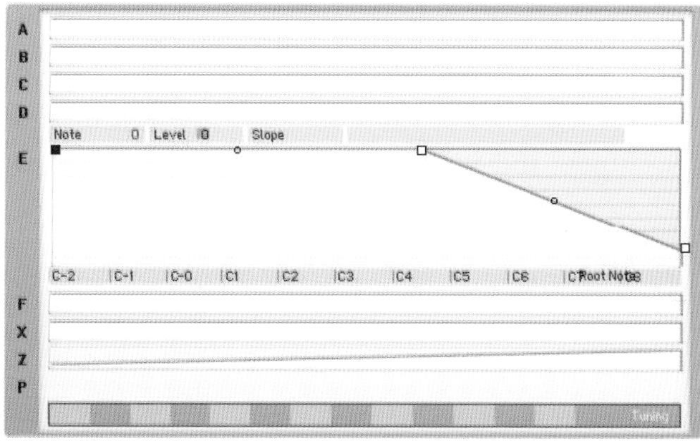

The graphic illustrates how Key Follow affects an envelope by virtue of keyboard notes.

That musical instruments get louder the harder you play them is a no-brainer, but here again, synths need an electronic assist, and that is called Velocity Sensitivity. Sometimes it's called *touch sensitivity*, but that could include behavior tied to pressure on the keys after a note is struck. The force applied to striking a key could perform a number of useful purposes. Strings, drum heads, and other instruments initially stretch and go slightly out of tune when played, and increasingly so with greater force; applying Velocity controls to the oscillator's pitch adds a touch of realism. As notes are played harder, they get brighter; here, Velocity attached to the filter is a typical approach. Of course, the most obvious Velocity control is to attach it to amplitude; the harder you play, the louder you get.

Some synthesizers will let you use Velocity to emphasize one oscillator over the other. That's an excellent technique for creating dramatic changes in timbre based on dynamic playing. Many sample-based synthesizers use Velocity-layered samples to re-create acoustic-sounding variations on timbre—for example, pianos layered with samples recorded at different dynamic levels. Sampled drums use this to great effect; quietly played snares sound very different from those that are bashed. As a MIDI guitarist, I often customize Velocity Sensitivity because the touch of a string is so different from that of a keyboard. There are several ways to do this, which I'll cover in a later chapter.

Everything in Modulation

Synths have a bunch of ancillary gadgets and techniques for building animated sounds, more than I can cover in one chapter. But I'd be remiss if I didn't talk about the Low-Frequency Oscillator (LFO). Like the Envelope Generator, it can add life to the Oscillator's pitch, timbre, or volume, but unlike the EG, it can be switched on and off or run free, creating rhythmic effects and more.

Remember those basic oscillator shapes we discussed a couple of paragraphs back? LFOs offer the same waveforms, but they are played back slowly at frequencies below the range of human hearing. Rather than add sound to the synthesizer, they modulate some other function on the synth according to their shape. For example, the smooth, continuous up-and-down motion of a sine-wave LFO routed to the pitch of an oscillator is often used to create vibrato.

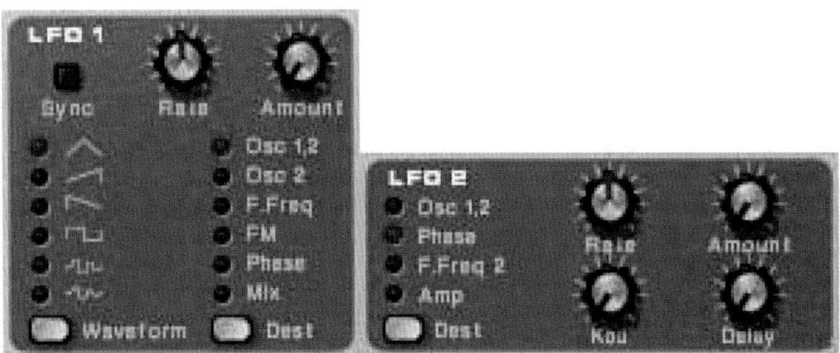

One of the typical uses for an LFO is to produce pitch changes (vibrato) in an oscillator.

Substituting a saw wave in the same example was likely the technique used to create one of the Star Trek "tricorder" effects. I've used the strict, up-and-down motion of square-wave LFOs to create one-finger trills. Applied to the filter, you can create wah-wah-type effects, and tied to the amp, tremolo is easy to produce.

There's much more to know about subtractive synthesis, but I have laid out the basic architecture for a technique that you'll find in most of the other synth types that appear here. It's a good bet that once you understand the principles, you'll be tempted to tweak sounds, and in doing so, dive down the rabbit hole of sound design.

Additive Synthesis

Whereas subtractive synthesis starts with a harmonically rich waveform and refines the sound by removing frequencies, additive synthesis builds sound by adding the simplest sonic elements. If subtractive synthesis can be likened to sculpting, additive synthesis is more like pointillist painting: detailed and complex. The technique derives from the work of Jean-Baptiste Joseph Fourier, who posited that any sound could be analyzed as the sum of multiple sine waves.

Drawbar organs are a simplified form of additive synthesis; the instrument's stops create different frequency sine waves, and altering the drawbar changes the length of the stop, varying its frequency. For the most part, though, organs are comparatively simple in their sound production. Fully implemented, additive synthesis is technically capable of reproducing virtually any sound with incredible realism. Because that kind of synthesis requires lots of computing power, additive synthesis usually combines some other synthesis techniques or a few compromises in design.

What are the compromises? For starters, sounds in nature usually consist of sounds that are not in any whole-number relationship to the harmonics; ladies and gentlemen, I give you the crash cymbal. In real-life acoustic sounds, each frequency has its own complex envelope; some frequencies die out over time, others linger a bit. One early additive synthesizer gathered harmonics into groups that you could route to one of four envelope generators. Almost every additive synth made commercially included a subtractive component to make sound design a bit easier. On the commercial realm, the Kawai K5000 series was a wonderful merger of additive and subtractive synthesis, and it shouldn't be too difficult to score one in the used-instrument marketplace, but I know of nothing currently on the market. The software instrument market, however, abounds with some fine synths that produce sounds that are worlds apart from conventional subtractive synths.

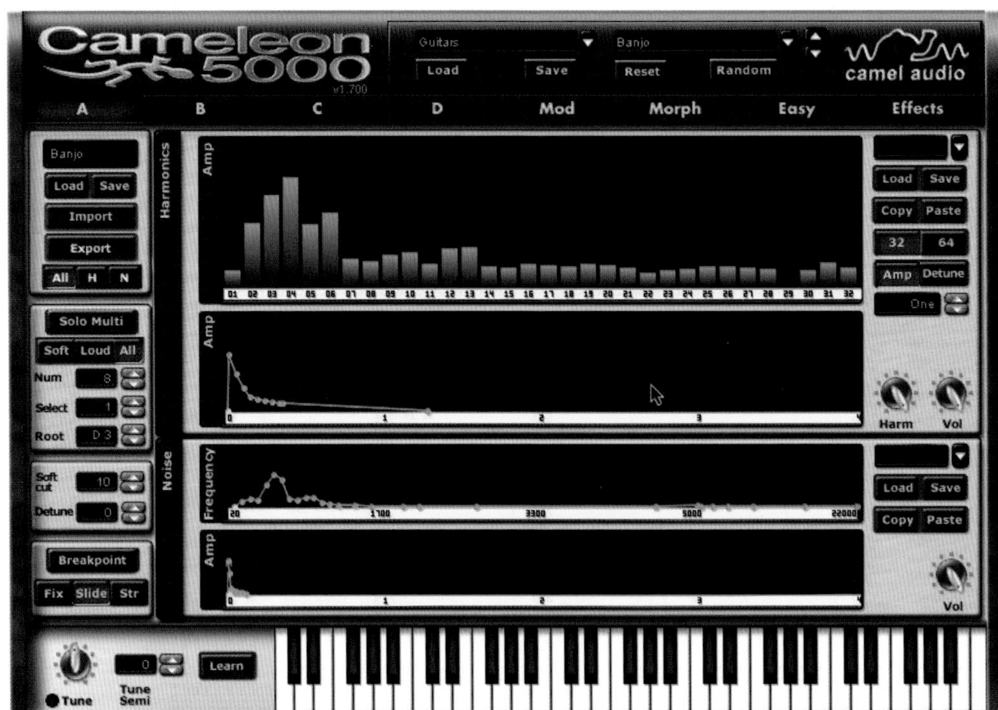

Here's a sampled banjo waveform reproduced in Camel Audio's Cameleon CA5000 additive synthesizer, with the fundamental at the left and harmonics to the right. I can click on any of the frequencies and adjust its amplitude, thereby changing its timbre.

Digital FM Synthesis

FM is an acronym for *frequency modulation*, which is nothing particularly esoteric; unless we're speaking in monotone, we modulate frequency in our conversations all the time. Vibrato is caused when we deliberately and repeatedly move a sound above and below a center pitch, and it is a good example of frequency modulation as it applies to synthesis. Even with the fastest human vibrato, our ears can register the variations in pitch. Synthesizers often create a vibrato effect by imposing the shape and speed of one oscillator (an LFO) over another oscillator. Shape influences the tonal character of the modulation, and speed controls the rate. That's all well and good, but as the rate speeds up, it causes the changes in pitch to occur more rapidly, until the waveform takes on the characteristics of a single, buzzy-sounding waveform. Once we create the vibrato at higher rates, the vibrato cycles are so close together that it creates *sidebands*—additional frequencies that combine to create a single, more complex waveform. If you have access to a synthesizer, you can easily demonstrate the phenomenon simply by finding a patch with vibrato, and pushing modulation depth and speed to the maximum amount; if you do this gradually, it's easy to hear the transition from wobbling pitch to a sound not unlike a dentist's drill. Once again, you can't hear the LFO, but its presence is made known through its effect on the normal oscillator.

FM theory divides the two categories of oscillator into *carriers* (the oscillator you can hear) and *modulators* (the oscillator creating the influence). Modular synthesizers used FM to some degree (in a simple analog form), and we can find it on a number of subtractive instruments, too, but it really came into its own with the Yamaha DX7, which took the concept much further than its older siblings.

The success of the DX7 spawned plenty of variations on the theme, but the basic premise is a system of six oscillators—Yamaha called them *operators*—whose signal flow could be configured in different ways to yield a varying number of carriers and modulators. Based on that signal flow (*algorithms* in Yamaha-speak), you could create sounds no other synth could create at the time; hyper-realistic bells, percussive synths, and electric pianos were the mainstay of the DX7. From the mid '80s through the '90s, you could hardly find a pop ballad that didn't start with the DX7's crystalline, sparkling take on electric pianos.

The DX7 grouped its complement of carriers and modulators into 32 Algorithms, depicted at the upper right of the keyboard's top panel. Carriers are at the bottom of each algorithm.

Unlike most synths of its time, the DX7 used no filters, but instead relied largely on the balance between modulator and carrier output (along with other factors) for shaping its sounds. There were a number of hardware successors to the DX7—the majority of which came from Yamaha itself, but Casio and Korg had some interesting variations on the theme. In fact, Korg sold a MIDI guitar system with a built-in rackmount FM synth, and Casio's last MIDI guitar had an FM synth built into the guitar itself! Digital FM's initial popularity has declined somewhat, but as of this writing, Yamaha has at least two hardware instruments in production, and there are numerous software instruments that rely on the technique.

Samplers, Sample Playback, and Wavetables

Take a subtractive synthesizer and replace the standard complement of saw, triangle, pulse, and sine waves with prepared digital-sound recordings, and you have a typical sample-playback synthesizer. Add the ability to record and add your own choice of sounds, and you have a sampler. Sampling is particularly adept at reproducing musical instruments, albeit in a sort of snapshot-based way, and that carries its own set of limitations; that six-second sample of Jimi Hendrix playing a single note will sound pretty silly if you are trying to build a lengthy solo with it.

Consider a sampled guitar: What would you need to play it convincingly? Guitars are extremely nuanced instruments; tone can vary based on distance between the bridge and the neck, how hard the note is played, and even what string the note is played on. Unlike keyboards, which can only play one note per key, guitars can offer multiple choices for the same note, and they all sound different. In theory, you'd need samples that can account for all that behavior.

Because sample-based instruments require memory to hold their samples, there are usually some compromises, and in many cases that's where the synthesis engines come in. For instance, Velocity can close a filter, simulating the softer sound of more lightly played notes, and open up to admit the higher frequencies and overtones of a sound that is played more forcefully. Another technique, called *round robin*, randomizes playback of a few different samples to help mask the repetitiveness of firing off the same sample every time you play the same note.

The evolution of the sampler into the virtual world has made many of these concerns academic; the computer's superior memory capacity and the ability to stream samples directly from disk has enabled gigantic, multi-gigabyte instruments that—when played well—are practically indistinguishable from the real thing. (See Chapter 11, "Composing with MIDI Guitar," for tips.)

When synthesizers hit the marketplace, there was a lot of debate in the music-technology community about whether they were really synthesizers or something in their own class. Once the gear started sporting filters, envelope generators, and other synth paraphernalia, the debate was over. To my way of thinking, samplers are essentially synthesizers with an unlimited source of waveforms. To that end, an enormous industry of companies is happy to sell you anything from pianos, drum kits, and entire orchestras to vintage synthesizers, Hollywood special-effects libraries, tortured metal and junk forged into fantasy instruments, and loops of all kinds— and in fact, just about anything that can move air is fair game for your sampler. And because it is a synthesizer, you can forge these sounds into anything your mind can conceive.

A sampled Dobro is only the start for this imaginative pad from Heavyocity Aeon; played back through Kontakt's powerful sample warping engine, you'd never suspect its origins.

Modeling

In the mid-'90s, the synthesizer world was buzzing (pun intended) with the idea that synthesizers could realistically emulate acoustic and electric instruments—not with a cumbersome load of samples, but by using processing power to reproduce the electronic and acoustic behaviors that produce those sounds. There are a few approaches to modeling synthesis. For example, analog-modeling synthesis starts with computer algorithms describing the actual components of an analog synthesizer. Plucked-string synthesis uses models of stringed instruments, and often details elements such as the stiffness of the strings, size of the resonating chamber, whether the string is bowed, played with a pick or with bare hands, and lots more. Yamaha may have been the first in the commercial marketplace with several physically modeled hardware (as opposed to software) synths. The VL1 was the first of their physically modeled synths out of the gate, and I recall seeing a demo set at NAMM in which two keyboardists were playing a saxophone duet. Saxophone may be one of the hardest instruments to duplicate on a synth, but I was pretty convinced. Several years later, Roland debuted the VG-8—not a MIDI guitar, but a virtual guitar that you actually played with a proprietary cable and your own guitar. If that seems silly on the face of it, consider that the VG-8 offered up a pretty convincing models of all sorts of electric and acoustic guitars at the tap of a pedal, held a number of interesting synth models, supported alternate tunings so you could switch to, say, DADGAD without physically retuning your strings, and hosted a good number of built-in effects. If that wasn't enough, you could build your own à la carte guitars from the components that the VG-8 modeled. A later software update added independently programmable string-bending intervals from the unit's foot pedal.

The editing section of Applied Acoustics String Studio, a physical-modeling synthesizer aimed at emulating stringed instruments.

The Line 6 Variax took the idea of guitar modeling, built it into the guitar, and added a deep software editor that let you store new sounds onboard the guitar itself. Since then, many companies have jumped on the modeling bandwagon, each with proprietary names for their approaches and spawning more acronyms than the Department of Defense. Modeling has expanded to cover drums, mallets, and even hybrid instruments. Banjo-accordions, anyone? Because modeled instruments have so many ways to play, they are covered in a separate chapter of this book (see Chapter 6, "This Year's Model").

Technically speaking, many of the synths I've outlined here are hybrid instruments; the technology has evolved enough to draw from several synth techniques at once. Still, some instruments are so outrageous in their versatility that they deserve special coverage in another section of the book. Because plug-in synths and processors are the most active proving grounds for hybrid instruments I've devoted a special chapter to plug-ins to help you navigate the digital jungle.

CHAPTER 5

Guitar Controllers and MIDI Converters

Guitars do things keyboards can't. How to make your synths play like a guitar. How guitars can use MIDI messages. Reading a MIDI implementation chart. Currently available MIDI guitar systems. How do computers fit in?

For all the awkward history with MIDI and synthesis, the expressive capabilities of MIDI guitar controllers can be considerably more powerful than those of your average keyboard; it just takes a bit of imagination and work. Once you understand that MIDI is almost infinitely malleable, your imagination can take it from there.

How many synthesizer solos mimic guitar sounds and techniques? It happens more frequently than you'd think. MIDI-equipped guitarists are in a unique position here: I have participated in many projects that required authentically played guitar parts, mostly for multimedia projects, musical arranger workstations, and musical auto-accompaniment programs in which an actual recorded guitar was not an option.

Keyboardists have a lot of challenges to overcome in order to get their synths to behave like a guitar. Consider how supple a solid funk rhythm played on guitar sounds; strumming up-and-down chords on a keyboard can be done, but it is often an abstract, tendinitis-inducing, unmusical experience. To belabor the obvious, rhythm guitar parts are best played by guitarists, and believe it or not, some synthesizer sounds work beautifully when strummed with a MIDI guitar.

Around the Bend

The next time you hear a synthesizer solo, pay attention to how many notes will sound at a time. Very often, synthesizer solos are monophonic because they are programmed that way, or because playing more than one note while using the pitch-bend-wheel can sound out of tune. Pitch bend is one of the most distinguishing techniques identified with guitar. Replicating the technique on synthesizers requires finer MIDI-data resolution in order to work convincingly.

Most MIDI messages work with a resolution of 128 possible values. If you are relatively skilled, your bent notes on a traditional electric, non-MIDI guitar will sound smooth and continuous, but if we were to slice that bend into 128 equal parts, they would sound stepped and grainy. For MIDI to get around this "zipper effect," Pitch Bend needs increased resolution. For that reason, Pitch Bend sends an additional byte that increases Pitch Bend resolution from 128 slices to 8,192: 4,096 slices above the center pitch, and 4,096 below (you do play downward bends, don't you?), which should be enough to smooth out the sound. Because of the way MIDI works, bending a note on a MIDI synth will send a stream of events, each event reflecting a minute change in pitch; that's a lot of data, and some MIDI guitars offer the option to thin Pitch Bend transmission, which should work for less bend-intensive performances.

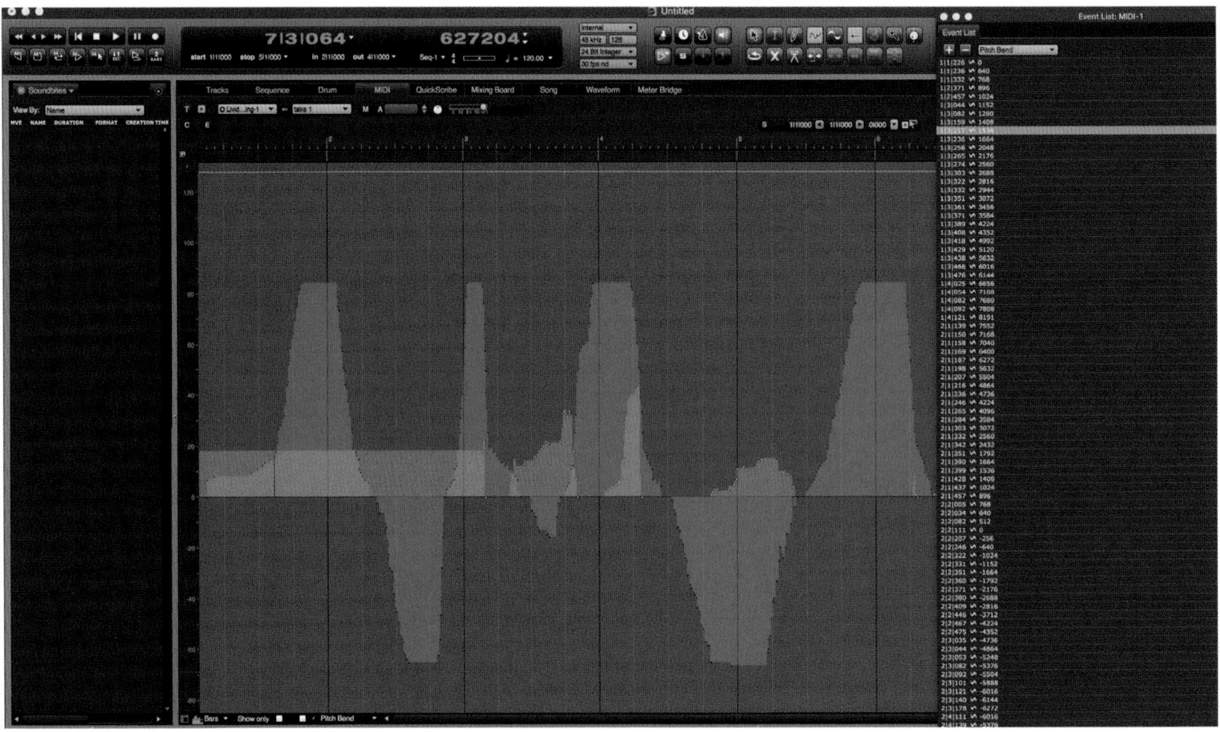

MIDI Pitch-Bend messages as recorded in Digital Performer's Event List. Notice the time frame for each event and the broad range of values.

The complexity of MIDI data notwithstanding, your job as a MIDI guitarist is considerably easier: You need to set a range for the amount of bend you want to send from your guitar, and make sure your synth agrees. In fact, this holds true with any remote controller, such as another MIDI keyboard or desktop controller gadget. If you plan to bend notes as high as an octave above or below pitch, your guitar controller's bend range needs to be set for an octave, and your target synthesizer needs to match that range in order to respond in kind. You'll have a couple of personal considerations in setting this up.

Not everyone bends notes the same way. How high up or down do you bend? I like playing blues, but I rarely bend notes more than four or five half steps. Just to be on the safe side, though, I set my MIDI guitar to bend up to six half steps and make sure that my target synth is set for the same range. If you like to do whammy bar dives, you'll need more, and many MIDI guitars and synths can accommodate up to a two-octave range. (I've even seen ranges of up to 32 semitones on some products.) Keep in mind that the greater the bend range, the grainier the bend may sound; despite MIDI Pitch Bend's enhanced resolution, you are stretching that resolution with every additional half step. Think of enlarging a photo; despite the number of pixels your camera supports, enlarged prints will be grainier than the original size.

There are times when you don't want or need to bend any notes; piano patches and pitched percussion sounds are two examples, but there are other considerations as well. In many cases, if you need to deliver consumer-oriented MIDI files for use in an auto-accompaniment program or keyboard, Pitch Bend data is often proscribed, partly because of data constraints and because it could confuse the settings of a synth with different bend ranges.

The ability of MIDI guitar controllers to send separate streams of data for each string is a huge advantage. As I mentioned in Chapter 3, the Axon converters allowed you to set up zones on the fingerboard that could send different MIDI messages. Zones could be set up vertically per string, or horizontally across the fingerboard, or both. There were some excellent demo patches in the Axon's presets, as well as a few goofy and useless setups. I recall one setup with brass and woodwinds transposed and set to play within their realistic ranges, making it easier to voice authentic-sounding horn-section parts. On the goofy side, there was one that changed randomly between synth patches for every note, and so playing a low E might call up a sax, while the F just above would play an electric piano, F# might play an accordion sound, and so on. I particularly enjoyed the real-time control just under my fingertips, though; it blended naturally with my guitar technique rather than forcing me to hit more pedals as I tried to play.

With the Pitch Bend settings properly set up per string, almost any synth sound can instantly become warmer and more human with the hand's natural vibrato. Speaking of vibrato, contrast the natural vibrato of your fingers with the synthesizer's LFO-induced vibrato; by comparison, the LFO is repetitive and unrealistic next to the human variations in vibrato.

Guitars and guitar controllers equipped with MIDI can do much more than simply play notes, due to the remarkable wealth of control options and flexibility of MIDI data. MIDI can provide guitarists with some impressive techniques for solo performance. For instance, you might think that all those ethereal, infinitely sustaining string and pad sounds will only last as long as your guitar strings vibrate. Think again: Using a keyboard hold pedal somewhere between your MIDI guitar and your synthesizer will let you send MIDI Continuous Controller (CC) number 66: Sostenuto. That pad sound will sustain as long as your foot steps on or latches that pedal. In fact, any subsequent notes played will not affect the notes you are sustaining, so you can solo, playing over sustained chords, if you'd like. Many guitar synths let you set up a second instrument of your choice for soloing—not a bad idea if you'd prefer something more responsive over the typically sedate quality of a slow pad. You can use that same capability to latch on to and sustain drum loops or other rhythmic parts. Many synths offer rhythm tracks that you can trigger with a single note, hit the hold pedal, and solo or comp over it.

It may not be obvious at first, but you can use the guitar's MIDI output to remotely set up different elements of your system. One of the simplest tasks is using your guitar to access different synthesizer sound programs stored in the synth's memory. One of the standard switches on MIDI guitar controllers sends Program Change messages.

I've spoken of the musical catastrophes caused by your guitar sending one range of Pitch Bend while your synth needs a different range to respond properly and stay in tune. Some MIDI guitar converters are able to transmit Pitch Bend Change messages in order to set up the receiving synth with a matching Pitch Bend range.

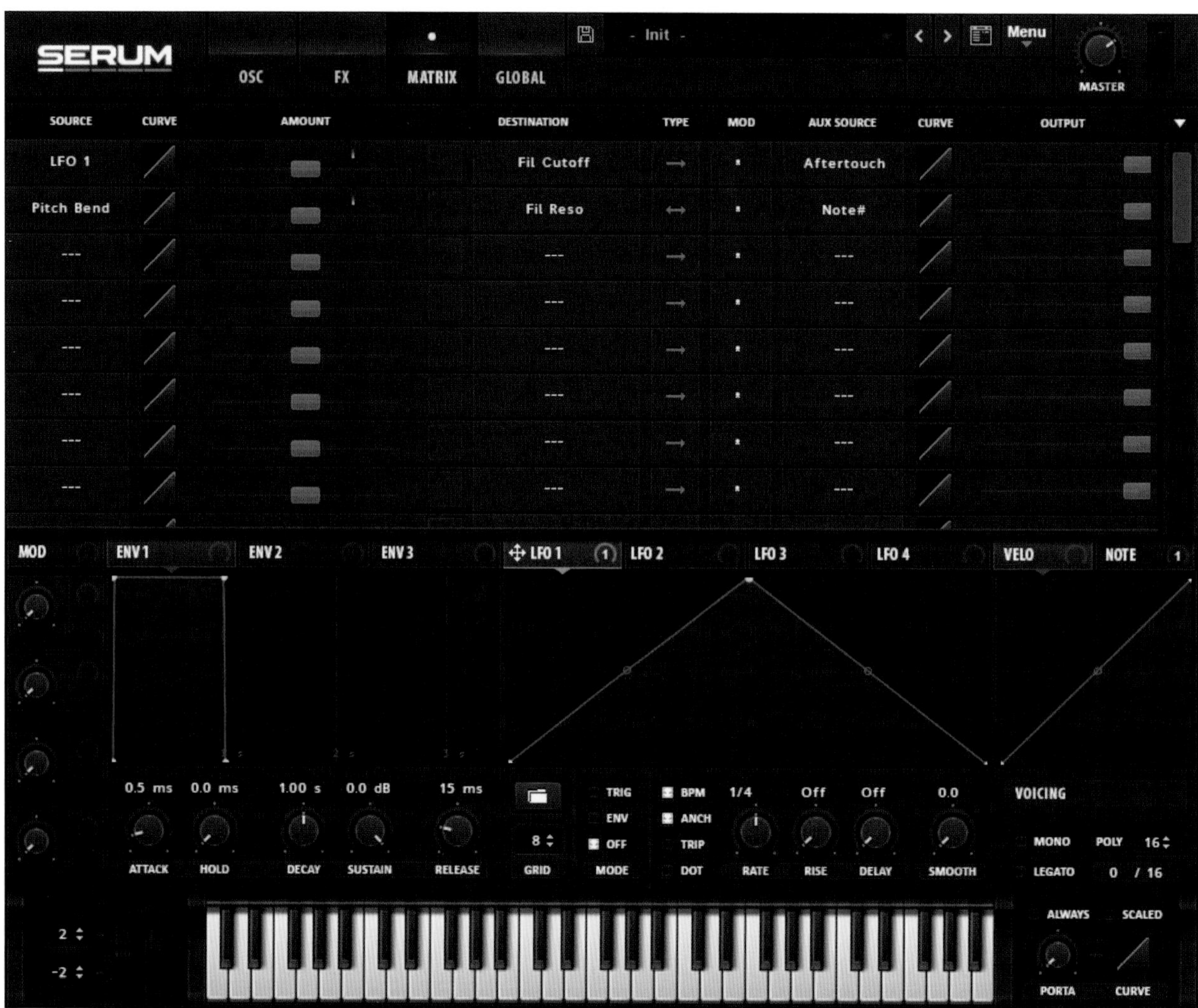

In this screen shot of XFer Serum, an LFO is controlled by CC 01 (Modulation). The LFO, in turn, is used to modulate a filter's resonance. The rate of the LFO is being modulated by incoming MIDI clocks, creating tempo-synced modulation.

There are so many things you can do from a MIDI-equipped guitar beyond sending note data, but even note data can perform powerful transformations beyond simply playing notes. The late, lamented Axon guitar was capable of sending MIDI Control Change data of any kind by virtue of MIDI Note Numbers. One of their presets controlled vibrato by playing higher or lower notes on the guitar. It was not the best possible use of the Axon's capabilities; the upper registers of the guitar produced a rather seasick-sounding pitch modulation, but that was just for demonstration purposes. It was easy enough to reassign the message that was transmitted to MIDI CC number 10, which typically changes a sound's pan position in the stereo field. A value of 1 though 64 would move the sound from the far left to the center, with 65 through 128 moving the sound to the right. That is only one of the many applications you could try. The possibilities are wide open. The target instruments themselves have numbers of ways they can interpret incoming MIDI data. For example, CC number 01 is commonly referred to as *Modulation*, and many synths use that to engage an LFO, which in turn modulates pitch (as I described the Axon Demo patch above). It's not difficult to tweak the synthesizer so that the same LFO can instead modulate a resonant filter, creating a repeating, automatic wah-wah effect. Furthermore, if the LFO can synchronize to an incoming MIDI Clock, the effect will fall in step with a sequencer track or a drum machine.

Not for Synthesizers Only

Of course, a guitar's MIDI control features can extend their reach well beyond synthesizers; the majority of professional effects processors have extensive MIDI capabilities, and there's no reason why your guitar can't be command central.

Many of the same elements that animate synthesizers are found in effects-processing gear; LFOs, filters, and other elements can also respond to MIDI data. In fact, if you aren't taking advantage of your effects processor's MIDI features, you are ignoring a large portion of the instrument's potential.

I find it convenient to, for instance, use CC number 01 to control modulation depth on phase shifters and flangers. In that case, you could route the message to the effect's LFO, which would produce an up-and-down cycle. Alternatively, output the guitar's CC messages directly to the effect's depth parameter. By sending a discrete depth value, you could adjust the phaser's depth to taste. The last example is also a great way to adjust the synthesizer's filter to control the overall timbre of the instrument. The important thing to remember is that as technical as some of this may seem, you can make some incredible music with a more intimate understanding of how MIDI works.

Reading a MIDI Implementation Chart

At this point, you are already on to some pretty cool feats of sonic legerdemain, but there's always a catch. For instance, one of my favorite MIDI controllers is *Aftertouch*, also called *Channel Pressure*. This MIDI message is so named because it is generated by varying downward pressure after the initial keys are played. It—as with just about any other MIDI data—can create virtually any response you desire in a synth: filter or pitch modulation, panning, and volume, to name just a few. You might be thinking that after-pressure on a guitar's strings wouldn't do much more than wear out your hands, and you'd be correct. But as we'll soon see, just about any MIDI command is assignable to any MIDI device, so you could generate Aftertouch from a pedal or control knob. That's important to know. What is also important is that not every synth sends or even responds to Aftertouch, and the reason is often one of cost. Sending Aftertouch from a keyboard requires sensors that are placed on the keybed, under the keys. This often adds considerable cost to less expensive synths, and as a result, many of the lower-end instruments

MIDI Implementation Chart

GUITAR SYNTHESIZER
Model GR-55

Date : September 9, 2010
Version : 1.00

Function...		Transmitted	Recognized	Remarks
Basic Channel	Default Changed	1–16 1–16	1–16 1–16	Memorized
Mode	Default Messages Altered	Mode 3, 4 (M = 6) x **************	Mode 3 x	Memorized
Note Number	True Voice	0–127 **************	x	
Velocity	Note On Note Off	o x	x x	
After Touch	Key's Ch's	x x	x x	
Pitch Bend		o	x	
Control Change	0, 32 1–31 33–63 64–95	o o x o	o *1 o *1 x o *1	Bank Select
Program Change	True #	o 0–127	o 0–127	Program Number 1–128
System Exclusive		o	o	
Common	Song Position Song Select Tune Request	x x x	x x x	
System Realtime	Clock Commands	o x	o x	
AUX Messages	Local ON/OFF All Notes OFF All Sound OFF Reset All Controller Active Sense System Reset	x x x x o x	x x x x o x	
Notes		*1 Can be received only through the Basic channel.		

Mode 1: OMNI ON, POLY   Mode 2: OMNI ON, MONO   o: Yes
Mode 3: OMNI OFF, POLY   Mode 4: OMNI OFF, MONO   x: No

From my Roland GR-55 Manual. (Photograph courtesy of Roland Corporation)

don't even receive the message. Different synthesizers respond to data in different ways. The original Casio CZ101 synthesizer—a very popular synth among MIDI guitarists at one time—was hard-wired to respond to MIDI CC 01 (Modulation) by producing vibrato only. Worse, it interpreted the message as a switch—vibrato on or off—when it should be variable. It can be disappointing and aggravating to find that an instrument you have purchased doesn't quite have the features you need.

Fortunately, MIDI protocol is very well documented, thanks to the MIDI Manufacturer's Association. Virtually every piece of MIDI hardware (and often software) provides a list of MIDI commands it transmits and receives and how it sends or responds to that data. This is called a MIDI implementation chart, and it's usually in the same place—at the back of the user's manual or in a separate document. It's also pretty easy to understand.

Let's examine some features of the MIDI implementation chart for the Roland GR-55 guitar synthesizer. Column one lists the MIDI function, followed by a column each representing whether the device transmits that function (Transmitted), whether it is capable of responding to that data (Recognized), and any particular conditions for that data (Remarks).

As indicated at the bottom of the table, a O in a column means that function is supported, and an x means it is not. So, for example, the first row tells you that the GR-55 can transmit or recognize data on any of the 16 MIDI channels. "Default" means what is available when the unit is powered up, and "Changed" simply means you can set it to transmit or receive on any basic MIDI channel. "Memorized" in the Remarks section means that settings to assign the unit to any given basic MIDI channel will be retained in the unit's memory.

Under Mode, you can see that the GR-55 transmits Mode 3 or Mode 4. As noted at the bottom of the page, these modes correspond to the MIDI modes, detailed in Chapter 2. As indicated in the Remarks section, you can set the mode of the unit, and it will be remembered. Note that Mode Messages are not sent or understood, which simply means that any external synthesizers will not receive messages to change MIDI modes, so if you want to change a connected synthesizer to respond properly, you'll need to do that in the synth's mode settings. Likewise, the GR-55 does not change modes from external messages. Peering down the Recognized column, you may notice that there are a number of features annotated with the x; this points to the unfortunate fact that the GR-55's built-in synth does not respond to incoming Note and Velocity messages. That means that you cannot use the GR-55 synthesizer for sequencer playback, and that the only way to trigger the GR-55 synthesizer is with the guitar connected to the unit via the 13-pin cable. System Exclusive is transmitted and received, and that's important if you want to save end edit patch data. As the unit has no built-in sequencer or drum machine, Song position and Song Select are irrelevant. As for Clock, the zeroes mean that the GR-55 can be synchronized to clock pulses sent from an external sequencer or drum machine; it can also serve as the master clock, rather than relying on an external clock-driven device. The unit has tempo-synched effects, too, such as delay, gating, and chorus. ■

Currently Available MIDI Guitar Systems and Components

MIDI guitar systems fall into two main types: à la carte component systems, in which you assemble your system from an assortment of controllers, guitar-to-MIDI converter units, and synthesizers; and guitar synthesizer packages, such as Roland's GR-55. The latter bundles a programmable floor unit with a self-contained synthesizer, effects, and MIDI output. These packages often bundle a divided magnetic pickup. Basic controls on the pickup include a pair of program bank selection buttons, a knob to regulate MIDI Volume, and a switch that toggles between a guitar audio signal with no MIDI being sent, MIDI data plus audio signal, and MIDI data only. Add your guitar of choice, and you have a turnkey MIDI guitar and synthesizer system.

Roland's most recent guitar synthesizer is a floor unit with a good-sounding sample-based synth, a decent number of modeled instruments, and programmable alternate tunings. One of the coolest features is that you can use the alternate tunings or create your own to play external synths.

Some manufacturers build guitars with divided pickups already mounted. Some, such as the ones marketed as "Roland-Ready," offer guitars with magnetic divided pickups premounted between the bridge and the guitar's bridge pickup; Fender's GC-1 is a genuine Strat that exemplifies this design.

Godin offers a range of guitars with piezoelectric pickups mounted in the bridge. Notice the programmable synthesizer controls mounted on the guitar top, near the neck. (Photograph courtesy of Godin Guitars)

Godin markets a line of "Synth Access" instruments that offer six individual piezoelectric pickups mounted in a saddle next to the bridge. Unlike the magnetic divided pickups, the strings sit directly on the piezoelectric element. The advantages to this kind of system include minimalized crosstalk between pickup elements, and the need to readjust the distance between strings and pickup is eliminated. This configuration arguably helps to improve accuracy in tracking. Another company, Brian Moore Guitars, specializes in guitars with built-in pickups and offers standard and customized instruments, including the iAcoustic guitar, and instruments with an additional USB port for shunting audio directly to computers.

Recently, Fishman released its TriplePlay system, which provides a pickup and control unit and built-in wireless transmitter with a USB receiver. Originally intended to interface strictly with computers, Fishman's TriplePlay bundles a generous complement of music software

Here's my personal MIDI guitar setup: The Fishman TriplePlay pickup and wireless transmitter is mounted in front of the bridge and feeding the receiver, which is inserted into the Fishman FC-1 foot controller.

and software instruments to get you started. More recently, the company released the FC-1 controller, which frees the unit from computer dependencies, adds programmable footswitches and jacks for additional pedals and for blending the guitar signal. The best part of this system is that it was designed in collaboration with Andras Szalay, who was largely responsible for the Axon Guitar-to-MIDI converters, and it's no surprise that this system tracks like a dream.

Guitar-like systems, such as the Synthaxe, have evolved into incredibly powerful MIDI controllers that forgo magnetic and piezoelectric pickups for switches and buttons arrayed along the fingerboard and string-like contacts on the body that let you strum and pick with arguably less ambiguity and more

The YouRock YRG1000 is a surprisingly affordable but well-implemented guitar-like controller. (Photograph courtesy of YouRock Guitar)

Harvey Starr's controllers offer incredibly deep MIDI control, including pressure-sensitive fret buttons, palm controllers, MIDI whammy bars, and much more. Starr will also build custom controllers upon request. (Photograph courtesy of Starr Labs)

speed when converting and sending MIDI data. Think of these as keyboards configured like a guitar. These are excellent interfaces to the world of MIDI for those who are more comfortable on guitar than they are with traditional keyboards. They run the gamut from very affordable, plastic-housed units, like the YouRock, to more expensive but deeply programmable high-end controllers, such as those from Starr Labs that place an ingeniously ergonomic array of trigger and control options beneath your fingers. Common to all these systems is a mode that allows tapping the fingerboard without picking the strings. You might find this to be the ideal system, fusing familiar guitar techniques with the unambiguity of a keyboard.

I never quite adjusted to the feel of the instrument; although the string tension is adjustable, it never quite felt natural to me. You will also miss out on the blend of synthesizer sounds with your guitar, a big piece of the electronic guitarist's art. Still, these are worthy additions for those who want to feed guitaristic MIDI data into a sequencer without much of the cleanup that traditional MIDI guitar involves.

Still less expensive is Jam Origin's MIDI Guitar software application, which simply takes your guitar's audio input, sorts out the frequencies, and generates MIDI data. You can tailor the software's response to your playing to produce more accurate and articulate tracking, and

For uncomplicated MIDI access to synths in your computer or mobile device, it's hard to beat Jam Origin's MIDI Guitar app, which translates the monophonic signal from your guitar's ¼-inch jack into polyphonic MIDI data.

considering how difficult analyzing notes from a guitar without a divided pickup can be, the program works exceedingly well. MIDI Guitar is available for computers as well as mobile devices. It is great fun calling up a synth in my iPad Pro without the need for an excessive amount of outboard MIDI gear.

I've outlined a number of ways to enable your guitar for the world of synthesis. These days, most of us have computers and mobile devices, but most of us rarely consider the tremendous advantages they afford the modern guitar player.

How Do Computers Fit In?

Computers are marvelous devices. As a powerful general-purpose machine, they can help balance your checkbook, stay in touch with friends, shop, watch video, and most importantly for us—they can support just about any musical activity you might need. If we narrow our focus to guitar, there is still a vast landscape of guitar-oriented software and hardware for the computer. For our purposes, let's take a quick look at software relevant to MIDI and guitar before we examine hardware. We can examine specific examples in ensuing chapters.

Guitar-Processing Software

Native Instruments Guitar Rig and IK Multimedia Amplitube side by side. Both let you set up anything from a simple guitar and amp to remarkably complex effects chains.

With the modern-day computer's processing power comes hardware modeling of electronic components, in which the computer simulates the behavior of an electronic device's tubes, transistors, capacitors, and just about anything else, with the ability to assemble the virtual components in a proper virtual signal flow. One of the logical outcomes of this is signal-processing software for guitar. The field is rife with delays, both digital and analog-modeled, amp simulators of all kinds, distortion, reverb, rackmount, multi-effects units, stomp boxes designed to emulate the most popular hardware models, and packages that let you build your own rack of effects or pedalboards. All the major digital audio workstation packages come with plenty of guitar-oriented plug-ins. In fact, in addition to standard stomp box models and effects processors, MOTU's Digital Performer actually provides an ambient virtual room with mics and amps. You have a choice of various condenser and dynamic mic models, and you can point them in any direction you choose, and vary your distance from the amps—which are modeled after popular amps and heads. The models and room ambiences sound terrific. Whether you are recording in a studio or a bedroom, the software allows you to capture the vibe of a well-regulated studio.

If you simply want to process your guitar without the added overhead of a DAW software host, many companies, such as ILIO, IK Multimedia, and Native Instruments, have you covered with stand-alone processor software that lets you build anything from a simple amp-and-cabinet setup to a huge rack filled with models of boutique processing gear and a boatload of great amps to play them through. The best part of these packages is that they can also be called up as plug-ins in your favorite recording software application.

Editor-Librarian Software

One of the beauties of synthesizers is their chameleon-like nature. As you run through the instrument's presets, you can usually get a sense of just how malleable synthesizer sounds are, and it's a safe bet that you will be tempted to dive in and try your hand at creating your own sounds. Creating, saving, and managing your own sounds are pretty easy tasks if you are working with software instruments because all the synth's parameters are on display, and the graphics help to provide a good sense of the instruments' signal flow. Saving your sounds inevitably organizes them in a folder of user patches, and these are generally viewable in the instrument's browser or, at worst, are a few mouse clicks away. If you are performing, you can load custom banks of sounds and arrange them according to your set list.

Hardware synthesizers pose a different set of problems. A good many instruments are menu-driven, with parameters buried under pages and submenus that you access through a single view screen. In those cases, programming can be a clumsy and counterintuitive deep dive through menus, submenus, and pages. Try as they might, few hardware instruments streamline the process or provide management of new sounds and banks like a computer-based editor-librarian. Editor-librarians let you load, create, edit, store, and transmit all synthesizer data. The best aspect of editor-librarians from a beginner's sound-design standpoint is that all the elements of the synthesizer's sound-shaping apparatus are on display, usually in a far more intuitive way than the actual instrument may provide. Elements that seem abstract are more tangible when displayed. A good example is the envelope generator; some editors graphically depict the contour of the envelope's development over time and give you the option of typing in a value or simply clicking on a point on the envelope and dragging. Is the sound supposed to have a slow attack? Click on the first peak of the envelope graphic and drag to the right to suit your taste. Does the sound linger too long after you release the keys? Drag the release point to

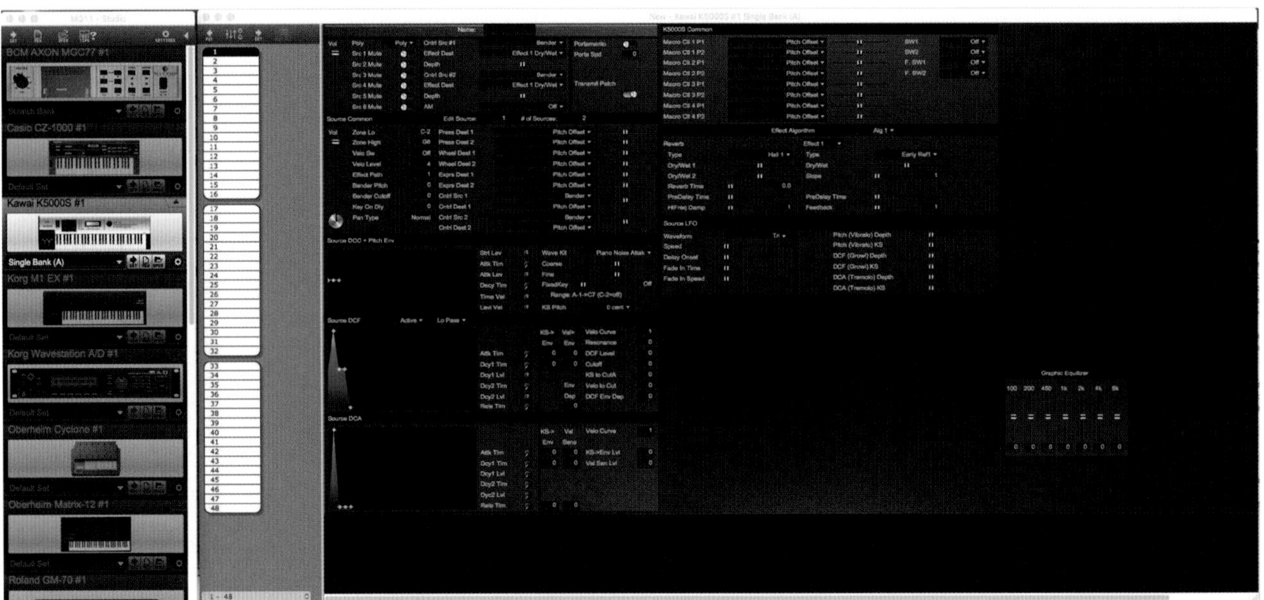

Screenshot of Sound Quest's MIDI Quest Universal editor-librarian. Selecting an instrument from the panel on the left brings up all of its editable parameters.

the left. At that point, you might want to navigate to the oscillator section to test out a different waveform; you are rarely any more than a click away on the software editor, as opposed to several pages away on a small display panel. All the changes you make are instantly updated on the synthesizer, so you can play the instrument and test your sound as you develop it.

Editor-librarians come in two basic types: single-device, which focuses on a single synth or device, and universal, which can handle multiple synthesizers and setups. There are only a few universal editor-librarians on the marketplace, and there are bound to be gaps in the number of instruments that are supported, so be sure to check whether all the devices you want to edit are covered.

If you own several synthesizers, universal editor-librarians offer the best bang for the buck. When I ran a full-time MIDI studio, I was able to retrieve all the settings from every synthesizer in use on a session, store it as a single bundle in the computer, and move on to my next session. When the client returned to resume that original session, I had only to load all the customized patches in the session and send them to their respective synths in one pass. The process took less than five minutes. That ability alone is reason enough to own a universal package.

If you plan to use only one or two synthesizers, the expense of universal software might be more than you want to pay. In that case, you have a wide field to choose from. There are plenty of commercial, shareware, and freeware editor-librarians supporting instruments past and present. If you just want to store synthesizer patches, there are a few software programs to store and organize raw System Exclusive messages. Generally, such packages have bare-bones user interfaces and require that you initiate any transmission of patch data from the instrument. That's a pretty simple operation, but not nearly as simple as requesting your patches directly from the computer.

Take Note

If you're a composer, work with a band, or gather other musicians to record your projects, you will eventually want to consider a music notation program. These range from simple, guitar-oriented tablature programs and chord-chart generators to complex, professional-level, publication-quality scoring packages. I could write volumes on any one of them; in fact, volumes have been written on most. See Chapter 12 for a few examples.

CHAPTER 6

This Year's Model

Why physical modeling? Guitar modeling, V-Guitars, Variax, modeling software examples.

Why Physical Modeling?

There are a number of reasons why the marketplace for synthesizers is dominated by sample-based, digital instruments. For starters, they are capable of detailed, realistic, and playable reproductions of natural acoustic sounds; if a keyboardist needs a piano for a club date, they will choose a digital, sampled piano rather than try to re-create one with analog synths or other means. Sampling is also great for reproducing drum kits, guitars, string ensembles, and more.

But sampling has its limitations. I'm oversimplifying, but you can liken sampled instruments to the illusion caused by a cartoon flip book. In that case, individual pictures comprise motion and action. With a sampled instrument, many samples create sonic movement. Think of each sample as a snapshot, a sound captured in every detail for a brief moment. As we've seen, though, naturally occurring sounds are variable, not static. Every time we hear that sample in all its perfection, we become less convinced of its authenticity. Samplers can successfully navigate problems such as these by adding more samples, longer samples, subtle variations on the original samples, and numerous articulations, but the cost is more memory and the additional storage space that sample playback often requires. Most significantly, though, creating a convincing emulation of a physical instrument requires a number of actions that are not physically related to the way the actual instrument is played. For instance, emulating the act of playing closer or further from a guitar's bridge would rely on keys that switch sampled articulations, the use of a modulation wheel or expression pedal, or some other form of modulation, whereas you would simply play a physical guitar closer or further from the bridge.

Computers excel at creating mathematical models, however, and modeled instruments are flourishing, partially because they require far less storage space, are less memory-intensive, and can often surpass samplers in re-creating the electronic and acoustic nuances of the instruments and hardware they are designed to emulate. For modeled guitars, the sound starts with the plucked string, whose original sound is passed through multiple filters, each designed to emulate the tonal characteristics of the target guitar by way of impulse responses—basically, a digital image derived from sampling a device, which is then superimposed over the original signal.

The way you pluck, whether picked or with bare fingers, affects the reproduction of the sound, which is reshaped by the modeling algorithms: Are the pickups vintage single-coil types? Is the guitar hollow, semi-hollow, or solid-body? To my way of thinking, modeled instruments have the edge over their sampled siblings. For one thing, many of the features that analog synths enjoy, such as pulse width and continuously variable waveshapes, are easily reproduced in modeled analog synths and are not dependent on more samples and other tricks. Several physically modeled software guitars realistically simulate the changes in tone when varying picking distance between bridge and neck. Natural variations created by dynamic playing in acoustic and electric pianos and guitars sound, play, and feel more continuous and natural with modeled instruments.

Maybe the most interesting aspect of modeling is the multitude of applications afforded to the modern guitarist, and they extend well beyond the role of traditional synthesizers. Arguably the most dramatic development from the guitarist's standpoint is guitar modeling, which debuted in the mid '90s with Roland's first V-guitar—or Virtual Guitar—the Roland VG-8, as described in Chapter 4. Since then, Roland and its subsidiary, Boss, have given us several variations on the theme. Roland dubs its virtual guitar (and other) modeling engines with the acronym COSM, which stands for *Composite-Object-Sound Modeling*. Two of its current instruments are the Roland GR-55 and the Boss GP-10. With V-guitars, you connect your guitar directly to the unit by means of a 13-pin cable—there is no MIDI involved. Instead, COSM processes your guitar playing in real time.

The major advantage of these instruments, in contrast to playing sampled instruments, is the direct translation and articulation of the guitarist's natural playing techniques. Playing harmonics elicits harmonics, bending notes and vibrato is continuous and smooth, and varying the picking hand smoothly and immediately alters the tone of the instrument without software-switching techniques. The Boss SY-300 is a modeling instrument of another stripe, and although it is not a V-guitar product it does some pretty impressive things with guitar. For anyone who has any experience with MIDI guitar or other guitar-synthesizer systems, playing the modeled sounds through these units provides a direct, tactile approach that few sampled, MIDI-triggered sounds can provide.

GUITAR ROLE MODELS

Modeling an instrument presumes that the goal is to emulate a specific instrument. As such, you will see models whose names bear a close resemblance to a hardware instrument, a brand name, a popular artist who has been associated with the instrument, or the provenance of a particular device's vintage. Unless instruments are licensed by the original manufacturer, the designers of the model are not allowed to name their creations exactly the same as the hardware instruments. Consequently, an MA28 is not a Martin D-28, no matter how close it may sound to the target instrument, and Lester's Banjo is not a Gibson Mastertone Granada banjo (even if it should have been named after Earl Scruggs rather than his guitar-picking partner, Lester Flatt).

How closely do the virtual guitars resemble their namesakes? Of those I auditioned, the resemblance was startlingly close. To level the playing field as best I could, I used initialized patches with all effects turned off on the Roland and Boss units. The acoustic instruments in the Line 6 Variax were a standout, but it's worth mentioning that if you prefer those extra-light-gauge-slinky strings and a low action, the response of the acoustic-modeled instruments being played on an electric guitar can require a bit of an adjustment in your playing dynamics. ■

Roland GR-55

The GR-55 is the current flagship guitar-synthesizer system of Roland's product line, but it is far more than a guitar synth, housing not only two oscillators of sample-based, subtractive-style synthesis, but a variety of excellent modeled string and synthesizer instruments, capped off by excellent amp and effects models as well.

Compared with earlier ventures into their COSM-based physical modeling, the GR-55 lacks some of the detailed "mix-and-match" capabilities of its predecessors; a modeled Telecaster is just that, with no ability to use pickups from another guitar type or to mount pickups in unorthodox places on the guitar. Still, the GR-55 provides a rich feature set with a variety of models and enough room to customize.

Acoustic-instrument models include steel- and nylon-string guitars, sitar, banjo, and resonator guitars. Dig deeper into the programming menu, and you'll find more specific sound-shaping parameters. For example, steel-string acoustic guitars subdivide into emulations of a Martin D-28 or Orchestra Model guitar, various Gibson acoustic instruments, and a Guild. Electric guitars offer several versions of Stratocaster, a Telecaster, an L4, and several others.

Overall, the models are quite authentic and respond in the same way real guitars do. Bending notes requires no special Pitch Bend adjustments; notes just bend the way you play them. Play a harmonic, and the guitar model will do the same. By contrast, MIDI guitar will simply read the pitch of your harmonic and play the appropriate Note Number.

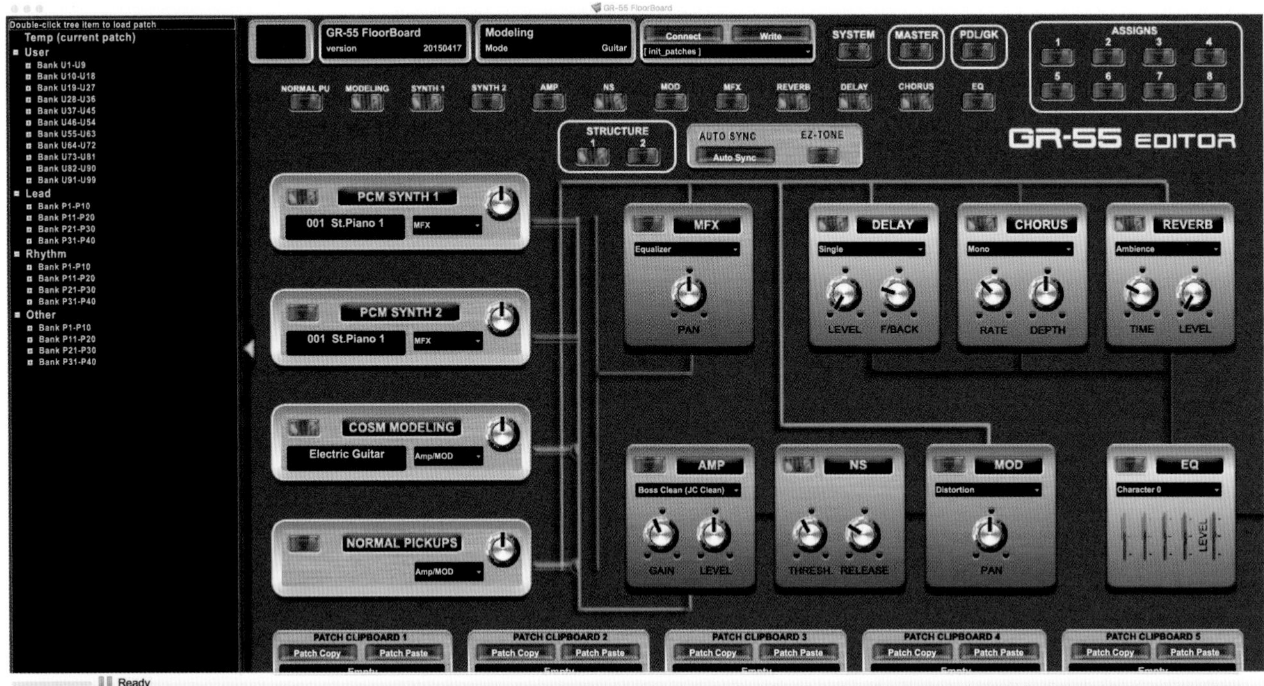

The inner workings of Roland's GR-55 guitar synthesizer as revealed in GR-55 Floorboard software, illustrating its combination of guitar models, coupled with a two-oscillator, subtractive synth, amp and effects modeling, and a sophisticated signal flow.

Die-hard guitarists might rail against the authenticity of the sound, and it may be difficult to argue that every detail of the sound and response is exactly the same, but in fact, the art and science of guitar modeling has advanced to the point where any debate on the matter becomes pretty trivial. To my admittedly biased ear, the modeled guitars create excellent and convincing replicas, if not resistor-and-screw-perfect copies. The original Roland VG-8 had pretty stellar-sounding electric guitars, but the acoustic models always sounded like poorly EQ'd acoustic-electric instruments: thin, overly resonant, and quacky (for want of a better adjective). Although I wouldn't trade a vintage Martin or Gibson acoustic for the GR-55, its acoustic guitars sound full-bodied and authentic. Anyone vaguely familiar with the sonic characteristics of different makes of acoustic guitar could easily identify the instrument, and they are good enough to be used in an exposed environment as well as in a mix.

The depth of programming varies with the type of instrument model selected. For instance, the basic settings for all electric guitars let you choose between front and rear pickup, or some combination thereof (you can assign controls to switch pickups), plus volume, and tone. By contrast, many of the acoustic models offer a Body parameter, which emphasizes the resonance from inside the guitar body; acoustic guitars, due to factors such as the type of wood, the quality of the build from instrument to instrument, the seasoning of the wood, and many other factors, can vary, even from models of the same manufacturer. As a result, you can dial in body resonance to taste.

Physical modeling on the GR-55 lets you adjust a variety of parameters, including the instrument's body cavity and resonance.

Synthesizer models are well-represented, too, with no fewer than a half-dozen different models to choose from, including Organ Wave and Analog GR, a pretty faithful impersonation of vintage GR-300-type tones. Basic settings are variable here, too: The Wave synthesis model offers a choice of saw or square oscillators and a Color knob, which is essentially a tone-control filter, whereas Analog GR has over a dozen different parameters—about as many as the original GR-300! As with the original GR-300, you can choose the synth oscillator, the oscillator plus distortion, or distortion alone. You'll find some typical synthesis controls in this group, but don't be surprised if you don't find a full ADSR; after all, the sounds will sustain for as long as the guitar strings resonate.

Of course, the basic settings are only the beginning of your sound-shaping possibilities. For instance, if you've ever thought about playing a 12-string electric sitar or a Guild acoustic guitar layered with piano and strings, this is your golden opportunity. In fact, most of the models—including synthesis types—offer a 12-string option, the only exception being the electric bass models. Apart from creating spot-on impersonations of typical 12-string guitars, you can also customize the tuning of each string, so designing a 12-string DADGAD-tuned banjo is a piece of cake, if that's your thing.

The instruments aren't the only aspect of the GR-55 that uses physical modeling; among the unit's signal-flow choices is an amp-and-speaker-modeling section that includes microphone models with both axis and distance-placement parameters. The modeled amp systems offer a surprising amount of customization, too. You can choose all-in-one amps or amp-and-cabinet combinations as well as different speaker models. Amp and mic models are titled as closely as legally allowable to the hardware that inspired them—for instance, SLDN models a particular Soldano amp, and TW is a Fender Twin type.

If the models aren't enough for you, bear in mind that the GR-55 includes two sample-based, subtractive synthesizers. You can use either or both, the sounds are quite good, and you have a very respectable set of sound-shaping tools, including full ADSR envelopes for filter and amplifier, with seven filter types.

The instrument also addresses the outside world. Naturally, you can blend your electric guitar signal with the physically modelled sounds and the sampled-content. MIDI output is pretty well accommodated, with a hardware MIDI Out jack and a bidirectional USB jack for MIDI and audio on the rear of the unit to connect to your computer. The USB connection comes in handy for saving and loading your patches, but because it both sends and receives MIDI, it's the ideal connector to play software instruments on your computer or mobile gadget. One extremely cool feature allows any alternate tunings used internally to be transmitted as MIDI notes to external synthesizers. Of course, any control switches and pedals can be assigned to outboard instruments independent of their internal functions. In that way you could, for instance, speed up a Leslie-type rotary effect on an internal sound while adding vibrato to an external synth or sweep its filter. Tracking is very good, and accommodating the instrument's response to your touch is easy. Bonus features include a 20-second looper that accommodates overdubbing and a second USB port that lets you load and play backing tracks.

As powerfully featured as the GR-55 is, it has a few points to consider: Its Pitch Bend range is fixed at two octaves, which works fine for its internal sounds but necessitates adapting any external MIDI devices to that range. There is no standard ¼-inch audio input for your guitar, so the unit cannot be used as a processor without a divided-pickup-equipped guitar and the requisite 13-pin cable. Lastly, the GR-55 provides no way to play its internal synthesizer sounds from anything other than your controller, so they cannot be played back from MIDI tracks in sequencer arrangements.

Boss GP-10

In contrast, the GP-10 Guitar Processor's Pitch Bend is fully adjustable from 0 to 24 semitones, and it can accommodate a standard quarter-inch guitar cable as well as the Roland 13-pin cable. The standard guitar input grants access to the GP-10's formidable effects, but not the instrument models; you'll still need the divided pickup and 13-pin cable for that as well as its MIDI controller features. MIDI tracking of external synthesizers and software instruments is excellent, which is important because, unlike the GR-55, the GP-10 has no built-in, sample-based synth. In lieu of the GR-55's hardware MIDI ports, the GP-10 furnishes a USB port to communicate with your computer as well as software and hardware synths. The GP-10 offers no built-in looper or audio-file player, but the rear of the unit has an Aux In jack, so if you have a CD or mobile audio player, such as an iPad or iPod, your backing tracks are good to go.

What distinguishes the GP-10 from its costlier sibling, however, is a slightly different selection of physically modeled instruments that are supported by a different, and arguably more flexible, feature set.

Foremost is the ability to bend modeled-guitar strings independently, in the manner of a pedal-steel guitar, with the unit's built-in foot pedal. Each string can be programmed to bend up or down by as much as 24 semitones. This feature is independent of alternate tunings and 12-string guitar modes, so the tuning possibilities are practically limitless.

The rear panel of the Boss GP-10 reveals inputs for a standard ¼-inch guitar cable, as well as a 13-pin cable for use with a divided pickup. (Photograph courtesy of Roland Corporation)

Second on my list is the ability to restrict the synthesizer models from polyphonic to monophonic performance. This has nothing to do with Mono mode for MIDI guitar; this simply allows you to play the instrument like an old-school, monophonic synthesizer, complete with swoops and glides between notes. This is a special treat to play on guitar, although it requires some modification of your picking technique—which I cover in Chapter 10.

All of the electric and acoustic guitar models populating the GR-55 are here; two additional modeled instruments grace the GP-10, a fretless guitar and a fretless bass, and these are realistic and expressive. Although the number of modeled synthesizers differs from the GR-55, the GP-10 has a separate class of models grouped under the Poly FX category that cover some of the differences. Whereas most of the GR-55 synth models have relatively scaled-back programming capabilities, GP-10's Oscillator Synth is a standout: It's a two-oscillator, analog-modeling, subtractive synth with resonant filters and three dedicated envelopes—a two-stage envelope for pitch and full ADSR envelopes for the filter and amplitude.

Boss SY-300

This comparatively recent addition to the Roland/Boss stable just might meet the textbook definition of guitar synthesizer, and yet there is no MIDI triggering of notes, no divided pickup, and no 13-pin cable. In fact, all you need to do is connect a standard ¼-inch cable from your guitar and you are up and running. What's more, the output is polyphonic, even though there is no need for a divided pickup.

Boss developers play the technology behind the instrument close to the vest, but they claim that there is no pitch-detection as you would find in a MIDI guitar. However, current products from other hardware and software companies can separate a polyphonic signal into individual frequencies for discrete processing in a number of ways; Celemony Melodyne and Jam Origin MIDI Guitar come to mind.

Because the sounds issuing from your guitar directly feed the synth engine, the SY-300 tracks accurately, with no need to set a Pitch Bend range, and without a hint of delay, all the while reflecting the nuances of bends, hammer-ons, pull-offs, harmonics, and other subtle guitar maneuvers, such as varying your picking hand's position between the neck and the bridge to affect the tone. It's not a stretch to think of the SY-300 as a very powerful signal processor, radically transforming the guitar signal through modeled analog oscillators, filters, and LFOs. Understandably, however, there are some guitar characteristics the SY-300 wasn't meant to handle. Because the device relies on your hands to sustain the strings, the amp and filter envelopes cannot sustain sounds indefinitely. For anyone with any experience with MIDI guitar or other guitar-synthesizer systems, that situation is usually remediable with a sustain pedal, but not on the SY-300.

The Boss SY-300 tracks guitar perfectly without need for MIDI or any special cables. (Photograph courtesy of Roland Corporation)

OSCILLATIN' RHYTHM

Where the GR-55 provides an audio-file player, the SY-300 provides a very simple step sequencer with a maximum of 16 notes per oscillator. There is no dynamic control or programmable duration for individual notes, so the patterns are simple, but you can link each oscillator's sequencer or program independent patterns to create some interesting polyrhythms.

In keeping with the basic ingredients of an analog synthesizer, the SY-300 furnishes a set of standard analog waveforms for its oscillators: sine, triangle, sawtooth, pulse, and a noise waveform. Pulse waveforms characteristically can sound anywhere from reedy or hollow, with all points in between, and the SY-300 is no exception, providing a variety of controls, including the LFOs to continuously vary the timbre. The noise waveform has a Sharpness control, which moves the noise to a more tonal focus, and with full-on sharpness produces a serviceable analog-synth choir sound. Additional parameters depend on the waveform choice and include ring modulation, which tends to add more metallic overtones, and oscillator sync, which creates a resonant, combed and swept tone. You can opt to process the straight guitar signal through any or all of the oscillators or through the filter settings (with limited LFO and amp controls), as well as through the unit's effects. Advanced parameters, such as ring modulation, synch, pitch, and envelope settings, are bypassed.

Here's a little secret: Although the SY-300 is marketed as a guitar synthesizer, it's far more versatile than that. Because your entrée to the unit is a single ¼-inch jack, bass, saxophone, violin, drum machine, synthesizer, vocals, loops, or even other tracks you have already recorded to your computer are viable signals for synthesizer processing. The unit offers several different ways to route audio, including one that can recycle computer audio through its USB port and back out.

SOUND REASONING

When auditioning synthesizers, it's natural to judge the instrument on the quality of the presets. By those accounts, you could be forgiven if the three aforementioned instruments disappoint you. I found that many of the presets were swimming in an excess of distortion and reverb. Fortunately, they are all programmable, and all have free editor-librarian software, so if you are wary of editing sounds from the front panel of the instrument, you'll love the software. There are some terrific sounds lurking in these instruments, all awaiting your development. You can download a dedicated GP-10 or SY-300 version of Tone Studio, editor-librarian software that communicates by MIDI through the USB connection to your computer. You can learn a lot by simply poking around and changing parameters; you won't damage anything, and the factory sounds are always at hand if you get into the high weeds. The software grants access to all editable parameters, so you can dig in pretty deeply and build your own library. Some of the sounds—even the overly saturated ones—might be a tweak or two away from something perfectly useful. There's nothing like the satisfaction of cooking up your own sounds, but even if you don't want to get your hands dirty, there's a sizable library of excellent sounds available online from Roland/Boss, as well as several excellent user forums.

Boss supplies the Tone Studio software, an editor-librarian with versions for the SY-300 and the GP-10, allowing you to create and store new sounds.

Roland supplies librarian software but no editor for the GR-55. Fortunately, you can download GR-55 Floorboard, an excellent freeware editor-librarian, from https://sourceforge.net/projects/grfloorboard/.

Line 6 Variax

Line 6 has a different take on virtual guitars: Why not build the virtual guitar software into an actual guitar? The convenience is undeniable: Simply plug your guitar into your effects and an amp, and you have access to a variety of guitars and tunings with the twist of a knob. Variax focuses on guitars and guitar-family instruments; you'll find no synths, samples, or even basses in their complement of sounds, but they have a few tricks up their sleeve that set them apart from the other modeling instruments I've mentioned so far.

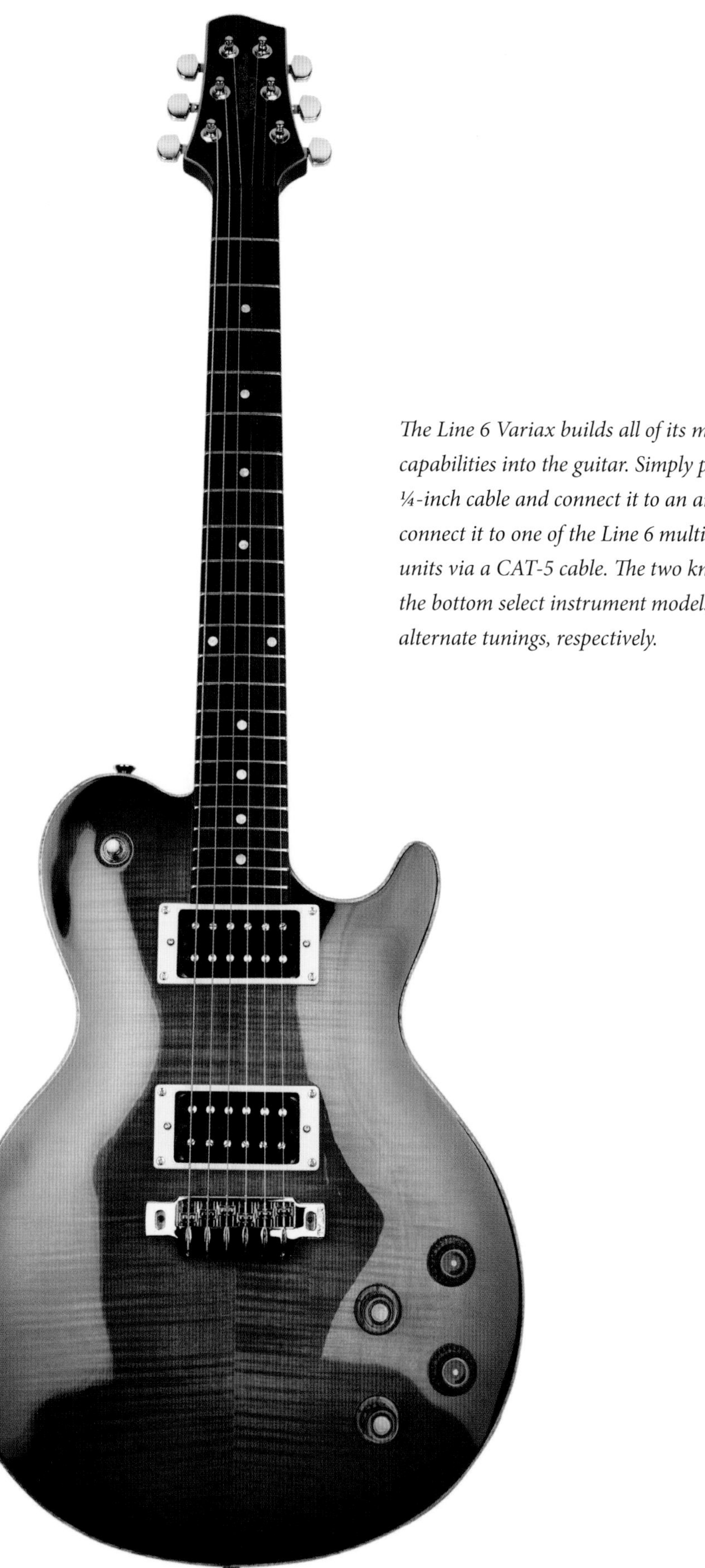

The Line 6 Variax builds all of its modeling capabilities into the guitar. Simply plug in a ¼-inch cable and connect it to an amp, or connect it to one of the Line 6 multi-effects units via a CAT-5 cable. The two knobs at the bottom select instrument models and alternate tunings, respectively.

Variax has no fewer than 14 electric guitars, 5 acoustic guitars, 2 resonator guitars (a Dobro and a steel-body), an electric sitar, and a banjo. You access these by a turn of the selector knob and the pickup selector switch, which of course also accesses the electric guitar pickups. A second selector knob changes tunings on the fly to preset or customized tunings, including 12-string versions of all instruments.

Line 6 offers several Variax guitars, ranging from the Standard, which is a Yamaha-derived, Stratocaster-like instrument, to several fancier guitars in their James Tyler line. Although the Variax Standard is the Line 6 baseline modeled guitar, I found it to be quite playable, with a solid build and plenty of models on hand.

All guitars in the Variax line share the same virtual guitar engine and the same controls. By contrast with current Roland and Boss V-guitars, Variax guitars offer a more mix-and-match approach that can produce some interesting custom guitars, angle each pickup 45 degrees in either direction, and move pickups between the bridge position and the neck—and even onto the neck if desired. It would be difficult to access all of that customization onboard a guitar; instead, all Variax models rely on Variax Workbench HD, an intuitively laid-out software application for customizing your sounds.

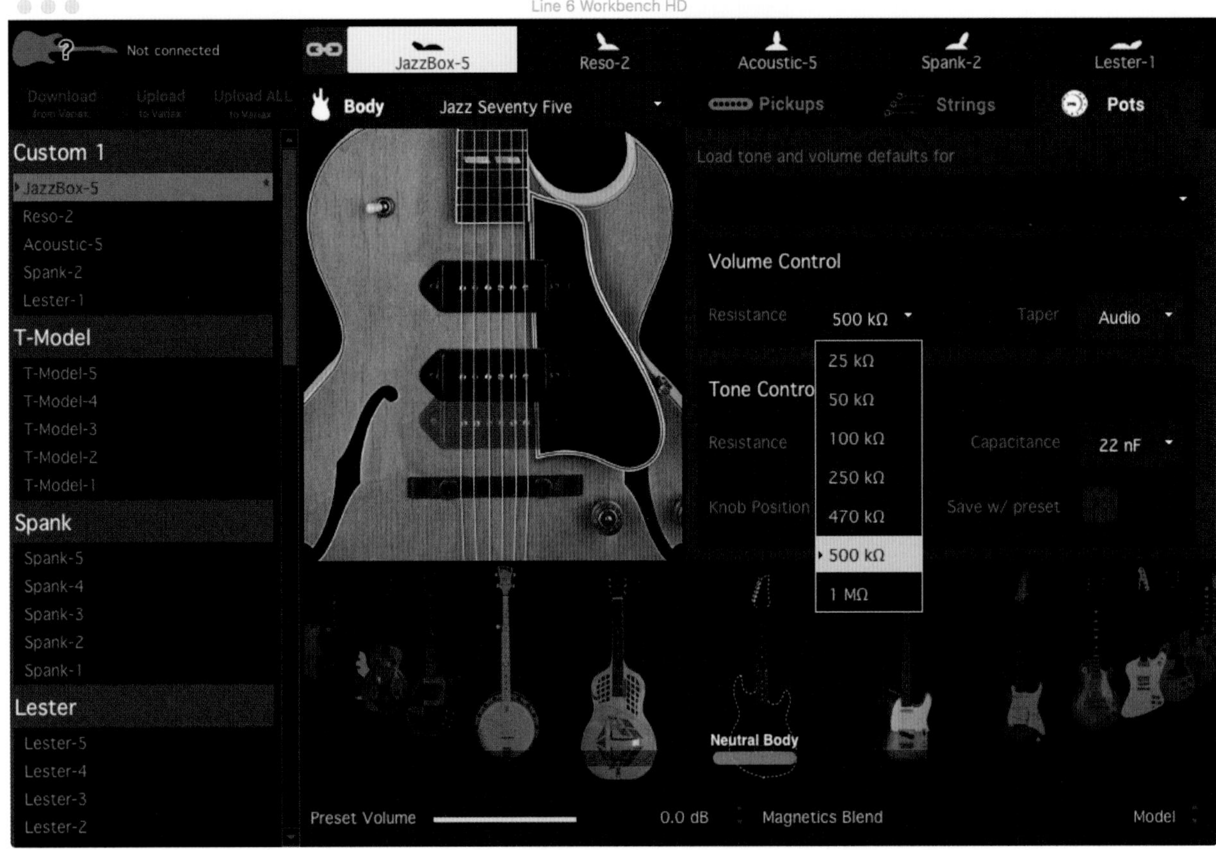

Variax Workbench is a software editor-librarian that lets you edit your Variax guitars on a detailed level.

Line 6 includes its proprietary Variax Digital Interface, which joins an Ethernet-type cable to a USB adapter in order to communicate with your computer. Once the software launches, it scans for the connected guitar and uploads the presets. Once everything is loaded, you are free to mix and match pickups or to drag a new guitar body to an existing pickup set, which you can then configure at will, add pickups to (up to three), and set up alternate tunings for. My wish list for future updates would have to include the ability to add pickups to the acoustic instruments. At this stage, acoustic and electric guitars aren't permitted to mingle very much. Quite often, what might seem unworkable in hardware is easily accomplished in the digital domain.

PROS AND CONS

Each of these systems has standout features, but choosing one depends on what you need. Roland's GR-55 offers the most versatility: guitar and synth modeling, a ready-to-play, built-in sample-based synth, access to external synthesizers through MIDI and USB, an audio-file player for self accompaniment, a looper, and excellent modeled effects, amps, and cabinets. On the debit side, you can't just plug in a guitar and enjoy the effects; you need a guitar that is equipped with a divided pickup.

The Boss GP-10 has no built-in sampled synth but enjoys USB and MIDI connectivity, great modeled sounds, more flexible modeled synths, a unique, foot-controlled programmable string bender, killer fretless bass and guitar models, and a terrific effects section that you can send any guitar through.

Also from Boss, the SY-300 offers a next-generation analog modeling synthesizer that you can play with any guitar and a standard guitar cable and enjoy accurate, lightning-fast response. Better yet, anything you can pass through the SY-300 is fair game, including bass, violin, saxophone, voice, previously recorded tracks—in fact, anything with a strong enough instrument-level signal—is fair game for playing the synth or just for passing through its admirable effects chain. Unfortunately, it will not help you sequence MIDI tracks or play other MIDI instruments—the SY-300 is not a MIDI guitar, and that's a serious limitation if you want to sequence synth parts with your guitar.

Likewise, Line 6 Variax instruments have no MIDI access other than editing, storing, and retrieving of patches on your computer. There are no synthesizer sounds, virtual or sampled. What they do have, however, is the most comprehensive selection of modeled guitars, with deep programmability and a wider selection of virtual guitars than the others. Plus, it's hard to deny the plug-and-play convenience of alternate guitars and tunings with no need for a floor unit or bulky 13-pin cables. The Variax also has no built-in digital effects, but before you dismiss it out of hand for that reason, consider that the Variax Digital Interface is capable of much more than storing and editing guitar models; it brings additional capabilities to the Variax in conjunction with Line 6's justifiably acclaimed effects processors (see Chapter 7 for more).

Soft Sell

Although we'll cover modeling a bit more in the software instruments sections, it's worth mentioning that there are a number of software instruments that model guitars, some with a great deal of realism. One standout is Applied Acoustics Strum GS-2. You might question the value of such an instrument when you can presumably play guitar, but the reality is that because MIDI is so pliable in terms of tempo and key, that it's a simple matter to lay down convincing guitar tracks in your sequencer for accompaniment, practice tracks, or even background parts.

Strum provides three ways to play. Keyboard mode is suited for single-string lines, and you can control common guitar articulations, such as hammer-on and pull-off maneuvers, legato-style playing, and note bending. Although it can serve quite well as a lead instrument, Strum's Keyboard and Loop modes are ideal for recording great custom rhythm parts. In Keyboard mode, you simply hold a chord, choose the inversions you want, and tap out single-key rhythms on the upper and lower octaves of the keyboard to play up-and-down strums, hand-muted rhythms, and bass notes.

In Loop mode, Strum loads a handful of preset rhythms stored as MIDI files; you can hold down chords, and the software does the heavy lifting for you, playing rhythm patterns and

Applied Acoustics Strum GS-2 is a software instrument that accurately models acoustic and electric guitars. The edit window provides some insights into the complexities of modeling acoustic and electric guitars.

arpeggios in real time, or you can drag MIDI files into the associated track to arrange them. It's worth emphasizing that GS-2 strums and patterns sound remarkably authentic.

Modeled guitars range from acoustic and acoustic experimental to electric clean, crunch, and distortion and electric DI. In some instances, the names of specific instruments are invoked, with titles like "Strat" and "Paul," but compared against the hardware units, they are more like generalized impressions of those instruments rather than true emulations. Nonetheless, they are utterly convincing as guitars, and there's plenty of opportunity to tweak sounds to taste, including a decent set of guitar-oriented effects, such as reverb, chorus, distortion, delay, and more. The software's logically laid-out programming section details how guitars produce sound, down to specifics such as the type of picks used (or choose fingers), playing position between neck and bridge (you can control this in real time), Non-harmonic string content, depth of palm-muting effect, choice of single-coil or humbucker pickups, and much, much more. Even if you are a seasoned guitarist, Strum GS-2 may be the fastest and most rewarding way to put great rhythm-guitar tracks together without picking up your guitar.

Other software offers plucked-string models, but GS-2 focuses on emulating guitars, whereas the others, including String Studio 2 and Tassman, are more generalized instruments. UVI Falcon offers plucked-string synthesis in conjunction with impulse modeling to create a bevy of fanciful, guitar-derived sounds, along with other sonic wonders, but rather than give away the whole show here, look forward to Chapter 9, which covers a selection of plug-ins and synthesizers in more detail.

CHAPTER 7

Guitar Processors

A child's garden of effects, reverb and delay, filters, dynamics, modulation. Multi-effects: hardware (rackmount) and floor units. Software: Guitar Rig, Amplitube.

A Child's Garden of Effects

Even though we may use the terms interchangeably, it's a good idea to distinguish *effects* from *processors*. Reverb, for example, is an effect; we can mix the output of reverb with the untreated (dry) signal. When processing the guitar with compression, or EQ, the entire signal passes through the effect and is altered. The confusion often arises because both effects and processors are part of an electric guitarist's signal chain, and in a sense, compression is often used as an effect to add sustain, punch, and snap to the instrument. Although an engineer might use processors as a mixing tool, guitarists often use them to sculpt their guitar's sound and responses.

Effects generally cover several important domains of sound: loudness (dynamics), pitch (frequency), timbre (harmonic content), and time (duration, repetition). Dynamics processors include compressors, limiters, expanders, or some combination thereof, and their function is to control loudness. Limiting stems from compression, albeit with extremely high ratios compared with the original signal. Used judiciously, limiting will keep audio peaks from distorting a signal.

Compression is generally used to balance relative levels of all content in a signal, and when used with guitar, it evens out the attack of strings, so that every note can be heard in a live performance. For guitarists, it has the added benefit of lengthening sustain. When used indiscriminately, compression will kill dynamics, and it's best used with a light touch. Expanders make the quieter parts softer, and the louder parts louder, thereby expanding the dynamic range. Distortion and saturation are also dynamics-based processors that boost a signal and introduce clipping and additional harmonic content into sounds.

Filters can process a variety of frequencies and functions, as illustrated by a few of the filter types available in the Guitar Rig plug-in.

Pitch- or frequency-based effects alter a sound's perceived pitch. Harmonizers are a good example. In the digital domain, the incoming signal is sampled, and the harmonizer adds a signal at a programmed interval. Originally, harmonizers simply played parallel intervals, but later versions can shift incoming notes to preset scales, or even use pitch detection or MIDI-note input to harmonize more adaptively.

Another popular guitar-oriented, frequency-based effect is the "whammy" pedal, which smoothly moves the sampled pitch of your instrument up or down by stepping on a pedal. More seemingly utilitarian applications, including pitch-correction applications, such as Antares AutoTune and Celemony Melodyne, can also be applied to more creative uses.

The tone knobs on your guitar are essentially simple filters; they determine whether your guitar's timbre will be warm and fat, jangly and piercing, or something in between. However, filters vary greatly in design and function, including EQ and the filters found in synthesizers, wah-wah pedals, and other devices. The basic operating principle is that filters allow certain frequencies to pass through unaltered, while other frequencies are amplified, attenuated, or eliminated completely. Thus, low-pass filters admit lower frequencies while attenuating higher frequencies, high-pass filters attenuate the lower end, and band-pass filters admit frequencies around a user-defined low-and-high frequency range. Filters often contain additional tone-shaping features, such as resonance, which emphasizes and sharpens frequencies around the defined cutoff frequencies. In EQ, this emphasis is usually referred to as Q.

Time-based effects include delay and reverb. Delay is simply programmed repetition of a signal—like an echo—which produces distinct repetitions of a signal, whereas with reverb, the repeated signal is spaced so closely together as to create a wash of reflections. Consider the difference in sound between shouting in a canyon, with a lot of open space, and shouting inside a cathedral, in which your shout reflects off of a number of objects in an enclosed space. Reverb is a more complex sound, reflecting the original signal and the rapidly growing density of multiple iterations of the same signal. Reverb and delay play an important part in the way our ears perceive a sound's distance and location. With less reverberation, the sound seems to be closer; larger amounts place the sound farther away. We can also move sounds around the soundstage by panning the signal.

EVERYTHING IN MODULATION

Of course, modern effects are capable of far more than simple static changes in loudness, frequency, timbre, and time. Modulation effects combine elements of synthesizer-like control over loudness, frequency, pitch, and timbre to further alter sounds in dynamic and evolving ways. For instance, the chorus effect combines a slightly delayed repetition of a signal with a cyclic change in pitch above and below the original signal. The cyclic nature of the pitch change is created by an LFO whose waveform shapes the output of the modified signal. Chorus provides an animated, beating effect to the sound, and often thickens and warms the tone.

PSP N20 relies on LFOs and other modulation sources to animate a variety of effects, including chorus, phase shift, and flange.

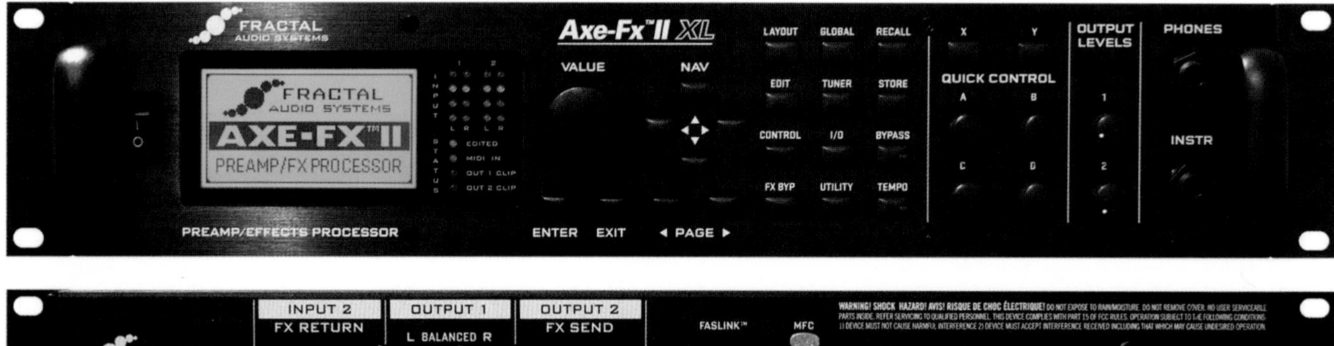

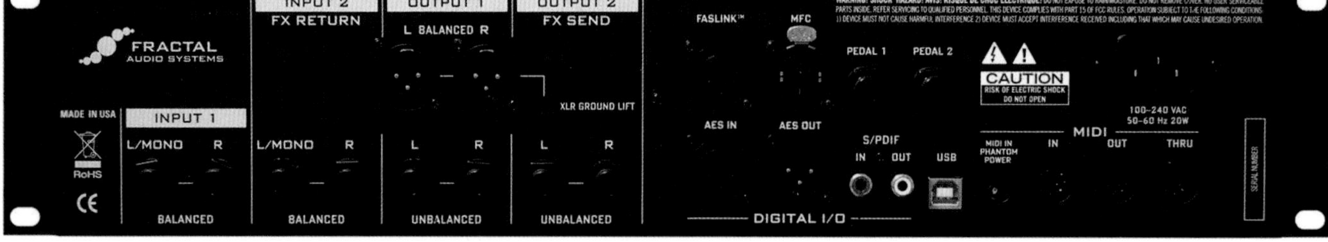

The front and rear panels of Fractal Audio's Axe FX II XL. Note the wealth of input and output options.

Phase shifters duplicate a signal and use an LFO to delay and modulate that signal in and out of phase with the original. *Phase* refers to the position at a point in time of a waveform's cycle, usually measured in degrees. When the signals are 180 degrees out of phase with each other, frequencies are canceled, creating a whooshing effect. Similarly, flanging works with the phase relationship between signals but adds a feedback effect to create additional signals and, therefore, more cancelations, or notches. In both cases, the effect relies on an LFO to create modulation.

Multi-Effects

The field of individual stomp-box effects is vast, and numerous books have been devoted to them. Rather than reinvent the wheel several times over in a single book, let's look at a few choice multi-effects devices that cater to guitar players.

Multi-effects units run in price from relatively inexpensive to very costly. The less expensive units can often sound surprisingly good and offer enough versatility for an entry-level electronic guitarist. As you might expect by now, there are strengths and limitations all across the board.

Most multi-effects units stop short of being a one-stop solution for stage and studio. Some simply provide a formidable lineup of effects and are meant to connect with outboard processors or an amp. You might find effects units with terrific reverb, warm chorus, raucous distortion, and mediocre amp and cabinet models. Other units have a hard-wired signal flow with little room for experimentation.

Fractal Audio Axe Fx II XL

Fractal claims that the unit replaces all of the technology between guitar, preamp, studio, and stage; from my time spent with the unit, I believe they make a strong case.

The first thing you may notice is that the two-rackspace unit is built like a tank. It is equally adaptable to stage and studio. The rear panel sports a comprehensive array of inputs and outputs, including left and right line-level jacks (in addition to the instrument-level jack in the front panel), an additional pair for the effects return, balanced and unbalanced left and right outputs, a second pair of unbalanced jacks for the effects send, and a pair of jacks accommodating footswitches or pedals.

On the digital side of things, you'll get S/PDIF and AES/EBU input and output (see glossary); a proprietary Ethernet-type link to connect with Fractal's MFC-101 foot controller; MIDI In, Out, and Thru jacks; and finally, a USB type B jack. The USB jack, as with the Roland

and Boss MIDI guitar systems, provides two-way communication of audio and MIDI data, as well as firmware updates via Fractal Bot software and Fractal's terrific Axe-Edit software. Even without the editing software, the front panel is remarkably easy to navigate, and the brilliant green LCD offers enough information to navigate the unit's deep feature set without an excess of manual hunting.

The Fractal Axe Edit software provides elegant editing of the Axe FX processor and reveals the unit's depth and complexity.

INSIDE THE BOX

The next thing you will undoubtedly notice is the character of the presets, in part a result of the careful and creative programming involved; sounds are remarkably animated, with blooming reverbs and rich, subtly sweeping chorus effects. Another factor is the depth of programming the unit affords. Among the unit's many claims to fame is its huge collection of modern guitar amp and speaker cabinet models. Add to that a bevy of guitar stomp-box and studio effects—each effect has a broad selection of models; a built-in monophonic, three-oscillator synthesizer; dynamics processors; and lots more.

The unit operates on a grid system, comprising four rows of independent (or interdependent, if you prefer) signal chains into which you can insert a seemingly limitless array (up to the limit of the unit's processing power) of objects, named *blocks* in Fractal-speak: amps, processors, effects, mixers, crossovers, and shunts. A shunt is nothing more than a conduit from one object through otherwise empty blocks to maintain a signal flow from input to output. Two of the device's great sonic wild cards are the Feedback Send and Return blocks with which you can route a signal from any point to any other point, breaking up the linearity of the signal flow from input to output and letting you connect and feed processors from one chain into another. You can mix and merge signal chains at practically any point in the signal flow. You can even insert an effects loop anywhere in the signal chain to bring in external effects, if you'd like.

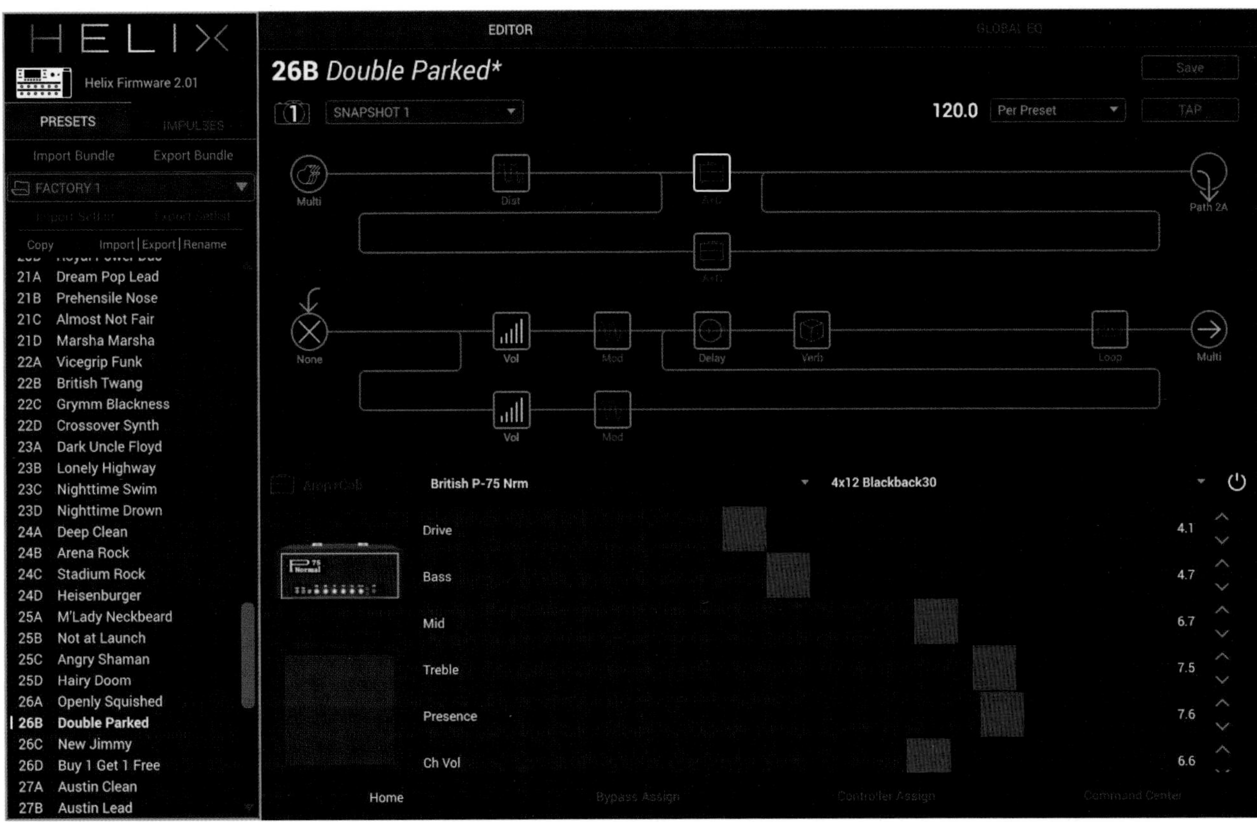

A screen shot of the Line 6 Helix Edit software. Helix provides up to 32 blocks per patch and a variety of ways to configure its signal flow.

One of the secrets behind the remarkable animated qualities of the sound is its rich pool of modulation capabilities, including LFOs, envelope generators, step sequencers, and even the envelope created by your picking hand; in short, a lot of synthesizer architecture is at play here. Many of the richest pads are every bit as impressive as those you'll hear from a synthesizer keyboard. Axe FX relies on impulse response files to accurately re-create the sound and feel of tube amps; in fact, you can dial in different preamp tubes from a handful of choices. For that matter, the factory settings offer nearly 250 amp types, over 100 tone stacks, and 100 cabinets, with plenty of room for your own impulse models. If that isn't enough, feel free to record a bit of your favorite amp and use Tone Match to emulate the sound of a favorite amp or recording. Fractal maintains a busy and creative online community sharing impulse responses and presets that you can always tap into through Axe-Edit software.

From the standpoint of onstage performance, Axe FX has a lot to like. Every patch has six scenes, which are different configurations of your patch's signal chain. The essence of scenes is that of a switcher box, so that you can easily enable and disable effects while playing. XY switching, by contrast, lets you switch between independent blocks with different parameter settings.

Line 6 Helix

Line 6 made their bones in the effects-processor community back in the '90s with the introduction of the POD, a kidney-shaped, floor-unit guitar processor, which is arguably the first commercial effects unit to take advantage of modeling effects. Before the pod, they produced the Flextone amp series, which could emulate a variety of amp and cabinet combinations.

The POD, however, was an extremely popular guitar effects unit due to its simple operation and easy customization via an array of knobs and switches on the unit's surface. The effects themselves were of very high quality and led to a line of individual stomp boxes based on physically modeled effects. Line 6 soon branched out into plug-ins and hardware variations of the POD theme in all sizes and configurations.

Helix, like Fractal's Axe FX units, is Line 6's attempt to build the complete guitar processor system, albeit with a different approach. For starters, Helix is designed as a floor unit. With the Variax Digital Interface, connected by a CAT-5 or Ethercon cable, the Variax guitar's modeling engine draws power from Helix, eliminating the need for the guitar's removable battery. The connection provides snapshot storage for easy recall of Variax settings, including the guitar model and tuning, as well as volume and tone knob positions. For hands-off control, you can move between two Variax models and tunings with one of the Helix footswitches or, of course, MIDI commands.

Happily, the communication works in both directions. The Variax volume or tone knobs can control Helix amp and effects parameters. You can treat Variax modeled and magnetic signals separately through independent signal paths, and either mix them together or send them through different Helix outputs.

PANEL OF EXPERTS

The topmost panel features a vivid, color-coded Main Display window clearly illustrating the patch components and signal flow through block icons on the Home screen. Depending on the context, other screens list parameters for the modeled effects and more. You navigate through the selection and editing process with a joystick which, again, depending on context, lets you move, copy, paste, and clear blocks. Other screens have unique action panels; for example, the Global Settings action panel lets you reset all global settings at once. A set of six knobs appears below the onscreen parameters; these offer direct access to parameter value edits.

At the far right, Helix's Expression pedal toggles between two groups of control functions, including, of course, volume and wah-wah as well as any additional effect parameters, MIDI Control Change messages, and amp settings you would like to sweep.

In the middle of all this are eight footswitches, each with a backlit scribble-strip-style display. The switches can be used for choosing patches in conjunction with the bank-selection footswitches to their left. If you choose, you can instantly change the footswitches' function to Stompbox Mode, in which the eight footswitches can toggle individual effects on and off, or with a bit of agile footwork, you can cycle through other models or assignments. To the right, two buttons pack a multitude of functions: The upper switch toggles between preset selection and the previously described Stompbox Mode; holding the switch down lets you edit parameters of selected blocks with your feet.

The rear panel offers a versatile supply of inputs and outputs, both analog and digital, audio, and control. From the left, two jacks accommodate expression pedals. A balanced output provides remote amplifier channel-switching and reverb on and off controls for your amp, and another jack sends control voltages to a connected synth via an expression pedal.

There are three different places to plug in a guitar: one standard guitar jack, an Aux In jack for guitars with active pickups, and most interesting of all, a CAT 5, Ethernet-style jack for plugging in a Variax guitar. That jack also powers the Variax modeling engine without need for the guitar's battery.

Thru its USB connection, Helix can serve as an audio interface to your computer, and to that end, you'll find an XLR input for connecting a microphone. The jack supplies phantom power for condenser mics. A bank of four sends and returns lets you bring external devices into the Helix signal flow, such as additional effects, synths, drum machines, and more. A pair each of XLR and ¼-inch outputs makes Helix eminently suitable to play through PA systems, guitar amps, and studio mixing environments. Speaking of PA systems, Helix's proprietary L6 protocol communicates with certain Line 6 speaker systems and amps—for example, with one of their DT-series amps, you can remotely select amp channels or reverb. The outlet accepts an XLR cable, and the output can also serve as an AES/EBU audio interface. If you prefer, you can use the unit's coaxial SP/DIF jacks to receive or send audio signal. Finally, MIDI In and Out ports receive and transmit Control Change, Program Change, and Continuous Controllers, as well as MIDI clock and System Exclusive messages.

Signal Flow

Helix defines signal flow as a path—of which there are two—and you can configure them independently in parallel, or in serial arrangements, or feed the first path into the second. For instance, you can run the output of one signal into a second amp model, or you can create more complex processing of the signal, such as sending the output of one path's amplifier into a filter and then into the input of the other path's cabinet.

Line 6 uses the same concept of blocks that Fractal uses for its objects. Blocks simply arrange themselves next to each other, which makes for simplified patch building but tends to limit the device to a more linear approach. Fortunately, apart from the modeling and effects, Helix also provides split and merge blocks, and options abound. You can arrange up to 32 blocks in a variety of ways.

The number of effects, amps, and cabinets is staggering, with a combination of effects modeled after classic gear as well as original Line 6 effects.

You will find, as you wend your way through this book, that much of the jargon that peppers this text are often features that products share in common. This is a key concept to intuitive operation of these devices, especially those that are not covered here. For instance, Scenes (as defined in Fractal's hardware) and Snapshots (in Line 6 lingo) are, simply put, ways of changing between different configurations of your effects unit's patches without disrupting your performance.

Comparing Axe FX with Helix is difficult, and perhaps unfair. To begin with, Axe FX costs several hundred dollars more than Helix. Both sound great, although the Fractal system has the edge in amp and cabinet sonics, and its reverb and delay have a sweetness and clarity that I've yet to hear in any other guitar effects processor. Both can import impulse responses, although Axe FX has a capacity for larger and longer files. Helix, on the other hand, has designed the unit with a built-in, versatile expression pedal, plus jacks to add two more pedals, and a control voltage out, letting you control analog synths and effects directly from the Helix foot pedal. Unless you already own or plan to buy a Variax guitar, it's a tough choice, and if you think I'm going to help you decide, guess again. Go to your local music dealer and try them out!

Having said that, I can now make your decision harder: Fractal offers the AX8 amp modeler, a pared-down, floor-unit version of the Axe FX, as well as the FX8, another floor unit minus the amp and cabinet models.

While you are shopping, don't overlook processors from T.C. Electronic, Eventide, and others. On the less expensive side, the Boss GP-10 I covered in the previous chapter makes an excellent, inexpensive, and compact processor unit, even if you just want to plug your non-MIDIfied electric in. There's a generous supply of excellent-sounding effects, and you have the ability to reorder the signal flow freely. (One of my favorite arrangements is a clean electric guitar with the chorus effect after the reverb for a nice airy and slightly surreal tone.)

As I write this, Boss has just released the GT-1, essentially the effects, foot pedal, and controls of a GP-10 minus the guitar models, in a battery-powered unit you can tuck into a backpack.

Native Instrument's Guitar Rig hosts an incredible collection of sound-shaping options designed for guitar. You can drag and drop components from the browser to the rack in virtually any order you wish.

Native Instruments' Guitar Rig

Not to be outdone by hardware, there are scads of software effects-processor systems for your computer as well as your mobile devices, and most of them sound great. Native Instruments' Guitar Rig Pro stuffs a universe of guitar processors, amps, cabinets, and more into an easy-to-use guitar package. The software opens as a virtual rack, with a browser on the left. That browser, depending on which button you choose, could contain individual components or fully set-up presets. Either way, you drag what you want from the browser into the rack.

Components are grouped by model type: Amplifiers, Cabinets, Delay and Echo, Distortion, Modulation, EQ, Special FX, Pitch, Reverb, and so on. Each of the categories offers multiple models, often fashioned after well-known hardware, along with some terrific Native Instruments originals.

Native Instruments sweetens the deal if you acquire Guitar Rig through a purchase of the Native Instruments Komplete package (more about Komplete later), which includes custom effects, amps, cabinets, models of revered vintage dynamics processors, and Reflektor, a particularly sweet-sounding convolution reverb with the ability to load your own impulse responses. Also deserving mention are the Control Room and Control Room Pro. These components are similar to Digital Performer's Live Room G, letting you select from a batch of amps, cabinets, and microphones—up to eight mics and five cabinets—which you can mix to create a blend of tones. Control Room Pro was added with Version 5, adding 29 cabinets, a Direct Injection (DI) box, many more microphones ranging from vintage to modern, and control over placement, phase, and room.

So far, the flow is linear, from top to bottom, as you drag models over to the rack, but you can reorder them any way you'd like, and then the Tools section of the browser breaks the linear scenario wide open and expands Guitar Rig's flexibility enormously. Split multiplies the signal into A and B channels, and you can create parallel, independent effects chains as well as mix the two together through Split's Mix Out. You can, of course, add multiple Splits and create more chains. Crossover lets you perform frequency-dependent splits with an adjustable dividing point between high and low frequencies. This is extremely useful when you want to channel the upper ranges of your guitar to one chain of effects and your low end to another.

I've saved the best for (almost) last. Container can hold a complete guitar rig, replete with amps, cabinets, effects, and splits of their own! It works in exactly the same way as the parent rack: Simply drag components into the container. You'll find a set of four control knobs; these can be changed to buttons and are assigned to parameters of components within Container. You can assign a total of 16 controls, and you can automate them in your host program or sweep them with MIDI messages.

Container offers a formidable list of cool, useful, and unusual presets, and we haven't even covered Guitar Rig's Preset browser yet. Suffice it to say that Container can be likened to Russian nesting dolls, with guitar rigs nestled into guitar rigs, up to the capacity of your computer's processor.

The final item in the Tool category is Master FX, which can provide a uniform sonic treatment for the entire rack and maintain a consistently processed output, even if you change programs. For example, if you are performing a set onstage and need a different set of effects, but perhaps you want to retain the overall reverb, Master FX will not change with the rest of the signal flow. The presets include delay and reverb and EQ and compressor, but you can add your own components as you would with a preset or Container. You'll also find Looper, which lets you record layers of tracks synched to the host's tempo or to Guitar Rig's metronome, and you can save layers or the composite track.

Now, About Those Presets

Click on the Preset button, and you'll find rigs arranged in categories, which include rigs gathered by use of a particular amp, bass amp rigs, and rigs suitable for specific musical genres, such as Country, Jazz, Ambient Music, Metal, Surf, and others. Another folder groups the virtual rigs by song, and here again, the litigious state of things prevents them from directly naming the songs, so instead, you might find Lotta Love, Crazy Randy, Jeff at Ronnie's, Foo Monkey Grat (if anyone can figure out what that one means, please contact the author), and the like. The only flaw I've found in this last category is that your results will vary with the guitar you use. If you've chosen the Jeff at Ronnie's rig and you've plugged in an ES-335 or even a Les Paul, you're not likely to nail the sound of that recording. That's true of any rig, software or hardware. And of course, if you don't have Beck's hands, your results may also vary. Nevertheless, there's plenty to tweak until you find the settings that work.

Yet another category groups by the use of particular effects, and these are divided into subfolders whose titles run the gamut from Abstract, Acoustic, and Animated to instrumental applications such as Drums and Vocals (yes, you can use Guitar Rig to process other sounds and instruments) to leads, effect-specific categories such as Reverb and Delay, and even mixer-dedicated patches.

There's more, lots more, but a detailed tour would be best accomplished with a second volume to this book. Suffice it to say that Guitar Rig Pro hosts a multitude of guitar sounds from straight ahead to wildly creative, and serves as well for a live rig as it does for studio recording.

IK Multimedia Amplitube Acoustic

As with everything else, there is a lively market for software-based guitar processors, especially in mobile devices. IK Multimedia has almost cornered the market in all things mobile, supplying software as well as hardware accommodating everything from iPhone to Android to iPad applications. I particularly recommend IK Multimedia's Amplitube, whether for mobile or computer applications. Amplitube, like Guitar Rig, offers scads of amps and cabinets as well as virtual stomp-box rigs and rackmount effects. These sound extremely authentic, and they provide a virtual room with an assortment of mics and top everything off with an eight-track recorder. Amplitude is vastly expandable with effects, cabinets, microphones, and more through in-app purchases, although it's irritating to audition a preset when you are ready to record only to find that some components require a purchase and a download. Amplitube acoustic for iPad offers clean, relatively simple recording and processing via its accompanying clip-on guitar mic. You get a choice of two solid-state and a single tube amplifier with gain, presence, and volume controls, along with bass, mid, and treble. Built-in effects options change for each amp, with solid-state being the simplest. You can fine-tune your tone with four-band EQ on the amp's right side. The latter two amps add a choice of hall, plate, and spring reverb along with a pair of digital delays, which can synch to tempo. In addition, you get stomp-box pedals you can assign to any of four slots: a compressor, one graphic, and one parametric EQ, a surprisingly effective 12-string guitar effect, and most interesting of all, an acoustic body modeler. You input the source type and the target instruments: Dreadnought, Classic, Jumbo, or Parlor guitar. I'm not convinced you'll be able to make an inexpensive Yamaha acoustic sound like an old Martin, but the effect is useful enough in that it provides some tonal variation. Bass Maker is essentially an Octave pedal, and its function is obvious and useful if you don't have the real thing handy.

Amplitube Acoustic, like most IK products, is expandable with online, in-app purchases. For instance, you can purchase Looper, or a complete eight-track recorder, or drum loops for the built-in drum machine.

CHAPTER **8**

What Is a Sequencer?

A brief history, explanation, and survey of major software sequencers. Choosing which works best for you.

Perhaps the strongest reason for the longevity and vitality of MIDI is the sequencer, a device that can record, edit, store, and play back MIDI data. Eventually, sequencers were able to perform those same functions with audio, and so the more inclusive terms *digital audio workstation* (DAW) and *digital audio sequencer* were adopted. Sequencers come in software as well as hardware versions; in fact, many modern hardware synthesizers have built-in sequencers. For our purposes, it's best to focus our attention mainly on software, which is of far greater usefulness to the guitarist due to superior audio- and MIDI-editing capabilities, as well as its capacity for expansion. It's also much easier to configure for guitar. One note to ponder: Other than performing, the digital-audio sequencer is the center of the electronic guitarist's world. A little historical perspective explains the sequencer's evolution toward the modern DAW.

Proto-Sequencers

Early in this book, I used the player piano to illustrate the differences between MIDI and sound. In a very simple way, player pianos illustrate one of the sequencer's main functions: the ability to play back previously recorded events that trigger a sound-making apparatus. We can trace the origin of sequencers back to ninth-century Baghdad and the invention of a water-driven organ that held barrels with pins that triggered notes, in much the same way a music box uses a rotating, wind-up barrel with pins that pluck its tines. There are records dating from the 13th century of a similar technique for automating carillon, the tuned bells you often hear in church towers, and the process extends to this day. Automatons—devices whose functions were mechanically automated—have survived from that time to the present day. Not too long ago, Pat Metheny recorded an album and toured, accompanied only by an automated symphony of actual orchestral instruments. Interestingly, the automation was guided by a MIDI sequencer and fed to mechanisms that translated the MIDI data to physical plucking, fretting, bowing, blowing, and striking actions that produced the music.

The earliest examples of sequenced synthesizer music date back to the '50s, using instructions encoded on wide spools of paper with holes punched in them, triggering an RCA Mark II synthesizer. Later-day analog sequencers created music by way of a series of sliders sending voltages to voltage-controlled-oscillators while they were synchronized to a clock. Presumably, additional sequencers with compatible clocks could link together and synchronize to play additional parts. Those types of sequencers were, as a rule, monophonic, and limited to relatively short, repetitive passages.

Of course, with the advent of MIDI and computers, sequencing supported polyphonic synthesizers along with an expanded set of musical gestures, including flexible note durations and velocity. It now became possible to easily link other synthesizers and drum machines to a common data stream. Because memory was limited and expensive, early hardware and software MIDI sequencers relied heavily on creating small sections of music, such as verses, choruses, and bridges (or even smaller parts) and accessing these sections as needed by drawing upon the computer's ability to instantaneously call up one section or another into RAM. The ability to reorder the music—add a chorus or two, replace a verse with a bridge, or other similar bulk-editing conveniences—worked great for pop and rock music, which often rely heavily on repetition. It was tremendously useful for situations where song form and length had to be modified quickly, but this was mostly inadequate for composers who wrote in extended forms, or those whose compositional style required a more linear approach. Additionally, every repetition of a passage was exactly the same, compositionally and dynamically. Conversely, change one event in a chorus, and all repetitions would change similarly. Nonetheless, manufacturers recognized the efficiency and ease of old-school, nonlinear, random-access sequencing and developed modern-day enhancements to the process. If you have ever produced music for fickle clients as I have, you'll understand the value of quickly reordering sections of a song.

Modern sequencers, on the other hand, offer a great deal more flexibility. As computer processing power and memory capacities grew, the sequencer took on more of the capabilities of a bona fide studio. In the early '90s, a California-based company by the name of Opcode developed the ability to record audio tracks side by side with MIDI data. This was a tremendous revolution in the industry, as it was the beginning of the completely tapeless studio. Displaying the waveforms for editing replaced jogging of tape reels back and forth and cutting tape with razor blades on editing blocks.

The resolution of recorded MIDI data improved immensely from a division of 24 parts per quarter note, to around 1,024 parts and greater, which helped MIDI lose the reputation of being stiff and mechanical-sounding.

Around the middle of the '90s, Steinberg introduced Virtual Studio Technology (VST), a plug-in format that enabled sequencers to host built-in, software-based instruments and audio processors and effects. This quickly developed into a growth industry for plug-ins, and the major developers of software sequencers soon followed through with their own proprietary formats, along with stand-alone synthesizers that didn't need to be called up as plug-ins in a sequencer host.

How Do Sequencers Work?

Every sequencer has four main functions: input, processing, storage, and output. In the modern-day sequencer, input includes the recording of MIDI events (most but not all sequencers can record audio, too). Processing is a broad field, which includes the editing, manipulation, and routing of data. Under this category, we can include plug-ins for processing MIDI and audio data, and even software instruments, whose sounds respond to the incoming MIDI data. Storage determines what you can do with the data, whether saving to a drive subject to later recall, loading a file into memory, naming and organizing, saving in a format suitable to another computer, and more. Finally, output is the ability to play back whatever is loaded into your software workstation. That could be for the purposes of auditioning tracks, overdubbing parts, transferring and saving the data as audio or MIDI files, or mixdown to a finished product. Mixdown can occur to another medium, for example, to a hardware recorder serving as a mixdown unit, or music can be bounced in its totality to a drive. Most sequencers these days even provide software for mastering.

BASIC EDITING TOOLS OF A MODERN SEQUENCER

Apart from the ability to record and play back audio and MIDI data, expect some basic editing tools from your sequencer.

For audio recording, you should be able to cut, copy, and paste regions of audio from one place in a track to another. Most sequencers let you snap regions of audio to a grid or simply drag a region until it feels right. Often, you will want to snip and move a region to provide a gap in which you can place another section. You should also be able to crossfade from one section of audio to the next to help bring about smooth transitions without jumps in sound level; adjusting volume in regions is essential. Beyond these basics, your tool chest will expand exponentially. Some sequencers provide the ability to slice or place markers in the audio and literally change the rhythmic feel of the music. Stretching audio to fit a new tempo without altering pitch or adjusting pitch without changing tempo is relatively standard in the major digital-audio sequencers.

MIDI editing encompasses all of the basic features of audio editing, plus a number of other essentials. Quantizing takes MIDI data and tightens up the timing. The ability to edit the Velocity of each note is essential, and better sequencers provide a number of ways to do this, which can change the dynamics of a performance radically. You might also want to edit the duration of individual notes, or move their start times to tighten up a passage. In days of old, the low resolution of sequencers left little question as to whether your notes were on time, early, or late. Now, with 1,024 divisions of a quarter note being the norm, you can exert your natural musical tendencies to push, lay back, or swing without worrying that you'll sound unmusical. Accordingly, quantizing usually offers a percentage parameter (how close to your goal of the nearest 16th note you want the notes to fall, for example); how intensely do you want to swing?

Much of the same sophistication applies to editing the Velocity of the notes. Velocity doesn't simply translate as loudness; in the acoustic world, sounds get brighter with harder playing; strings go out of tune and back after stretching. In MIDI, any number of things can happen with Velocity; for instance, harder velocities can trigger a different sound or affect the speed of a sound's attack.

Of course, MIDI is vastly more than just note data. Look for tools to smooth Pitch Bend or Modulation data. You might want to be able to unclutter your view and look at one type of MIDI event at a time; better sequencers offer data filters to let you focus. Some sequencers provide a logical editor feature, which lets you define criteria to select for editing—say, for example, you wanted to select all MIDI notes under a duration of a 64th note with velocities less than 40, only between E3 and F#4, from bar 3 to the third beat of bar 17. You'd be surprised at how such seemingly finicky editing capabilities can come in handy. I'm hardly scratching the surface. ■

Feature for feature, you can expect just about all of the major sequencers to be roughly equal in outcome, and what one sequencer advances will likely be matched by the rest over time. As a guitarist, what matters most is how guitar-friendly the software is, and whether its workflow is compatible with the way you create music. I have not found a single sequencer that lets you approach it with a MIDI guitar as easily as you would with a keyboard, with support for independent string bending—at least, not without a few mildly inconvenient workarounds. The good news is that once you have set up your sequencer, you can always save that setup as a template file. From there on, it's a matter of finding the music-creation programs that best fit your workflow. Do you like to develop music from small ideas and repeated phrases, or do you have a song form in mind and need to work in a more linear style? Maybe you want to collaborate with other musicians and need to rearrange ideas on the fly. Perhaps you like to develop ideas with loops. With all of the aforementioned features in mind, let's look at a few of the major examples of software sequencers.

Ableton Live (Mac, Win)

If you like to build songs in smaller sections, a loop at a time, from phrases to measures or longer, you just may have found your match, because that's Live's most central feature. Live fronts two main windows. The Session View is a nonlinear interface populated by columns of Clip buttons for each track. A clip is a cell of data that can hold anything from a single note to a meaningful phrase to an entire performance of a single instrument. Clips for any given instrument or audio track are arrayed vertically. Each horizontal row of clips comprises a scene, consisting of musically related data from the other tracks. In more musical terms, a scene could be a verse, a chorus, a bridge, or even a one-bar fill with all the tracks that constitute that musical moment.

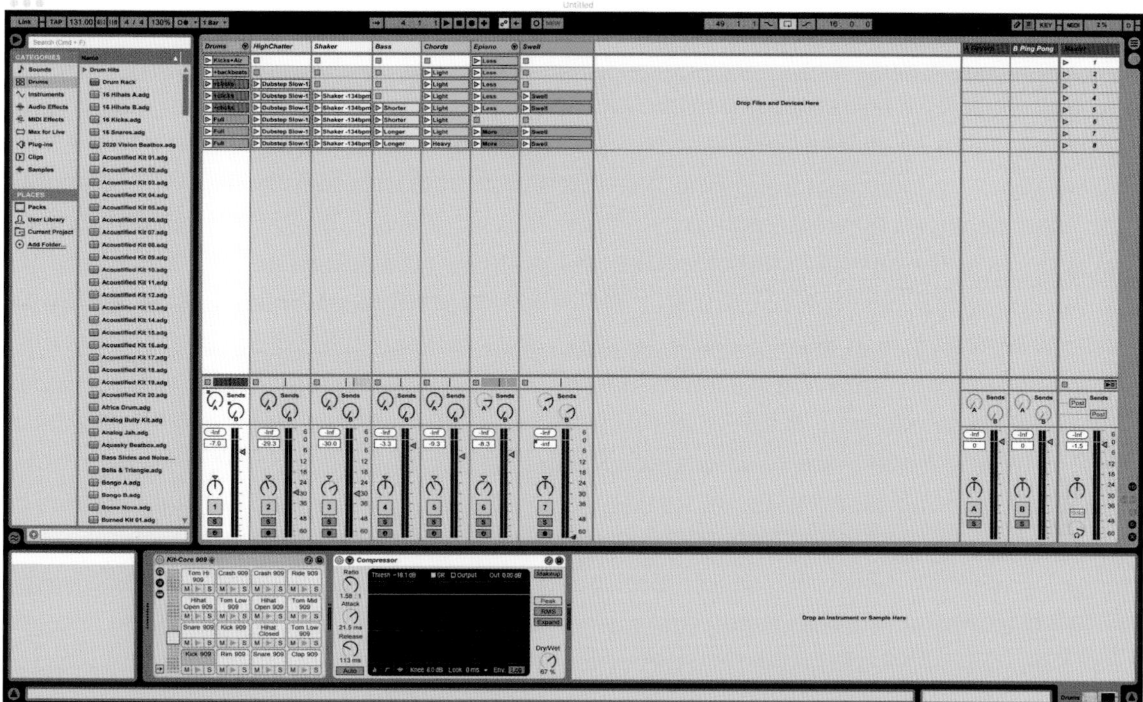

Ableton Live's Session view presents a modular, loop-oriented approach to song structure. Each small square represents a clip of audio or MIDI data.

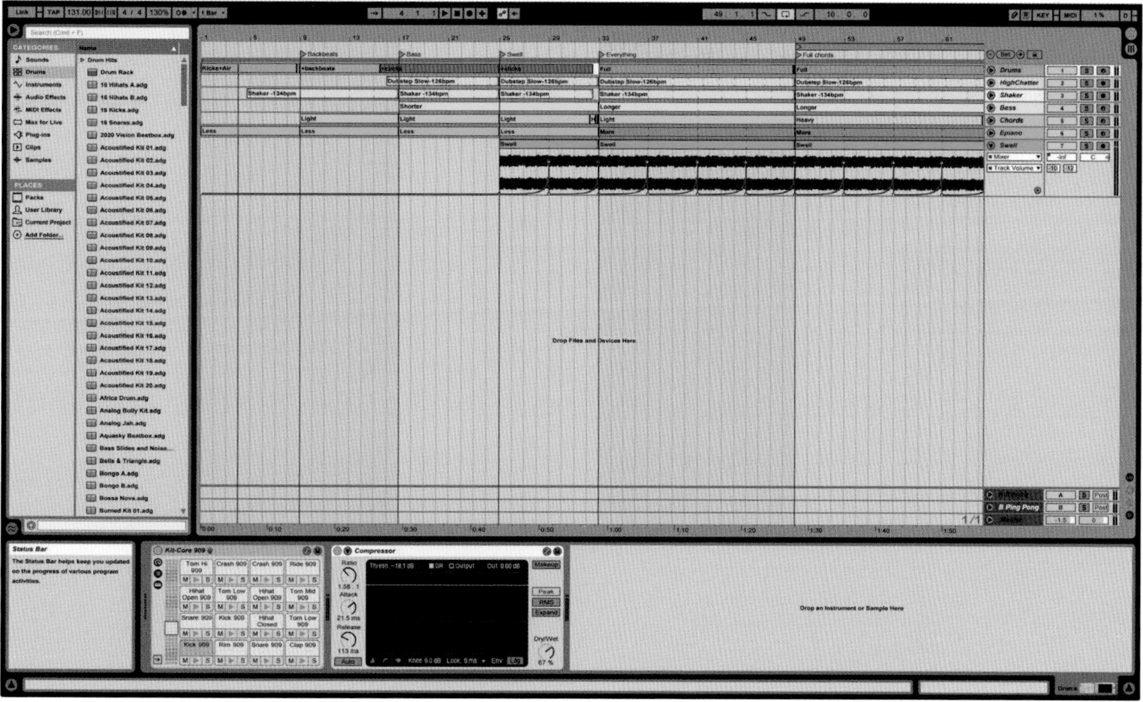

The Arrangement view in Ableton Live provides a linear approach to song structure.

Hit your computer's Tab key, and you are looking at the Arrangement view, which presents the more familiar, linear, timeline-oriented view, albeit with track assignments on the right-hand side of the screen. You can work in either mode; your clips show along the timeline. You can work strictly in the Arrangement view if you'd like, or move back and forth between views as the spirit moves you.

If your work style favors clips in the Session view, you assemble the song in whatever order you choose. Clips from one scene can play in other scenes. For instance, if one of the track columns is devoted to bass, click on another clip in that track column, and while the rest of the scene plays, the new clip will temporarily replace the one previously playing in that scene. It's a great antidote to the repetitiveness of looping tracks. One of the beauties of this approach is that it can be improvisational or a construction kit toward a specific goal. Finally, when you wish to commit your work to a final song form, you click the Arrangement Record button and assemble the song by launching different scenes and clips; Live will then record your moves for posterity.

If you need to edit your tracks, Live provides a good supply of audio editing amenities, including excellent pitch- and time-warping features. You get a modest set of tools for fixing up MIDI tracks, although as a MIDI guitarist, I miss some of the more detailed capabilities of other DAWs. For instance, a Logical Editor feature which lets you select notes of minute duration and weak velocities would make it a simple matter of weeding out unintended notes and other data that MIDI guitars sometimes send. You can weed out those imperfections note by note, but in a session where good takes are marred by less-than-perfect playing, getting to those details quickly can be a major time-saver.

All of Live's instruments, processors, loops, and other resources are on display and instantly accessible from the left-hand browser, which you can stow away at your convenience. Live's collection of instruments is formidable and includes a couple of samplers, analog and other physical-modeling synths, a neat and simplified but very capable FM synth (see Chapter 4), an instrument rack, where you can combine multiple instruments and, of course, access your own collection of third-party virtual instruments. You'll also find a bevy of effects and loops, and plenty of amp and cabinet simulators for dressing up your guitar's audio tracks.

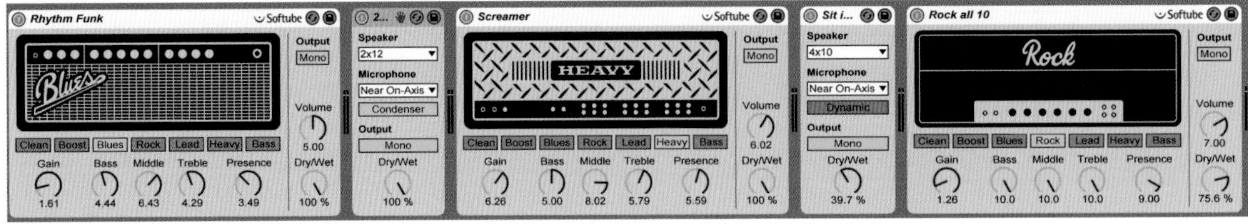

A random sampling of Ableton Live's amp and cabinet models. You simply drag and drop them from Live's browser onto your guitar track.

Ableton's site hosts a generous number of add-on sounds and patches that you can download—many for free. Optionally, if you decide you want to design your own MIDI- and audio-processing tools, synthesizers, and other plug-ins, you can add Cycling 74's Max for Live, a programming environment that is integrated into Live. It comes with a large number of presets you can use immediately. All in all, Live is a versatile approach to digital music creation.

MOTU Digital Performer (Mac, Win)

From the standpoint of guitar-oriented plug-ins, looping, editing, and especially MIDI, Digital Performer's (DP) features have made it my go-to recording software. Audio recording for guitar extends beyond the typical guitar-amp processor and stomp-box design. DP features Live Room G and Live Room B, plug-ins that provide virtual guitar recording rooms for guitar and bass respectively, replete with amps and cabinets, microphone models, and an adjustable room ambience that adapts realistically to the choice of mics and their placement. You can arrange up to four channels of microphones. Channels one and two are mono, independent mics; you can place them in the rear, on- or off-axis near or far, or use an omnidirectional mic. Three and four are a stereo pair and offer a variety of stereo mic techniques for placement.

MOTU Digital Performer is loaded with guitar-oriented plug-ins, including a choice selection of stomp-box models.

Digital Performer's Live Room G plug-in is a virtual ambient recording room tailored for guitar and replete with virtual amps, cabinets, and mics.

You'll find a slew of additional plug-ins for cabinets and stomp boxes. Custom '59 is exceptionally tasty, with models of vintage Fender and Marshall amps. ACE-30 models different versions of the popular Vox amp to reflect changes made to the tone circuitry. Stomp-box models are titled to resemble the original hardware—for example, Clear Pebble sounds (and looks) like the Small Stone, Electro Harmonics' vintage phase shifter, scuff marks and all, and Diamond Drive emulates Voodoo Labs Sparkle Drive distortion pedal. MultiFuzz models Craig Anderton's Quadrafuzz, which divides the input into four independently processed frequencies, producing a range of sounds from subtle and warm to aggressive and monstrous.

ACE-30 is patterned after the Vox AC-30 amplifier and offers a choice of modern or vintage circuitry.

You can focus on the guitar-oriented stomp-box emulations (there are many more), but you might miss out on some of the more creative plug-ins that MOTU has in store, including Megasynth, which is the equivalent of plugging your guitar into an analog subtractive synth, and Sonic Modulator, which uniquely combines pitch, amplitude, delay, and filter effects in one plug-in. What's more, DP maintains preset virtual rigs combining stomp box and other effects, arranged by application (Clean, Classic, Country, Blues, etc.) that you can load into the guitar track's channel strip.

Polar is a looping recorder app within DP's already remarkable virtual recording facility. Polar offers a slew of creative applications. It's ridiculously easy to use, and each pass is recorded to RAM and layered with the original track. You can save passes as Soundbites (DP's term for

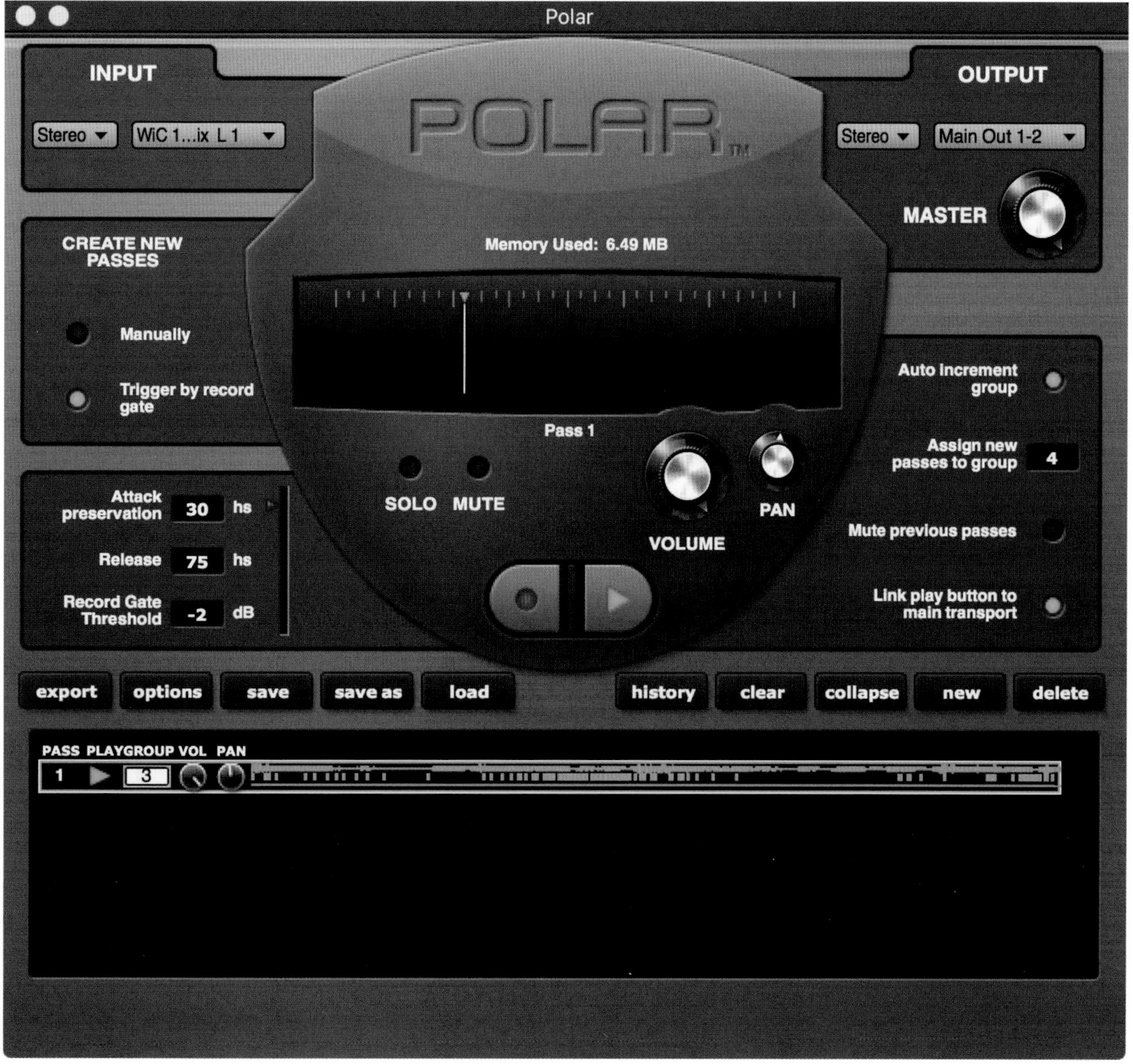

Polar is MOTU's unique loop-recording and overdubbing plug-in.

audio segments) and choose which passes to keep or discard. You can also record loops to new tracks as you play them.

As an environment for MIDI guitarists, DP tunnels through some of the editing hurdles that plague other sequencers. Setting up an effective, Pitch Bend–ready recording environment still requires a bit of forethought. Because DP records MIDI strictly on a single-MIDI-channel-per-track basis, you must enable simultaneous recording of multiple tracks and assign each of your controller's strings to its own track input as well as a single destination to each string, but once done, you can save your setup as a template for instant recall. Although DP can't record more than one MIDI channel per track, it can combine MIDI data from several tracks into a single editing window, so you can enjoy uncluttered editing of all strings in a single view, without having to jump from track to track. Though the individual string-per-track arrangement seems fiddly, it bestows a few major benefits that other DAWs cannot duplicate, such as alternate tunings for your MIDI guitar without retuning strings. (I explain track setup in detail in Chapter 15.) Of course, in certain instances (particularly when emulating pianos and other keyboards, you may want to disable Pitch Bend entirely—in which case, you can record all strings to a single track.

DP has a number of great tools for de-glitching MIDI. Select a region from any window—as long as you select the proper track—and you can fix things up rapidly. You can split notes into separate tracks by a variety of criteria, including pitch, duration, range, and velocity, and either move them to another track or just remove them.

On the surface, DP is primarily a linear sequencer, but it offers capabilities for nonlinear, piece-by-piece music creation that rival those of Ableton Live. The Song window lets you build projects in any way you like, from small parts and individual tracks to entire sequenced songs. Just take any portion of a project, from the entire sequence to a few notes, or a riff in a track, and convert it into what DP calls a Chunk, and drag Chunks into the Song window's timeline.

One of the great advantages for the performing electronic musician is that you can drag a list of sequences into the Song window and create your entire show's set list of backing tracks. In

A detail of the Digital Performer Song window in which Chunks, comprising sequences and smaller portions of a sequence, can be freely arranged into new song forms.

the Chunks window, you can even access them in nonlinear form, and jump from song to song at will by sending a MIDI message or using a key command.

DP offers several virtual instruments, including a simple virtual sampler, an FM synth, a drum machine, a synth bass, an analog-modeling synthesizer, and its flagship instrument, MX4, which combines analog modeling with wavetable synthesis and provides elegant modulation schemes that breathe life into the sounds in unique ways.

If notation and scoring are your thing, DP provides Quickscribe, a full-featured notation window. You can print out charts or even sequence tunes entirely in Quickscribe's windows. DP supports MusicXML, a music notation file format supported by many other music-notation and production applications. You can import your music into a dedicated notation program, such as Finale, or load a MusicXML file into another DAW, such as Apple Logic or Steinberg Cubase.

A detail of Digital Performer's Quickscribe feature, which provides built-in notation for tracks, parts of tracks, or the entire sequence. You can create an entire sequence from the notation alone.

I've used every popular Mac-based sequencer, and I instinctively turn to MOTU Digital Performer when I want to get the job done.

Apple Logic Pro X (Mac)

Logic Pro X originated on the Atari ST computer in the '80s and garnered plenty of attention for editing and creative features that were well ahead of the curve at the time. Now exclusively an Apple property, Logic continues to enjoy a robust feature set.

Unique to Logic is the Environment window, which includes the Environment, a graphic programming window for customizing MIDI and audio input and output. You may never need to use it; the default setup of the program hides it unless you choose Advanced Tools in Logic's Preferences window.

Three distinct Environment windows float over Logic's main window: Mixer, Keyboard, and Mapped Instrument. You may never need to use Apple Logic's Environment; nevertheless, it offers advanced MIDI and audio processing.

VIRTUAL CAMELS

Logic is graced with a number of terrific-sounding virtual instruments, among them a few physically modeled keyboard staples, such as Fender Rhodes and a Wurlitzer-inspired electric piano; a virtual drawbar organ; a full-featured sampler; several modeled analog synthesizers; a powerful drum-kit designer; and Sculpture, a deeply programmable modeling instrument that covers a number of acoustically generated synthesizer. More recently, Apple purchased Camel

Audio Alchemy, a sophisticated synthesizer that draws on a number of synthesis techniques and is capable of breathtaking animated tones. In all, Logic is well-stocked with a generous variety of terrific-sounding instruments.

Better yet, Logic's built-in virtual instruments are supremely easy to set up for MIDI guitar. Click on the bottom arrow of any Logic instrument and a small menu of settings appears; among these, and of most interest to the MIDI guitarist, are pull-down menus for MIDI Mono Mode and MIDI Mono Mode Pitch Range. Still better, it's equally simple to record all six MIDI channels to a single track.

Logic's collection of guitar-oriented amp and processor plug-ins is on a par with that of Digital Performer, but perhaps even more extensive and certainly more colorful. You can choose Pedalboard from the Audio FX menu, and a virtual on-screen pedalboard along with a tray filled with stomp boxes—a full complement of fuzz, phase shifters, flangers, chorus, and delays, wah-wah, echo, and more, once again modeled after familiar hardware units—are at your command. Simply click and drag them onto the board in any order you choose.

Logic's Pedalboard hosts a wealth of great-sounding (and colorful) stomp boxes. Drag and drop pedals from the browser on the right into the main pedalboard area in any order you choose.

Amp Designer is equally easy to use: You get emulations of vintage, modern, and boutique amps and cabinets as well as a variety of mics, and as with Digital Performer, you can change mic position and distance from the amp cabinets. These are not named after specific cabinets, but their graphic design should provide a few clues to their origins.

A great convenience is Logic's Library browser, which harbors a generous supply of presets that combine amps, pedalboards, EQ, and additional effects to create a range of finished guitar sounds that run from conventional and practical to huge and completely outré, with all points in between.

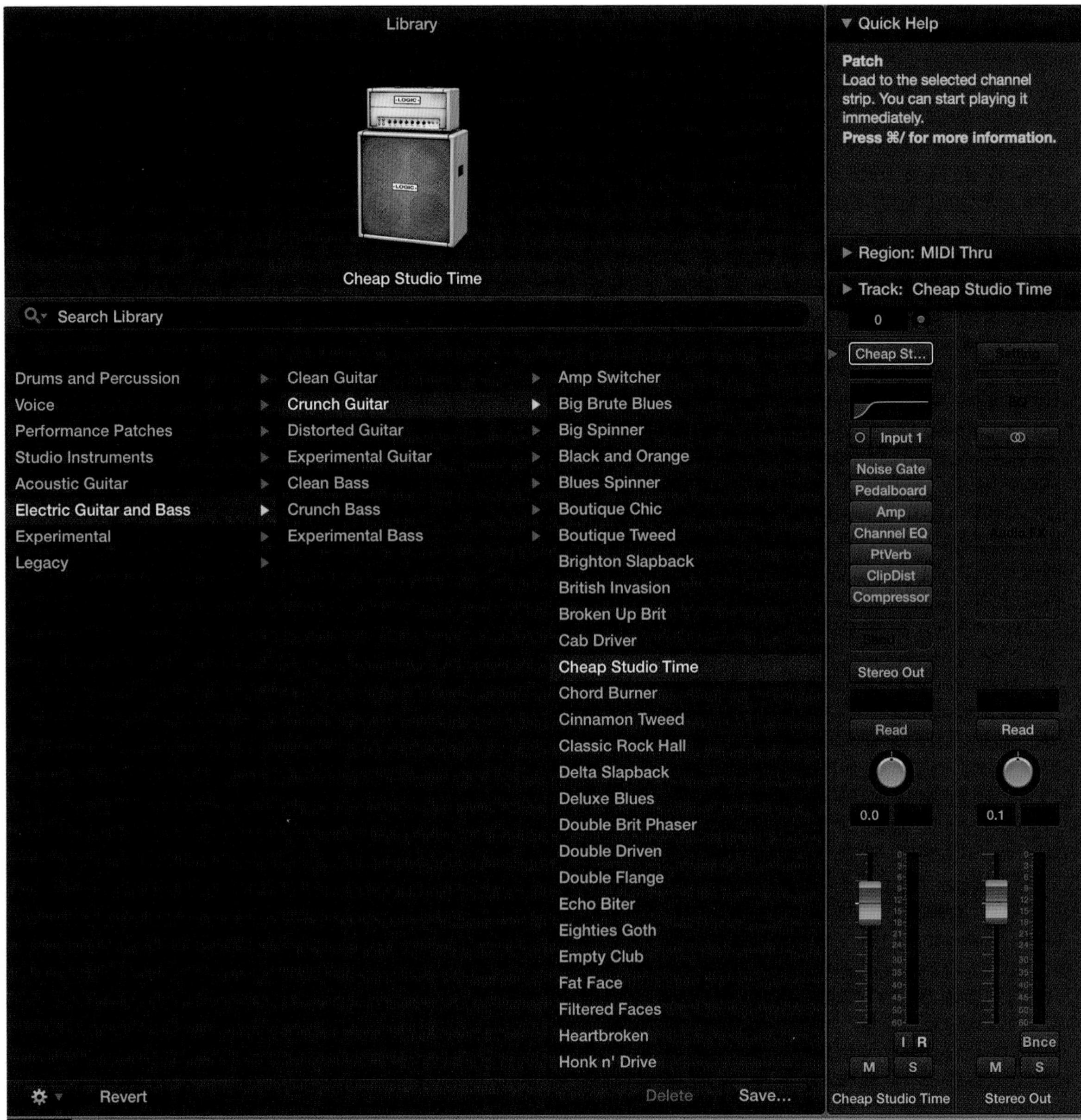

A hefty supply of presets comprising amps, pedalboards, EQ, and additional effects are available from the Logic Pro X Library window.

CLEANUP

Logic's editing tools are incredibly powerful. The MIDI Transforms window may require you to do a bit more work at first, but once you've mastered it, you can make it jump through some powerful hoops. To edit MIDI notes, you describe the data and the conditions, such as location, duration, velocity, a range, and more. You could program a Transform that looks for all notes with durations between 40 and 120 ticks that only fall between beats three and four and delete them, move them to a separate track, or shift their pitch up or down by an octave. Once you've set that up, save it, and you can recall it at any time. Granted, that is an edit you might not want to use very often, but again, selecting and deleting all notes with a value of less than 120 ticks might be a great way to clean up your performance. Of course, Logic's MIDI Transforms are not restricted to notes. In fact, just about any MIDI data you can think of can be edited, thinned, scaled, deleted, or created.

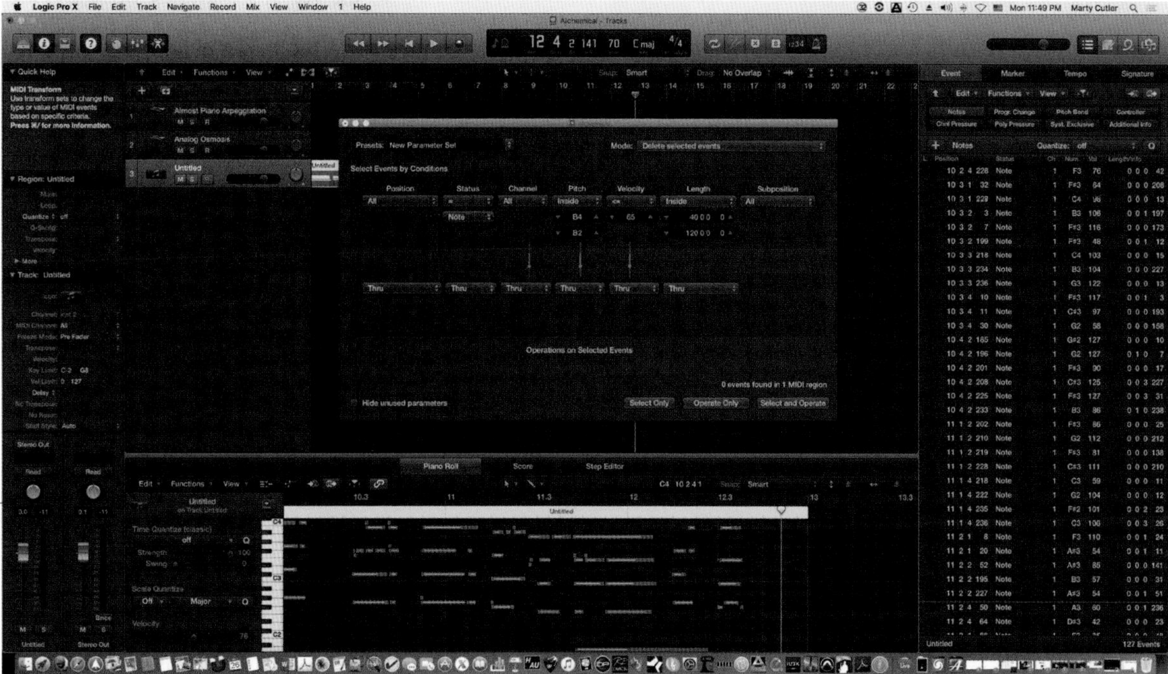

I have customized Logic's MIDI Transforms window to delete any notes between B4 and B2 with MIDI Velocities lower than 65 and durations between 120 and 40 ticks. You can set up parameters and transform practically any type of MIDI data.

When you consider its guitar-friendly features, super-high-quality virtual instruments, and plug-ins and its remarkable bang for the buck ($200, downloaded from the App Store), Apple Logic Pro X is a top contender in its eminent suitability for the modern guitarist. One important point to consider: Apple Logic is the only DAW in my list that is exclusive to the Mac; all others are cross-platform.

Steinberg Cubase Pro (Mac, Win)

Cubase has a multitude of great-sounding plug-ins, a Logical Editor that easily rivals that of Logic Pro X, and the ability to record multiple MIDI channels on a single track. Unfortunately, the only built-in instrument that can support more than a single MIDI channel is their Halion Sonic SE sampler, as contrasted with all of Logic's synths. Of course, there are scads of third-party software instruments that support a multitimbral setup. We'll discuss a handful in Chapter 9.

Cubase has a multitude of great-sounding plug-ins, including LoopMash 2, and a powerful Logical Editor that works in the same manner as Logic's Transforms window.

Cubase's built-in synths and drum machines sound gorgeous and are easy to program. It has a variety of creative audio apps not found in the other programs—LoopMash is a piece of work with its ability to combine disparate music loops into a single groove.

On the audio side, Cubase also offers some nice-sounding guitar amp–modeling plug-ins, although they are not quite as parameter-laden as those of DP and Logic. For some, that may be less daunting; others may find the lack of detailed editing frustrating.

Setting up audio for Cubase can be somewhat fiddly, depending on your circumstances. If you use a second audio interface, such as the USB ports of the Roland GR-55 or the Boss GP-10, you will need to create an Aggregate Device in Apple's Audio MIDI Setup app; this combines any inputs and outputs you plan to use from multiple devices. Cubase is a remarkably deep program with great instruments and tools.

Presonus Studio One Pro 3 (Mac, Win)

A relative newcomer to the digital recording world, Studio One is remarkably streamlined and mature, largely due to its extensive implementation of drag-and-drop techniques. The efficiency of setting up a track by dragging a software instrument or effect plug-in (for example) is infinitely faster and more preferable to menu diving, selecting from a pop-up window, or other standard operations. Most everything you need is tucked away in a tabbed browser: Instruments, Effects, and Loops categories help you to focus as you skim through your immediate resources. Click on Files to navigate through your entire computer if you need to look elsewhere or if you want to load songs or presets without having to click outside Studio One. Whatever you find in the browser, simply drop it onto the main arrangement area and you have set up a track. Anything you need to fine-tune the track, such as MIDI channels or the like, are available on the left-hand side of the window. Volume and pan position are on the left. Care to dress up your synth or audio track with some reverb? Hit the Effects tab, find a reverb, and drop it onto the same track; the reverb's panel pops up, and you can select the patch you like.

Plug-ins suited for guitar include the cleverly titled Ampire XT, an amp-and-cabinet plug-in whose neat user interface packs a generous choice of amp heads and modeled speaker cabinets and mics with variable positions. Stomp boxes include wah-wah, tube driver, EQ, modulation, pan, tremolo, delay, and reverb. All but the first two can be individually switched to pre- or post-cabinet. You can't reorder the effects chain in the stomp box section, and as the modulation effect covers flange, phase shifting, and chorus, you can choose only one, but don't let that worry you, because Studio One provides a boatload of high-quality effects, and you can arrange them all—including Ampire—in an FX Chain, a workspace where you can link any and all effects, including third-party plug-ins. Here, you are not restricted to any order or even signal path; FX Chain handily provides splitters that you can add at any point in the chain. It bears repeating that you can accomplish all this with drag and drop.

Perhaps Studio One's most dazzling implementation of drag and drop is the Scratch Pad window. A click on the Scratch Pad button divides the window in two parts, with the Arrangement window on the left and the Scratch Pad on the right. You can drag around a region of single or multiple MIDI and audio tracks, drop items into the right-hand window,

Studio One Pro's Scratch Pad brings drag-and-drop ease to rearranging songs. You can also drag instruments and effects onto tracks.

and edit and move parts around to your heart's content without affecting the original track. In almost any other scenario for so drastically rearranging music, you would need to undergo a ton of cutting, pasting, saving (always saving), and sweating to make sure nothing was lost on the way to your new arrangement. Here, just drag, drop, and move things around to taste. It is incredibly liberating. One more: Simply take any section of MIDI or audio, drag it back to the browser, and you will automatically create a loop in the process—brilliant.

For all of its workflow brilliance, Studio One comes up a bit short on the MIDI-recording side of things. It's strictly a single-channel-per-MIDI-track operation, so you'll need to set up a template, as you would need to do with Digital Performer or Live. As with DP, you can shift-click and combine your six-track performance into a single view for editing. Unlike Digital Performer, however, Studio One MIDI-editing commands are limited. If you need to clean up the occasional glitch misfires that MIDI guitars are heir to, be prepared to hunt and peck. The most frustrating aspect is the Delete Short Notes command; there is no inkling in the software or in the documentation as to what constitutes a short note, and I have had to undo frequently because Presonus's idea of a short note differs from mine. I have stopped using it in favor of picking out tiny notes manually. Studio One is sorely in need of a Logical Editor in the fashion of DP, Logic, and Cubase.

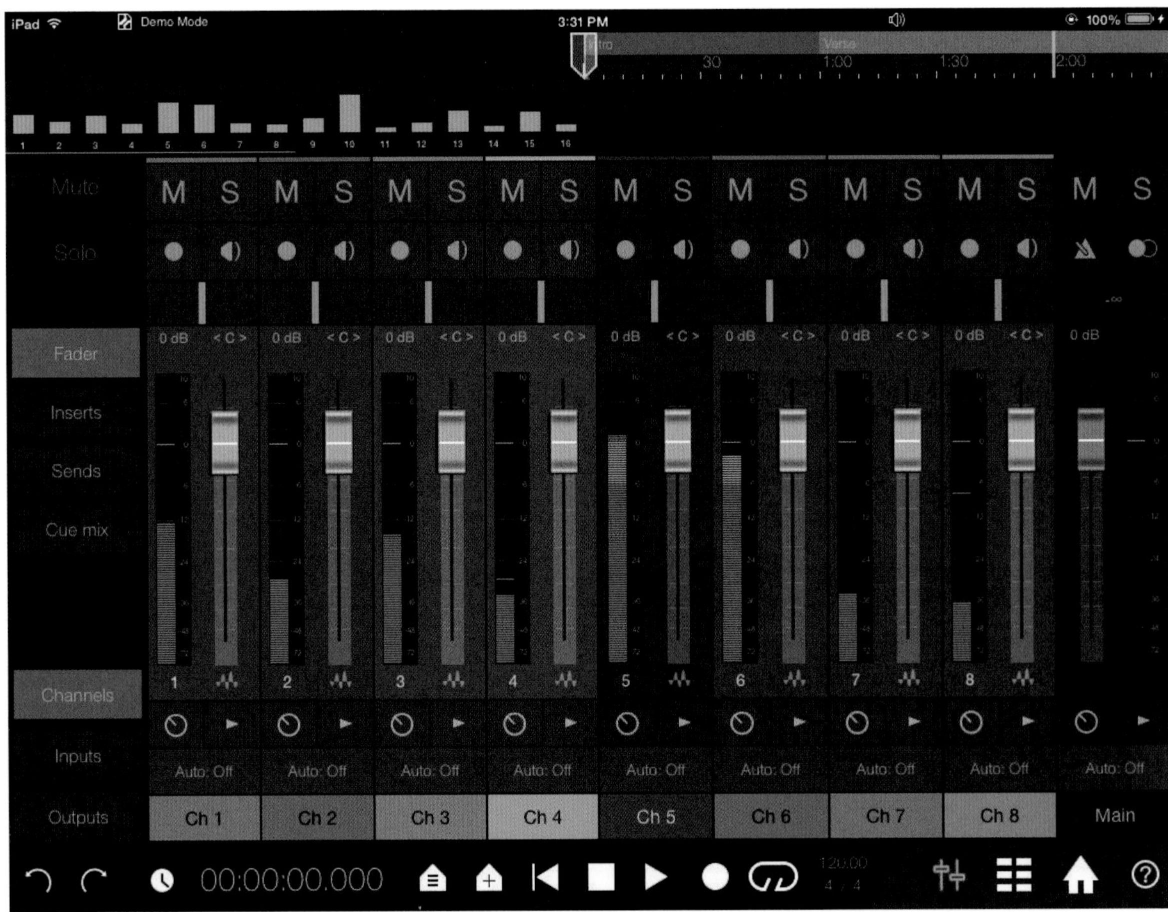

The free Studio One Remote app is a remarkably comprehensive remote controller, letting you mix, load, and set up plugins and automate the recording process from your iPad.

Studio One has lots to recommend it, despite my reservations. If you have an iPad, the Studio One Remote app just might tilt you in its direction. It is easily the most comprehensive DAW controller I've yet seen, and it's free. With a single touch, you can look at and edit channels, inserts, and sends; add inserts and busses; edit faders; open the Channel Editor; record, play back, bounce, or nudge events; add automation; and so much more. All this up close and comfortable, without squinting at the monitor.

Propellerhead Reason (Mac, Win)

Reason is a hybrid offspring of a DAW and a virtual analog synthesizer studio. It presents a rack of some really powerful synthesizers, a couple of samplers, drum machines, loop players, and processors as well as virtual control voltage (CV) inputs and outputs with MIDI splitters, audio splitters, pattern sequencers, and arpeggiators. You can create monster sounds and effects with the Combinator, which harbors multiple instruments and processors and adds its own controls, and lots more. Reason is a closed system in that it can load only its own synths and third-party instruments specially designed for its system, but the great news is that it can be easily set up to work in conjunction with any DAW that supports a protocol called ReWire—and that's practically all of them. Anything sequenced in Reason can be synchronized to another DAW, and its processors, mixer, instruments, and effects can serve as a passive rack full of studio gear. Its audio outputs can be called up in the host program, and you can access its virtual instruments

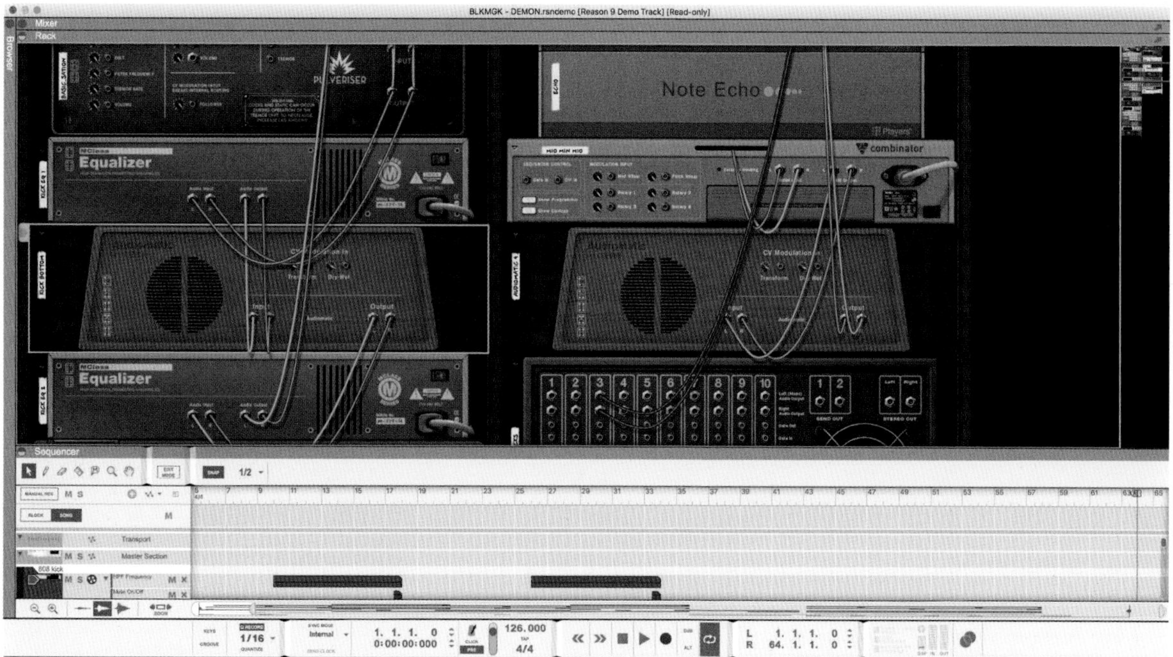

A rear view of Propellerhead Reason, displaying the virtual cabling of its many effects, synths, splitters, and other devices.

by MIDI from the master sequencer. This is particularly handy because you can edit the MIDI data in (for instance) Digital Performer, even though the data is triggering Reason. Reason has many things to offer, but deep MIDI editing for guitar is not one of them—as it is limited to only one MIDI channel per string. Another issue to contemplate, if you are considering Reason as your sole music-production software package, is that its plug-ins are Rack Extensions, a Reason-derived format that many third-party developers have not completely adopted. On a positive note, however, Propellerhead rigorously controls the quality of its plug-ins, making it a robust program that hasn't ever crashed in my use, and that's been over a decade. Other positive aspects include the huge library of sounds, samples, and third-party synths and effects they have amassed. Reason is a self-contained and flexible monster of a compositional tool.

Avid Pro Tools (Mac, Win)

If one software program has become an industry standard, it is Pro Tools, which has been widely adopted for use in major recording studios across the country. One reason for this is its remarkably streamlined editing workflow and elegant editing and comping tools. *Comping* derives from the word *composite*, meaning that a track is the composite of regions of multiple takes. In the days of analog tape, this was usually done by physically splicing the best bits together—for example, a guitar solo derived from multiple takes. Pro Tools offers a Clips window in which you can define pieces from multiple takes, drag them to the Clips list, and rearrange your tracks by dragging them into whatever order you choose.

Pro Tools 12 HD supplies a "lite" version of Eleven, their amp and cabinet plug-in. You get a choice of modern and vintage-style amps, as well as a pair of 4-by-12 virtual cabinets. These sound very authentic, and cranking up the gain produces a realistically graduated crunch. If you like what you hear, you can spring for the full version, which contains many more amps and cabinets along with a programmable virtual mic setup. As with Reason, Pro Tools uses AAX, a proprietary plug-in format. The good news is that it is supported by nearly all third-party software developers, and installations almost invariably include an AAX version.

MIDI guitarists may find a few hurdles to exploiting the technology's full potential. One is that Pro Tools MIDI tracks are single-channel only. That means you need to set up a track for each string. You can group MIDI tracks, but you can't edit all input from your MIDI controller in a single view, which makes tracking down items for cleanup awkward.

Take Your Pick

It's hard to go wrong when choosing a digital audio workstation, but as a guitarist, you have a different focus on the software, and a few more things to think about than the average keyboardist or engineer. There are a handful of other excellent programs out there. Cakewalk Sonar (Windows only) is an amazing program that rivals any that I've mentioned. Bitwig Studio looks extremely promising and flexible. FruityLoops—Windows exclusively—also has a number of devotees of its somewhat unconventional modular style.

Keep in mind that most of the applications I've mentioned offer trial software, and in some cases, you can find fully operational, pared-down versions at a reduced price. Avid Pro Tools and Presonus Studio One offer free, downloadable versions, which may be all you need to get your virtual feet wet. In many cases, audio hardware for computers bundles special editions of recording software that may meet your needs; you might not need all the features in the flagship version of the software. Be sure to search the internet for free, open-source DAW software, too; there are a number of free and shareware programs out there that are worth investigating.

CHAPTER **9**

Plug-Ins and Software Instruments

Plug-in formats: AU, VST, and AAX versus stand-alone, guitar-friendly features. An overview of popular software.

It's likely that the first images this book may conjure are rack upon rack of guitar processors, mixers, and synthesizers. While that's not an unrealistic picture, virtually all of that has moved inside your computer, iPad, and even your phone—and it can sound fully professional. In fact, many virtual instruments outstrip hardware instruments, feature for feature.

In Chapter 4, I described some of the fundamentals of synthesis and outlined the various methods synths use to shape sound. When software instruments first hit the scene in the '90s, the older, slower processors could barely keep up with the intense calculations required to generate synthesizer sounds in a musical way. One big problem was latency: the delay caused by the need to read data into Random Access Memory (RAM) before it could be processed and output. To be sure, professional instruments that utilized samples in some form or other, such as the New England Digital Synclavier, were in use as far back as the early '70s. The first personal-computer-based instruments to arrive were primarily sample-based and were stored in a chip on a computer soundcard. Because these were often sold as part of a general-purpose computer system and the samples were short and not numerous enough to produce more than a general impression of the original sound, they weren't all that useful to professional musicians, and were barely acceptable to hobbyists. Around the same time, Roland mapped out a system called General MIDI, by which synthesizers maintained a compatible library of sounds so that musicians who shared projects could expect a consistent performance with respect to instrument types, transposition ranges, drum assignments, and the like. This called for (for example) a bank of pianos, followed by a bank of chromatic percussion, followed by organ, guitar, and bass, and so on. Each bank had consistent types of instruments arrayed in the same order of program changes, and so piano banks started with Acoustic Grand Piano, through several varieties of acoustic and electric instruments, culminating in Clavinet—which isn't a piano, of course, but needed to be accounted for in the scheme of MIDI composition. In sum, when using General MIDI synths—no matter which one—program 1 would always load an acoustic grand piano, program 17 would always load a drawbar organ, and program 106 would always call up a banjo. General MIDI first appeared in the marketplace in hardware synthesizers, such as Roland's Sound Canvas series.

Many computer companies started to incorporate this protocol into their sound cards, and as processors sped up and RAM became more plentiful, more attention was devoted to higher-end sound devices that drew upon sample libraries. The late '80s and much of the '90s were the heyday of sample playback instruments and samplers, some of them branching off into less literal, more creative corners—instruments such as the Roland D-50, which derived sounds from a combination of attack transients ranging from plucked string attacks to bags of nails striking a pipe, and digitally generated, analog-style waveforms. The Korg M-1 succeeded this with an equally eclectic choice of sounds and higher-resolution, multisampled instruments, among other features. Still, realistic emulation of acoustic and electric sounds was the dominant goal; keyboardists wanted realistic re-creations of acoustic piano more than billowy pads with sparkling high-frequency motion.

Meanwhile, Yamaha made a brilliant sortie into nonsampled realms with the VL-1, the world's first commercially available physical-modeling synthesizer. Targeted primarily at realistic brass and woodwind sounds, the instrument's realism and expressiveness was startling, especially when held up against the comparatively static nature of sample-playback synthesizers. Yamaha soon released module versions of the VL series, and eventually, the physical-modeling engine found its way into a sound card.

By the mid-'90s, computers could provide enough processing power and memory to re-create the internal processes of synthesizers; that is not particularly surprising when you remember that synthesizers had largely gone digital by that time. Some of the early adopters were Seer Systems Reality, which combined sampling and sample playback with a variety of modeled synthesis types, and Bitheadz Retrosynth, which was an analog-modeling synthesizer. Around 1996, the German music software company Steinberg introduced its Virtual Studio Technology (VST), featuring Cubase VST, a DAW that integrated MIDI sequencing, audio recording, and built-in software effects, processors, and synthesizers. The race was on.

As I write this (20 years later!), the number of software instruments is overwhelming. In order to accommodate multiple computer platforms and audio engines, several plug-in formats were developed. Apple devised the Audio Units (AU) platform to accommodate its acquisition of Logic from its original company, Emagic, and to support developers within its own operating system. Digidesign developed its own cross-platform audio technology, Real-Time Audio Suite (RTAS), which later gave way to AAX, and Windows offered DirectX, which was later supplanted by Steinberg's Virtual Studio Technology (VST). Of these abbreviations, AU, VST, and AAX have survived—all of them are supported in virtually all software instruments. That is beneficial in the same way that General MIDI is beneficial, in that a sequence created with a software instrument or effects plug-in on the Mac will sound pretty much the same on a Windows computer. In fact, several cross-platform DAWs, such as MOTU Digital Performer, can host AU and VST plug-ins under the same virtual hood, ensuring compatibility when a composition is ported over to the other platform.

With current computer technology, software instruments and effects plug-ins have achieved capabilities you would be hard-pressed to find in a hardware device. Samplers can stream multi-gigabyte audio from disk, and synthesizers have more and better envelope generators and LFOs. And with the computer doing the heavy lifting, more complex, hybrid, multi-engine synths are making amazing inroads. Let's look at some instruments on offer and the features that favor guitarists.

Spectrasonics Omnisphere 2

A hybrid synthesizer of the first order, Omnisphere 2 enjoys the expert programming of Eric Persing and Diego Stocco, among other masters of sound design. The instrument furnishes a logically organized user interface that encourages exploration, making it simple to tweak and undaunting to dig deeper into. All parameters are logically arranged within a multiple-page system.

All parameters are logically arranged within Spectrasonic Omnisphere's multiple-page system. You can access very deep editing without ever getting lost.

The springboard for many of the instrument's great sounds is its stellar library of sound sources. Omnisphere is most definitely *not* a sampler, yet the sounds reflect the state of sampling art, imbued with animation and attitude. Conventional sounds mingle with ethnic instruments, burning pianos, banjos and guitars played with an EBow, hang drums played with electric toothbrushes, vintage synthesizer tones and wavetables, vibrating light filaments, and a galaxy of other sounds ranging from conventional to outré. Few of them sound anything like you'd expect because of the recording and processing techniques used to capture and shape them, but also due to Omnisphere's formidable synthesizer capabilities.

At the core of Omnisphere are two multiple-engine Layers, each with its own oscillator section, filter, envelopes, effects, and more. Oscillators start out as real-time, generated wavetables or sample playback. Select the A or B Layer and then click on the magnifying glass icon: Each oscillator is bolstered by waveshaping, FM, ring modulation, granular synthesis, and other techniques, along with a Unison mode, which multiplies the oscillator, letting you produce anything from natural, detuned chorusing to wildly inharmonic timbres. One of Omnisphere's unique capabilities is its Harmonia feature, which layers up to four additional oscillators that you can assign to different frequencies, detune, and, in conjunction with the wavetable oscillators, independently assign to different waveforms. Technically speaking, a single Omnisphere patch can deploy up to 24 oscillators.

Omnisphere's granular controls break up the oscillator sound sources and synthesizer wavetables into small grains whose pitch, duration, envelope, and position in the stereo field can be easily altered to create fascinating, animated timbres that travel far afield from their source.

All of this is tied to a deep but intuitive subtractive-synthesis engine with a stunning array of high-pass, band-pass, low-pass, and scads of other specially designed filter types. The envelope generator is a piece of work in itself; it defaults to a simple ADSR type, but right-clicking at any point in the envelope produces a drop-down menu that lets you insert another stage, a pulse shape, a spike, and lots more, in addition to a handle that lets you drag and create your own envelope segments. I could rhapsodize an entire chapter's worth about Omnisphere's synthesis capabilities, but suffice it to say that Omnisphere 2 is the very argument in favor of software instruments over their hardware kin. My only wish is that Spectrasonics would release a standalone version of the synth, but Omnisphere supports all plug-in formats, so it can easily load into a DAW or just a less processor-intensive, freeware host program.

CREATING A MONO MODE MULTI IN OMNISPHERE

Omnisphere 2 is eight-part multitimbral, so it is more than suited for MIDI guitar. To make the six-stringer's life easier, opening the Multi tab defaults to a mixer window, from which you can assign your independent parts to each mixer channel. From there, you can assign your choice of patches, MIDI channels, any of eight individual outputs, levels, pan position, and sends to four virtual effects racks. There are several different modes of operation within the Multi frame, but this one is the location to quickly and easily save basic Mono Mode setups for MIDI guitar.

Our goal is to create a simple Multi patch with the same sound on all six MIDI channels. I'm selecting Omnisphere because it's laid out in a way that makes the process clear and as simple as possible; you may have to do a bit of hunting and pecking on other devices, but this should lay out the basic groundwork for you, regardless of the synth you choose.

Load Omnisphere into your host program. I recommend a host program with low CPU overhead, such as JU-X Software's Hosting AU <http://ju-x.com/hostingau.html> for several reasons: You can load it quickly, it can support all MIDI channels on a single track, there's no finagling extra MIDI tracks, and most importantly, Omnisphere requires a host program.

Once you have loaded Omnisphere, you should be looking at the default patch: an initialized, no-frills (and boring) sound. It doesn't sound especially impressive, but for our purposes, it will work just fine. On the right side of the panel, locate and click on the rectangular Solo button; it will now be highlighted in blue. If you play the patch now, you will notice that it can play only a single note at a time. Next, navigate to just below the Glide buttons and locate the Bend Down and Up menus; set each to 12 semitones (or whatever you find to be a comfortable range on your guitar controller). Now go to the upper-left,

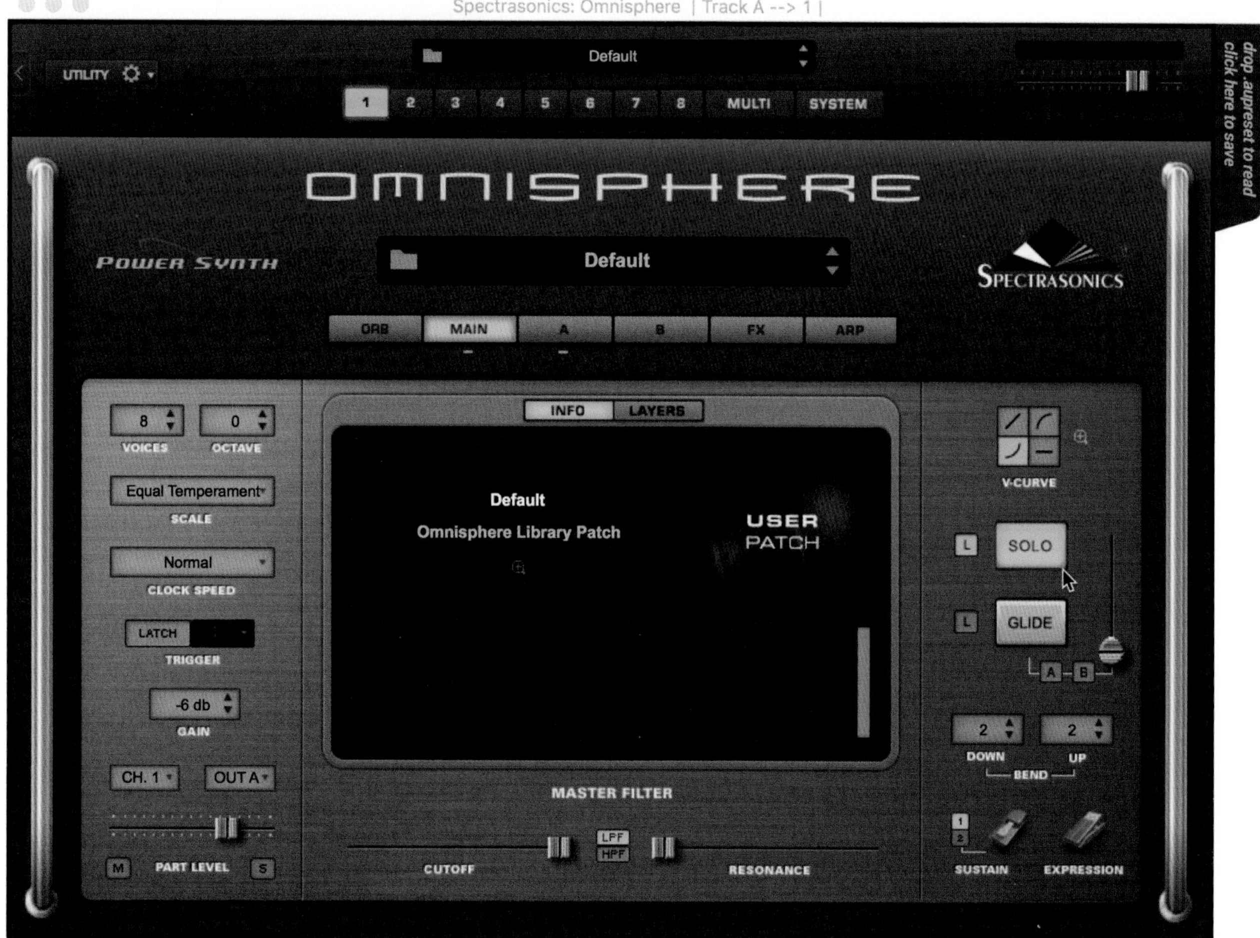

Omnisphere's Default Patch and Main screen. I have clicked the Solo button, indicated by the blue highlight and the computer's arrow pointer.

metallic-gray corner of the instrument's virtual rack to find the pull-down menu marked Utility; drag down to Save Patch As and click. A dialog box will pop up, and you can name the patch whatever you choose. Then save it in the User folder, which will be the default folder when saving your own patches. The User folder contains a number of subfolders with descriptive titles to help organize your own creations, and you can create your own subfolders. Congratulations! You've just done your first bit of synthesizer programming!

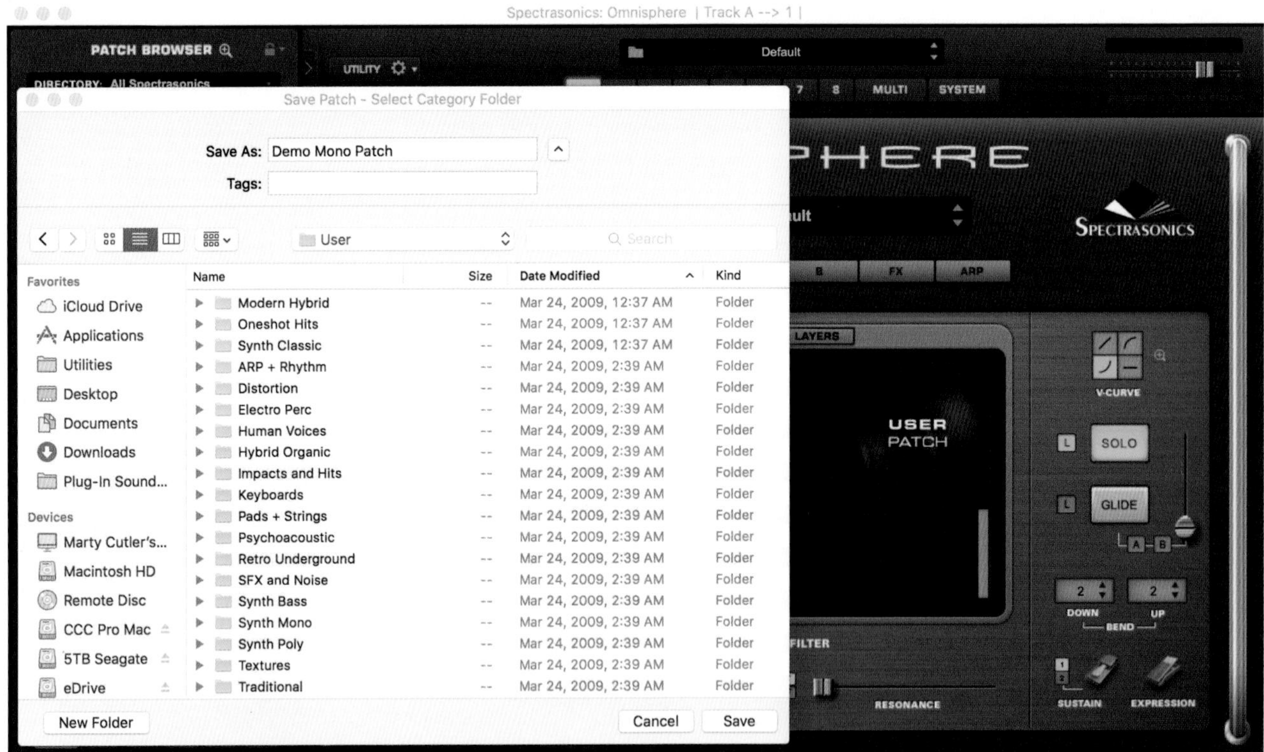

Name and save your edited patch to the User folder. Spectrasonics has thoughtfully provided a selection of subfolders to organize your patches by category.

At this point, all you need to do is navigate your way to Omnisphere's Utility menu, at the upper left of the main panel, and select Clone Part 1. Look at the Multi to examine your handiwork. In the topmost center of the instrument, locate and click on the button marked Multi, directly to the right of the Part buttons numbered 1 through 8. A Mixer page will open. You will notice that your patch is replicated in all eight parts of Omnisphere. Make sure that your patch occupies each of the first six slots, and that parts one through six are consecutively assigned to MIDI channels 1 through 6. You can again navigate to the utility menu and save the Multi with the name of your choice; once again, you will find categorized folders and the option to create your own. Congratulations are again in order; you've just programmed your first Multitimbral patch (or Multi).

In all probability, your guitar has six strings; you're probably wondering what you can do with those two extra parts. Options abound. You can assign them to the same MIDI channel as other strings as a layer, choose a completely different patch—for example, a

Omnisphere's Multi page can hold parts for up to eight independent patches. Here, each part is assigned a separate, consecutive MIDI channel.

bass sound—and assign the remaining two slots to the bottom pair of strings by matching their MIDI channel assignments. For that matter, notice the Level, Pan, and Aux knobs; experiment with these. You can always recall your original patch as long as you've saved it. To get some inspiration, poke around the Factory Multi presets.

Given the breadth and depth of Omnisphere's sonic capabilities, you may wonder why I had you create a rather homely patch and then assign it to six separate parts. The reason is to focus on assigning patches for a MIDI guitar setup. You want to assign a part to each string. As I've discussed earlier in the book, Pitch Bend will affect all notes on a single channel, and for MIDI guitarists to get around that issue, each string should be assigned to a different MIDI channel. In case you are wondering why I would restrict the patch to only a single note at a time, pick up your guitar and play a note acoustically on the first string, then—on that same string—play a second note while trying to sustain the previous note; you will always cut off the previous note. Assigning each string to Solo (or Mono on other synths) mimics that behavior and prevents sustained, ringing notes from running together. It provides the additional benefit of minimizing the glitches that may come from less-than-clean playing. Given that understanding, you can now set up your own MIDI guitar Multis with any of the factory presets or your own creations.

Another aspect of Omnisphere's versatility is that its proprietary Steam synthesizer engine is compatible with other virtual instruments in the Spectrasonics line, including Trilian, an instrument focusing on the many varieties of acoustic, electric, and synthesized bass. Spectrasonics' most recent virtual instrument, Keyscape, can also be played within Omnisphere or as a separate plug-in, but there are compelling reasons for the former. Keyscape focuses on a massive collection of keyboard instruments, some of which are extremely rare, and all of which have gorgeous and often unusual tone. It's a perfect match for Omnisphere 2. Keyscape shows up in Omnisphere's browser, and a quick trip to the Spectrasonics website authorizes Omnisphere to use it as a satellite program. The benefits should quickly become obvious. The Keyscape interface provides customized tweaks for each patch, but they are tweaks; you can't get down to the sound-design nitty-gritty in the same way Omnisphere 2 provides. I could use Keyscape's sounds as is and hardly bat an eye, but the temptation to dig deeper and use the sounds is always there, and it was heartening to click the little x next to the instrument logo and discover the full Omnisphere engine lying behind the curtain. You can easily combine Keyscape layers and oscillators with Omnisphere's existing library or use its Granular engine, Harmonia, and other remarkable sound-design resources. As I was finishing edits for the book, Spectrasonics released Keyscape Creative, a free, add-on sound library for Omnisphere, drawn from Keyscape as a sound source. Any resemblance to traditional keyboards is purely coincidental.

Additionally, bringing Keyscape into the Omnisphere fold gives performance benefits, among which are Omnisphere 2's arpeggiator, Live and Stack modes, and my favorite: Multi. ■

Arturia Matrix-12 V

If you are looking for vintage analog sounds, Arturia's collection of vintage instruments is a good place to start. Its stock-in-trade revolves around its faithful software re-creations of the most revered vintage synthesizers and keyboards. The Modular V is a stunningly accurate modeled Moog Modular, and Stage-73 V captures all the crunch and funk of the Fender Rhodes stage and suitcase pianos.

In keeping with the needs of the electronic guitarist, Arturia's Matrix-12 V demands a closer look. The instrument dominated the airwaves in the mid-to-late '80s with its broad timbral range, covering squelchy synth basses to warm, creamy pads to screaming leads and aggressive brass tones. For some, the Matrix-12 was the last great analog synth of its time.

Whether your DAW of choice is Cubase, Pro Tools, or Logic—even if you just want to play the instrument without the encumbrance of additional software—Arturia has you covered with support for VST and AAX (Mac/Win) and AU (Mac only), as well as a stand-alone version (Mac/Win).

Matrix-12 V's two oscillators are versatile; you can select up to three waveforms to mingle in oscillator 1, and as many as four in oscillator 2, with a noise oscillator added to the selection of pulse, saw, and triangle waves. The pulse wave's width produces a hollow-sounding square wave with the knob set at the center, and bright, nasal tones at either extreme end.

Although each has its own amp and envelope, the oscillators share a filter, which has no fewer than 15 different filter types, including the unusual-sounding phase filter, which shifts the phase of the waveform's harmonics and is capable of producing beautiful and subtle timbral motion. You can regulate the strength of the filter on each oscillator's VCA. If you want to add some grit to your sounds, FM turns oscillator 2 into a modulator over oscillator 1, or you can apply frequency modulation to the filter.

As you might expect from the instrument's name, you will find a rich matrix of modulation, distinguished by a lag generator, which, by changing the data rate between two points, can reshape modulation sources; and ramp generators, which provide additional linear modulation. These are great when applied to vibrato generated from the modulation wheel, as they can gradually increase the amount of vibrato, rather than turn it all the way up instantly.

Guitar Multitudes

Rather than descend into the rabbit hole of modulation tricks the Matrix-12 V can do—and there are many—let's return to our guitaristic point of view and examine how the Matrix-12 V pans out. One look at the instrument's Multi page should provide some clues. You can allocate the instrument's 12 voices to any of the 12 Voice slots; the original Matrix 12 synthesizer only offered six voice slots, by the way. Arturia manages to pull off the seemingly contradictory task of remaining faithful to the original design of vintage instruments while adding features more suitable to modern needs. It may be a coincidence, but it is worth noting that there are exactly twice as many voice slots as there are strings on a guitar. Whether by intention or by design, Matrix-12 V makes it easy to set up a multitimbral guitar in some very creative ways. For starters, each voice can be assigned to one of six zones, and each zone has an assignable MIDI channel. Each voice also has a Detune parameter, so you could copy voices 1 through 6 to 7 through 12, assign the same sound, and then detune one voice slightly against the other to create a beating effect, but why stop there? You could layer a different patch in the second six voices, or a different patch for each of the slots, or perhaps transpose one group of patches to an interval of your choosing. Each zone has a low and high note limit, so you could program an instrument that only plays in the low range and another that, say, starts at middle C and plays higher. Naturally, you would want to explore panning the instrument's voices across a stereo field. But there are other possibilities, too.

Similar synthesizers (albeit without the Multi section) include AIR Vacuum Pro and Applied Acoustics Ultra Analog 2.

Arturia's Matrix 12V is a great analog-modeling synthesizer, with sounds that are faithful to the original instruments, and updated features befitting a modern software instrument. Its Multi page provides convenient programming for MIDI guitar.

Native Instruments' Kontakt

In its preteen years, sampling, though widely accepted by electronic musicians, was regarded as a separate entity from synthesis, primarily because it lacked some of the core ingredients of synthesizers of the day. Generally, the first commercially available instruments could capture and play back audio with little else to recommend them: no filters, no envelope generators, and often not enough memory to build dynamic sound or accurately re-create an instrument's full range. As RAM and storage became cheaper and digital technology matured, samplers were able to adopt full synthesizer architecture in addition to their audio-recording capabilities, and sample-playback instruments became the preeminent design in commercial keyboards.

With the advent of virtual instruments, samples could be stored in the computer, loaded into RAM, and processed through virtual synthesizer processing. As faster processors and drives became affordable, sampled content could be read from the drives on the fly, without the need to load them entirely into RAM, freeing memory up for other functions. That process is known as *streaming*, and it became widely adopted, the net result being that virtual sample–based instruments could work with larger samples, and more of them.

My very first sampler was Akai's S612, which had a top sampling frequency of 32kHz of 12-bit audio, all of 128 kilobytes of RAM, and no storage save for an optional drive that could save two samples at a time to quick disks. Editing was minimal. And with a maximum sampling time of up to eight seconds, it was hardly good for anything beyond an occasional snare replacement or an orchestra hit.

Contrast that with Native Instruments' Kontakt (Version 5.3, as I write this), in which instruments comprising hundreds of megabytes are routine, and multi-gigabyte sounds are becoming less and less rare. Furthermore, Kontakt is multitimbral, letting you load as much sample content as your computer's CPU will allow, and at up to 24-bit, 192kHz playback. In addition to supporting the three major formats, Kontakt launches as a stand-alone instrument.

The factory content is generous, running from meat-and-potatoes band and orchestral instruments to inspiring, hybrid libraries that (for instance) place unorthodox upright pianos whose enormous sound chambers are built into the wall of a hotel, and tempo-synchronized loops of Cuban, African, Balinese, and Indian instruments alongside playable kits and instruments.

West Africa is a particularly enticing library with a detailed, tasty sampled kora; you can play it from your guitar, or press the Play button and select from a number of performance loops, or do both. If you want a less repetitive performance, there's a knob to select variations, or you can

West Africa is one of many delightful factory sample libraries for Native Instruments Kontakt, as evidenced by the number of libraries displayed in the browser on the left. Because of its prodigious multitimbral capabilities, you could assign loops to the lower strings of your MIDI guitar and an instrument to the higher strings.

trigger fresh variations with lower-pitched notes that are outside the range of the instruments. If your guitar controller has a Hold function (most do), you can sustain loops for as long as you like while you play over them. You'll also find a generous supply of percussion-ensemble performances you can play with in the same manner. In general, emulative instruments are detailed and emotive, and hybrid, synthetic sounds are rich and animated. Kontakt has an enormous cadre of third-party developers, supplying everything from percussion libraries derived from junk and banging on dumpsters, to hyper-realistic virtual orchestras, to exotic and haunting pads derived from field recordings of desert winds blowing through phone lines.

Art and Architecture

The heart of Kontakt is a freely configurable, modular, subtractive synthesizer, loaded with an à la carte menu of filters, envelope generators, effects, sample editors, and scripts with which you can define how Kontakt will play back samples. You can play back one-shot drum samples or foley sound effects with no filters, loops, or envelope settings, or you can record grooving rhythm-section loops and deploy Kontakt's Time Machine module so your loop can synch to tempo without changing pitch, or try the Tone Machine to change the pitch of the loop without losing its natural sound, as it would with conventional pitch-shifting methods.

You could spend your entire musical life exploring Kontakt's presets, but one of the best parts of sampling is the ability to roll your own. As with virtually all software samplers, Kontakt has no live sampling facility; you will need to record your samples in your DAW software, a mobile device, or a hardware digital-audio recorder that lets you transfer your recording to your computer. Once you've loaded them into your computer, Kontakt can access the samples, and you can use its sample editor to assign the sounds to the proper keys and take it from there. There's a dazzling lineup of options, but don't be intimidated; Native Instruments provides some of the best manuals around.

As a compatible sound source for MIDI guitar, Kontakt makes it pretty easy to set up a quick and dirty Multi and get to work. Select a patch from the browser on the left and drop it onto Kontakt's virtual rack. It will already be assigned the first MIDI channel, and subsequent patches loaded in will take on the next consecutive MIDI channel; you can confirm that by looking at the left side of the instrument, under its title in the virtual rack.

Next, look just above and to the right, and you'll see an indicator that reads *Voices*. This indicates how much polyphony is being used when you play. Directly to its right, you'll see a parameter labeled *Max* and a small window with a number to its right. You can click and drag down or use the up and down arrows to the left to change the value. Those options are a bit slow, so simply double-click in that window and type the numeral 1, and then repeat the process for all six consecutive channels and patches. You have now effectively put Kontakt into MIDI guitar Mono mode. Save the Multi and you are ready to roll. Of course, in Kontakt, you can load as many patches as you like and make some amazing splits, layers, and far more complex patches.

An acoustic upright bass Multi I created in Kontakt. Each part is assigned a consecutive MIDI channel—one for each string of my guitar, and each string matches the pitch-bend output of the guitar.

Another sampler with equally powerful capabilities is MOTU Mach5, which in version 3 adds a variety of synthesizer engines, including analog modeling, four-operator FM synthesis, modeled percussion, modeled organ, and more. You can build monstrous sounds in Mach5 by stacking and splitting oscillators. Mach5 is remarkably intuitive to set up for MIDI guitar: Create as many parts as you like, select a part, and add a patch from the browser.

Mach5 is supported by an ever-growing collection of sound libraries, and it's compatible with the large collection of great sounds from UVI, a company that has amassed excellent libraries ranging from emulations of vintage synthesizers to a two-volume set of sampled children's toys. Don't overlook MOTU's own batch of great libraries, such as Ethno, a brilliant collection of instruments from around the globe, or their Symphonic Instrument, comprising brass, woodwind, and strings in solo and ensemble settings as well as orchestral percussion, historic instruments, and much more. While you're at it, check out the Bob Moog Foundation's Encore Soundbank, which features some of my sound-design handiwork among the work of some luminaries in the synthesizer world.

Native Instruments' FM8

When Yamaha's DX9 and DX7 synthesizers hit the musician's marketplace, they took the world by storm, largely because their crisp, detailed, and often crystalline tones were such a stark contrast to the prevailing warm and fuzzy sounds characteristic of analog synthesizers of the day. Digital FM sounds were not subject to the tuning issues of overheated analog circuitry and were therefore more reliable on stage. Anyone who lived through the '80s will doubtless have heard the DX7, with its hard-edged bass sounds and its crystalline and glassy electric pianos dominating practically every ballad on the airwaves.

For a quick refresher course on FM synthesis jargon, please refer to Chapter 4. The DX7 (and most digital FM synthesizers of the day) had no filters, and because programming the instrument led to a labyrinth of submenus, musicians had a hard time grasping the instrument's user interface, which offered minimal real-time control. Additionally, coming to grips with the use of algorithms to shape your sound was daunting. Almost singlehandedly, the complexities of the DX7 gave birth to a cottage industry of synthesizer programmers who could provide fresh sounds for the instrument.

Yamaha had many variations on the theme over the years, but its most successful incarnation is the Native Instruments FM8. The 8 in the instrument's name refers to the instrument's complement of eight operators, as compared to six from the DX7. The DX7 offered 32 different algorithms to configure the operators into carriers and modulators; FM8 offers 64 and adds the ability to create your own. To the DX7's only option of sine waves, each FM8 operator can be any of the 32 waveforms on offer. Native Instruments didn't stop there, though; one of the operators can serve as a multimode filter, complete with resonance and multiple-segment envelope generator.

The result is an often breathtaking collection of sounds with swirling harmonics and unexpected evolution from one characteristic to the next. If FM synthesis seems intimidating, you can use the instrument's Easy/Morph interface, which boils the most significant tweaks down to a single page, with sliders and knobs assigned to characteristics such as harmonic and brightness, along with envelopes governing any timbre and amplitude changes over time and an effects rack with buttons to simply engage your choice from a generous rack of effects. Morph is simply an axis with four points and snapshots of the sound with different settings. Dragging a mouse through the plot creates major changes in the patch sound.

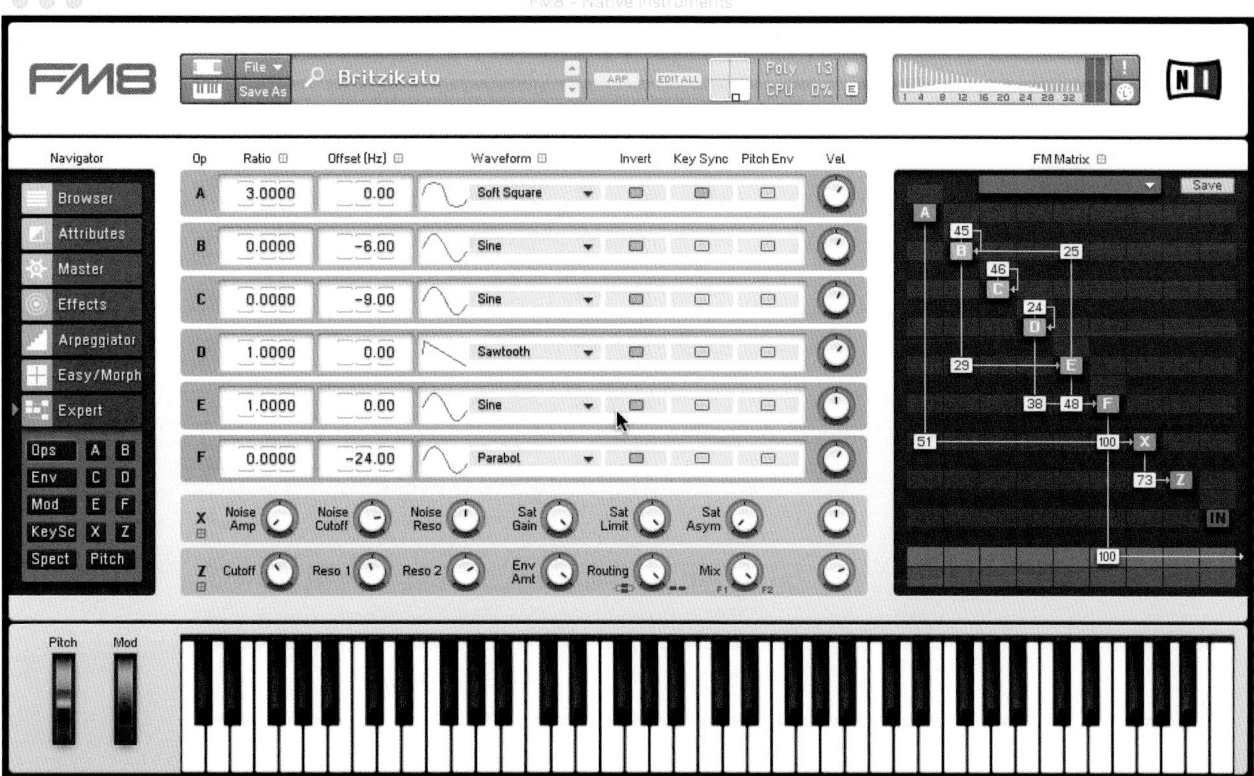

Patterned after Yamaha's DX7 synthesizer, Native Instruments FM8 uses extreme frequency modulation and a complex matrix of operators to create complex, animated sounds.

FM8 can nail the classic sound of the DX7 or sound like nothing you've heard before. Its timbral variety is truly vast. If you're feeling nostalgic—or just need to re-create DX7 sounds—you'll be overjoyed to know that there are countless DX7 patches all over the internet, and FM8 can import and play them, as well as those of its ancestor the TX-81Z, so your sonic options are practically limitless.

As a target instrument for your guitar synthesizer, FM8 is limited to input from only one MIDI channel, but surprisingly, its processor overhead is extremely low, and you can load up a half-dozen separate instances of these in any host program and set the Pitch Bend as desired. That's good news, because FM8 is eminently suited for blending with your guitar signal. Its crisp response and nearly limitless selection of tones can form some great hybrid electric and synthetic tones. For a unique hybrid of modular analog and FM synthesis, look into U-He Bazille.

LinPlug Spectral

Theoretically, additive synthesis—because it deals with the raw building blocks of sound—should enable us to conjure up perfect replicas of naturally occurring instruments and sounds simply by constructing them from sine waves. The reality is, of course, that so much more comes into play beyond the static reproduction of sound, and the computational horsepower required of additive synthesis to create sounds that change over time is enormous, and probably prohibitive, certainly in a commercially available instrument. Add to that the arduous and counterintuitive process of conceptualizing a sound, sine wave by sine wave. That didn't stop manufacturers from trying. Kudos to the sound-design team for the late, lamented Kawai K5 synthesizer, whose acoustic piano patch produced a startlingly realistic attempt. As they say in the business, though, "Close, but no cigar." As much as the patch was imbued with many of the properties of an acoustic piano, it wouldn't have fooled anyone in an exposed musical environment.

Nonetheless, additive synthesis—or at least the core principles behind the techniques—guides a number of instruments that can produce sparkling, unusual sounds. Today, a small number of plug-ins use additive synthesis as a springboard for creative design. Most modern-day plug-ins combine additive and subtractive principles and usually assign groups of oscillators that collectively form components of a sound's harmonic structure. Because almost all natural

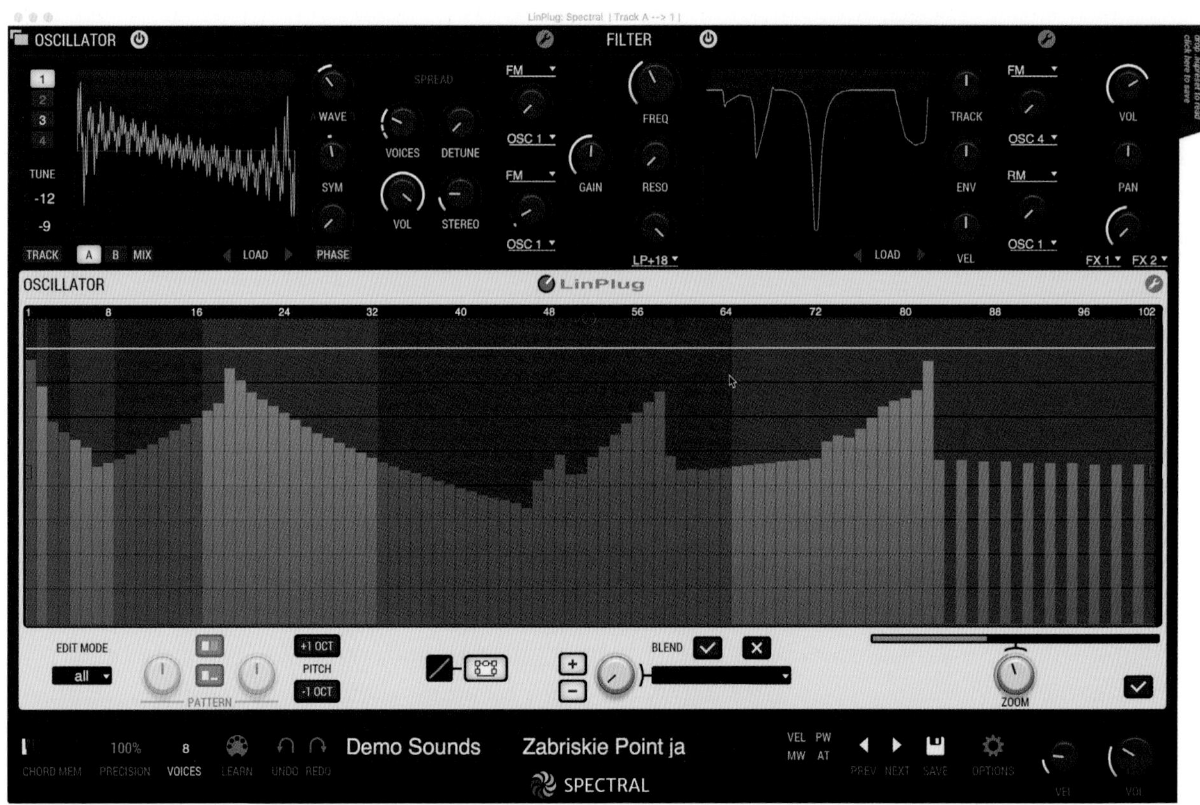

LinPlug Spectral is a four-oscillator hybrid of additive, subtractive, and FM synthesis. You create waveforms by dragging over the harmonics (represented as individual bars in the lower pane of the window).

sounds possess a great number of frequencies falling outside the harmonic series, a compromise might include the ability to detune groups of harmonics.

One of the finest plug-ins of the lot is LinPlug Spectral. If you are intent on playing meat-and-potatoes sounds, such as acoustic piano emulations or spot-on tenor saxophone solos, from your guitar, the world of plug-in instruments offers loads of resources for you, but Spectral isn't one of them. Spectral's strength lies in the ability to create sounds no analog synth or sampler can produce. Add subtractive synthesizer components, and you can even emulate classic analog instruments. Spectral can do that and so much more.

Four oscillators, each with its own signal path, let you create waveforms by clicking and vertically dragging individual bars representing harmonics ranging left to right, from high to low. Spectral retains a pool of preset waveforms that you can load as starting points, too. You select an oscillator to edit by clicking one of the small, square buttons on the left of the instrument panel. Each oscillator also features an A and B button, to switch between different states of its waveform; you can even load two completely different waveforms for each oscillator. A Mix button lets you blend or morph between the two states.

There are a number of ways to alter the waveform, including phase, symmetry, and the number of voices. As with Omnisphere, the number of voices is almost like creating additional oscillators that you can then detune to create a thick, natural chorusing effect. Knobs for simple amplitude modulation (AM) and FM are great for creating clangorous overtones that a basic harmonic series couldn't normally produce. You can also use a pull-down menu to change the modulation type to phase modulation, which is similar to FM. Each of the oscillators sports a resonant multimode filter, and the options here extend well beyond high- and low-pass filters. As with the preset waveforms, the filters have a drop-down menu with a library of filter types you can load, but even more intriguing is the ability to hand-draw filters using the same techniques you use to draw the oscillator waveforms. Along with a deep matrix of modulation tools, filters can create anything from rhythmic, glassy bubbles of sound to shape-shifting pads with coruscating upper harmonics darting in and out.

If you're thinking that Spectral is only good for ear candy, take another guess. It also excels at punchy keyboards and basses as well as rounded, slowly moving pads and aggressive lead sounds, and the sounds are filled with motion and life. As a MIDI guitar sound source, you'll need a powerful computer, because Spectral is strictly a single-channel synth, and loading six separate instances of the synthesizer could likely push your computer's CPU to the limit. The good news is that by selecting a somewhat lower-resolution sound quality, you might have an easier time of it, and the reduced sound quality is still not bad, but that doesn't leave much room for other instrument plug-ins.

Korg Legacy M1

When the M1 was released in the latter part of the '80s, it caused quite a stir, and with good reason. The sounds were distinctive, thanks to its whopping (for its day) 4MB library of meat-and-potato sounds, including brass, guitars, pianos, organs, strings, and drum kits, among a palette of plucks, pops, poles, and anvils, mixed with unusual sounds created with digital signal processing (DSP) software. Drum kits were unusual in its day, but Korg supplied several full drum-and-percussion kits, making it an essential component in what was one of the first commercially available synths to offer a comparatively sophisticated onboard, eight-track sequencer. It was also one of the first synth keyboards to offer Multis, which manifested themselves in split and layered and crossfaded sounds that sparked people's imagination; this synth could sound big! The M1 also sported a 512KB-capacity card slot, and Korg used it to host a sizable number of ROM cards with fresh samples. You could also purchase blank cards and use them to store your own programs or sequences.

M1 sounds turned up everywhere: film scores, pop hits, jazz recordings, and pop ballads. Eventually, as memory grew less expensive, the M1 was supplanted by instruments with a larger complement of samples and effects—many of them from Korg—but it's interesting to note that some of the core M1 sounds survive in the memory of some of the company's most powerful synthesizers. Despite its comparatively tiny memory, the Korg is a triumph of creativity over size.

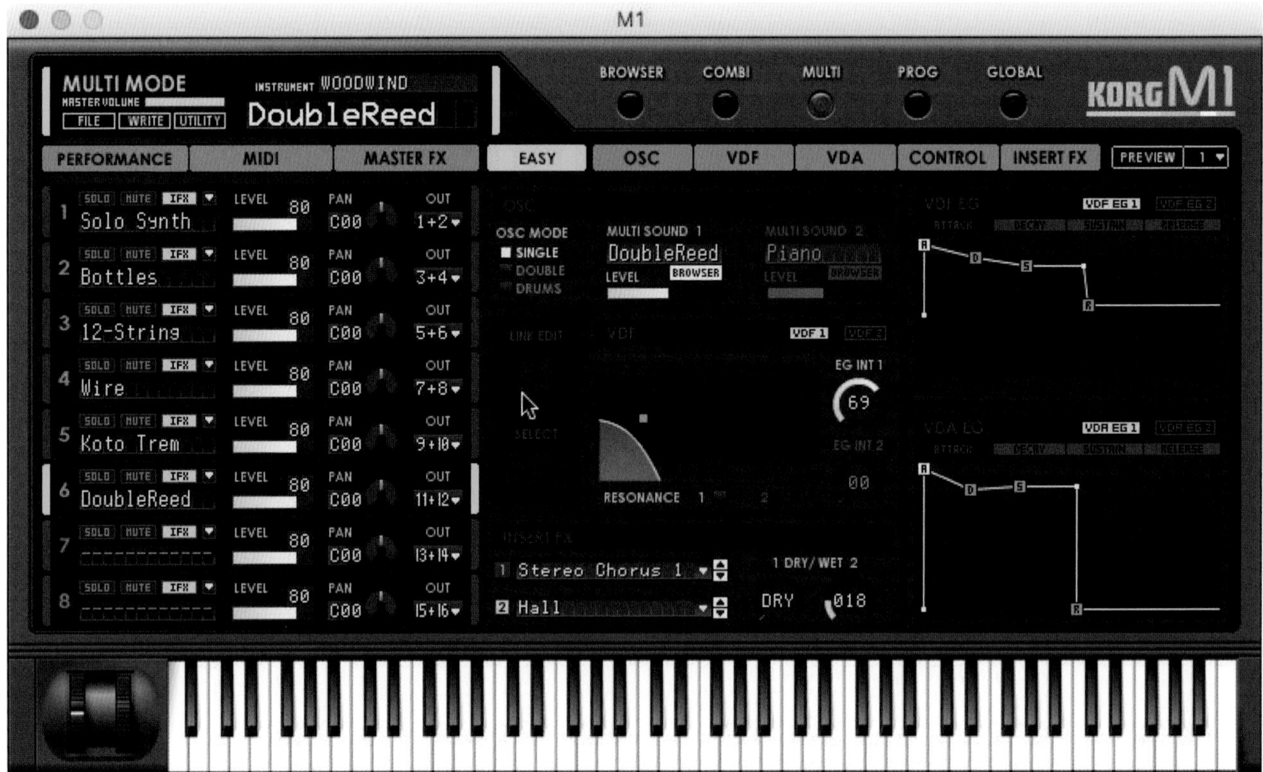

The Korg Legacy M1 includes all of the classic sounds of its hardware sibling and adds an easy-to-arrange Multi page.

As someone who has extensive programming experience with the M1, I can safely say that if you think it's difficult to eke out fresh sounds with its limited sound set, think again—especially as regards the software version. The Korg Legacy M1 contains all of the sample data from the M1 expansion as well as all of the ROM card samples from the company's T-series synthesizers (which eventually replaced the M1). Add to that a resonant low-pass filter, and you have a terrific-sounding shape-shifter of a synthesizer that can also provide you with a real-world-sounding rhythm section.

For all of its sonic versatility, though, its inclusion in this book is due to another feature: The Korg Legacy M1 is a killer instrument for MIDI guitar. The instrument has an interesting and versatile division of labor. It can be set to play in Program mode, strictly a single patch at a time. Combi mode is a Multi, but it's designed more toward splits, layers, and, in general, ways of building a more complex single instrument. Multi Mode, however, is a feature added to the software M1, replacing the onboard sequencer of its hardware predecessor. Here, you have eight separate channels you can use for assigning to your guitar's MIDI input, and you can handily change each channel to monophonic response.

Plenty of synths out there offer unique sound-mangling approaches, and many of them can double as effects processors for your guitar signal. Another synth worthy of serious investigation is Xfer Records Serum, a wavetable synth with an exceptionally deep but intuitive modulation system and the ability to import your own wavetables.

As long as I am touching on the subject of creative sound design, I'm compelled to mention one of my favorite synthesizers of all time: Native Instruments' Absynth. Now at version 5, this synthesizer started its life in the late '90s. Its longevity is partially a result of its continued development, and it is a telling index of how good this synthesizer actually is that it's still at the top of my go-to list for intriguing, attention-getting, and most importantly, *musical* instruments. As with Spectral, its stock-in-trade is not letter-perfect acoustic instrument clones; instead, it excels in the thing synthesizers do best: sounding like a synthesizer.

At this point, I'll abandon any pretense at editorial neutrality to make a couple of enthusiastic recommendations. Anyone seriously contemplating a dive into synthesis and guitar processing needs to at least take a long look at Native Instruments' Komplete bundle. It may seem counterintuitive to offer several different upgrades to a package that implies completion, but other than a DAW, Komplete Ultimate may be all you'll ever need for a . . . complete music-production and performance system. I've already discussed the Kontakt sampler and FM8, and I've mentioned Absynth, all of which are part of the Komplete package. Among other software, you'll receive Massive, a wavetable synth with a meaty, complex sound; Battery, a drum-machine-oriented sampler; and Reaktor, which blows the roof off the collection's value. Reaktor is at heart a construction kit for synthesizers, effects, and event processors. If you've ever wanted to design your own audio effects or build your own synthesizer, Reaktor is as good a place to start as any. Reaktor is a blank slate with models of audio-processing and event-processing components. You can drag these components into the main window from the browser and link them together from input to output. With version 6 come Blocks, which combine multiple components into a single function, such as oscillators with FM or other kinds of modulation.

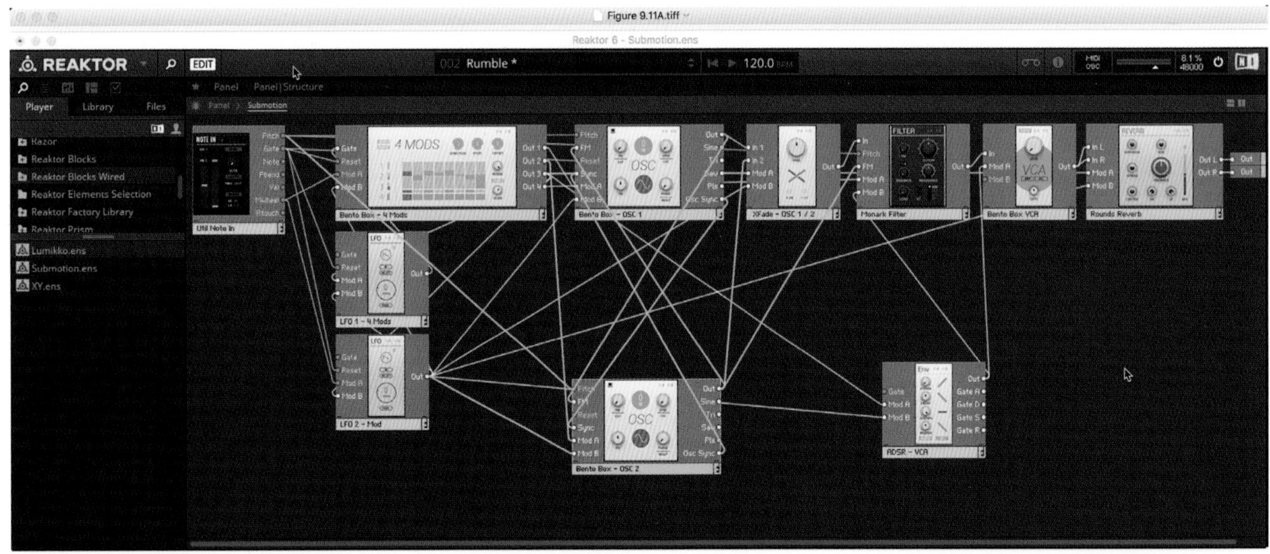

Two views of a software synth in Native Instruments Reaktor. You can link Blocks—preset synthesizer components—and build your own instruments. If you aren't interested in designing your own virtual instruments, Reaktor has a vast library of synths, samplers, drum machines, and effects that are ready to use.

If building your own effects or synthesizers is too much for you, don't worry; Reaktor comes with an enormous grab bag of pre-assembled synthesizers, effects, and gizmos of all kinds, ranging from step sequencers and self-playing drones, to reverb, distortion, analog and physically modeled synthesizers, and instruments you probably never knew existed. If that isn't enough, there are online user groups that post their own creations for free download, and many of these are terrific-sounding. Additionally, periodic updates often include new, Reaktor-derived plug-ins from Native Instruments, and these invariably range from unique and very useful to spectacular, and you can deconstruct them to create your own variations. Effects range from wildly modulated mashups of filters, gates, and sequencers to more conventional reverb and delay units. As with the effects, Native Instruments releases its own stellar synthesizer creations. Komplete Ultimate seems a bit pricey—until, of course, you account for the truly enormous number of synthesizers, sounds, and resources: 87 individual products, and roughly half a terabyte of content. I recommend you go to the Native Instruments website, check the demos, and download trial versions.

CHAPTER 10

Guitar versus Synth: Who's in Charge Here?

Adapting synthesizers to guitar, guitar technique, and programming. Working together to improve tracking.

If you've been reading this book from the beginning, it has probably dawned on you that guitars and technology might not be as comfortable a marriage as you might think. A major part of this book deals with MIDI, an unambiguous protocol that attempts through binary code to describe technical gestures by which we control devices that react, to ultimately produce sounds we call *music*—in our case, we are doing this with guitars, the instrument of Nigel Tufnel. All the same, with a decent understanding of how MIDI works and how guitars are played, exploring the music in music technology can become second nature.

Envelopes Rule

I've been harping away about the guitar-friendly features of this or that synth or sequencer. But it is also important to realize that some things are just lost in translation. This actually happened: I was in a music store and saw someone getting ready to play a Roland GR-707. He became completely frustrated by the instrument's intermittent response. I wasn't close enough to see him play, but strangely unmusical wisps of the synthesizer wafted through the air. Finally, I got a little closer to find out what the problem was, and sure enough, the guy complained about how bad the tracking was. He started playing speed metal riffs to make his point. Of course, he was playing a slow-moving pad, as if he thought the synthesizer would automatically follow his playing to the letter. That goes to illustrate my first principle of MIDI guitar. Say it with me: "Envelopes Rule!" Remember, synthesizers use controls to determine how quickly they attack or fade out, and we need to play according to the way the sounds are set up. This shouldn't come as a surprise to anyone who has tried to play 240bpm bebop on a tuba. Although by now I'm reasonably certain that someone will pick up a tuba and prove me wrong, you can't play speed metal or any other solo that depends on rapid-fire picking with a patch that has a slow attack without making drastic alterations to the programming. The concept of envelopes has another implication if you are trying to emulate a realistic performance of an acoustic instrument. If we turn my tuba example around, you will not convince anyone that you are emulating a realistic tuba performance.

Of course, there's the possibility that you might just like the tone of the patch, and that could form the basis for a solo instrument or a pad with a more rapid attack. Excellent—you're on your way to becoming a creative programmer! With the caveat that you might not like the result of your altered instrument, you can do this and remember that you are not breaking anything, that you can always go back to the original patch and start over. Perform these edits with your MIDI guitar connected so you can get a tactile impression of the instrument's response to your edits and your playing needs. Keep your manual by your side (or online) so you can locate the parameters you need to edit. A quick re-reading of Chapter 4 wouldn't hurt, either.

First, let's examine two reasons why your synthesizer might be responding sluggishly to your neo–Van Halen solos. I'm assuming that you are working with a subtractive-type synth with typical envelope generators. Most synthesizer patches shape their sounds with two envelope generator types. One controls the shape of a sound's amplitude. It might be called a VCA, recalling the good old days of analog synths with voltage-controlled amplifiers, or it could be labeled DCA, referring to a digitally controlled amp; Korg calls its amp envelope generator a VDA (*V* standing for *variable*). Regardless, the *A* in the envelope's nomenclature is usually your clue that it controls the sound's loudness over time.

Next, start by calling up the patch you need to edit and accessing its envelope parameters. I'm using the Korg Legacy M1 to illustrate the process because it has a relatively easy-to-understand architecture and because it covers the parameters we need to examine. For purposes of clarity,

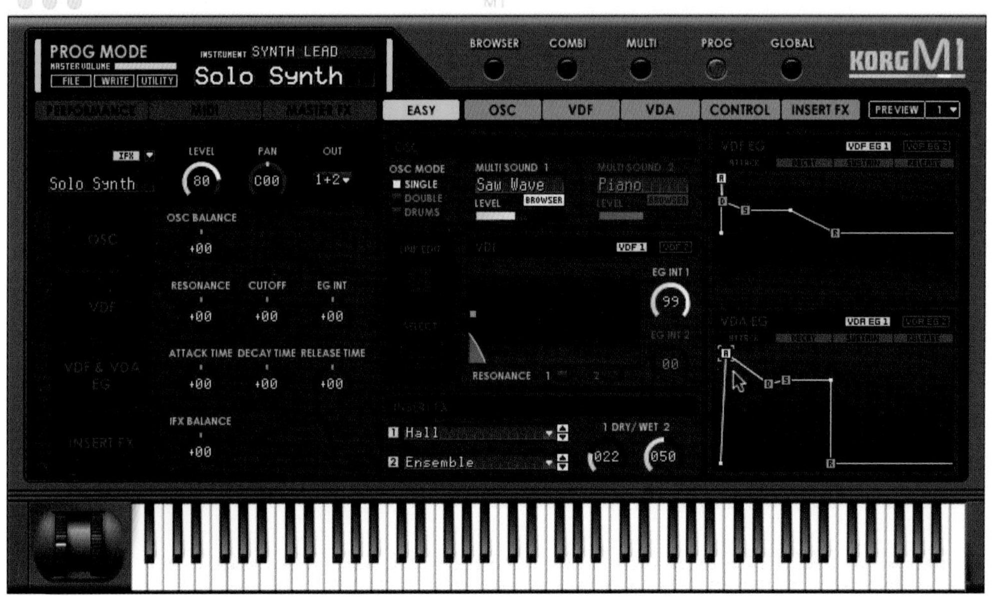

The cursor points to the Attack parameter in the Korg M1 Amplitude Envelope Generator; click on one of the small rectangles to change the way the sound develops over time.

let's start by clicking on the Easy tab. The two aforementioned envelope generators sit on the right-hand side of the graphical user interface (GUI); topmost is the VDF (yes, Korg's acronym meaning *variable digital filter* instead of DCF). First, let's focus on the VDA. You will notice four small rectangles positioned on the line graphics. The lines plot the program's changes in amplitude (vertical axis) over time (horizontal axis). They might be a bit small to read, but the rectangles represent the ADSR parameters of the sound program, and they are also virtual handles you can grab with a mouse click. In reality, the Korg's envelopes are slightly more complex than a simple ADSR, but the rectangles handily mark the more familiar aspects of the envelope. Notice that the first line, which represents the attack time—the time it takes to reach its maximum amplitude—is canted rightward, meaning that it takes some time to reach its full volume. If you are content with how the rest of the sound develops over time and simply want to speed up the attack, just grab the first handle of the four and tug it leftward until you are happy with the response time. If the response time is still sluggish, look at the filter envelope in the VDF, just above; notice that in my example, the attack time is very slow there, too. Grab the rectangle for the filter's attack and move it leftward until the sound responds properly. One word of warning: Be especially ginger with the filter settings. A lot of the program's tone rides on how bright or muted it is, and drastically altering its timbral contours might ruin the patch you are after.

At this point, the sound may respond to your playing, but you might find that the attack, while speedy enough, sounds a bit harsh, or that its speed causes the patch to articulate every glitch and accidentally triggered note you play. In those cases, consider that you may have a bit of leeway in the instrument's attack time—and this is where having your MIDI guitar controller connected is handy. Back off on the attack time just a tiny hair until you are satisfied that everything sounds and performs the way you want it to. The response may feel a tad squishy but will still track your musical gestures. For a long time, Joe Zawinul's lead sound was an alto saxophone sample with a somewhat softer attack than your average lead, but it was an excellent foil for his very unique and profoundly human solo style.

We are not done yet, though. Another aspect of making a sound respond quickly is whether it gets out of the way of your next note soon enough. To that end, look at the release tabs on each envelope; dragging them to the left shortens their time. Here again, being judicious keeps the sound from cutting off prematurely and sounding too staccato.

And yet, we are still not quite through—and I guarantee you will be glad you were patient. Having gone through all this, here's your reward, and it's a genuine enhancement to expressive playing. Just about all modern synthesizers in existence are *velocity sensitive*. To many, that simply means that the harder you play, the louder you sound, but in the world of MIDI and synthesizers, Velocity is capable of controlling much more. Using our Korg as an example, we can first click on the VDA tab and locate the cryptically abbreviated Vel Sens section, and with it, the equally mysterious EG Time parameter. The former stands for Velocity Sensitivity, and the latter stands for Envelope Generator Time. Increasing the EG Time value allows us to change the attack time by how forcefully we play. That means that a lighter touch lets you play with a softer, more pad-like effect, and bearing down produces a more aggressive tone that will let you indulge your speed-picking fantasies. Varying your touch between both poles yields very expressive results. Once again, congratulations on your programming ventures.

I've highlighted the Velocity Sensitivity (Vel Sens) with a rectangle. Here, you can set how your picking dynamics affect the intensity of the envelope, the speed of the envelope, and the polarity of the effect.

MONO MADNESS

Despite the importance of enabling independent string behavior so your synthesizers will respond more like a guitar, there's a world of benefit to learning how to play a guitar like a synthesizer, too. The late Keith Emerson was renowned for his solo on the tune *Lucky Man*; the sound of that gliding, swooping, and monophonic synthesizer caught the ear of many a listener. Another good reason to play sounds monophonically has to do with emulation of wind instruments. One of the dead giveaways of unconvincing emulative solos occurs when one note lingers into the next note—show me a wind player who can do that! Mono synthesizer programs ensure that the release of one note does not run into the next. They often have the benefit of portamento, the ability of a sound to glide in pitch to the next note. They can also be programmed for a legato response so that the sound of the attack doesn't retrigger with every note—so your patch doesn't sound like a typewriter.

Working a monophonic sound for expressiveness doesn't necessarily come naturally to guitarists—even those who can spin out flowing, single-note lines. Nonetheless, a competent steel guitarist already has the proper techniques at hand (pun intended) to achieve similar results by integrating a technique called *blocking*. Speaking as a lapsed steel player (another intended pun), I can acknowledge that the techniques required for a guitarist to master blocking may not come immediately, but with practice, you'll gain the control you need.

Blocking, as you might guess from its name, is the technique of damping notes with your picking hand. That's an important technique for steel players in particular because the instrument's setup provides an enormous amount of sustain. One of the beauties of the instrument is its ability to play long, slow-moving chords smoothly, and yet particular country music styles often require short, choppy, almost banjo-like arpeggios. A lot of the ability to vary the style so drastically lies in the player's picking hand.

Try this: On your picking hand, curl the pinky, ring, and middle fingers under and into the palm of your hand. You can grasp your pick of choice (I usually use a plastic thumb pick, which stays in place with less gripping) between the sides of your index finger and thumb. Your hand should be in a relaxed position roughly a quarter-inch or so above the strings. The idea is to be in position to play notes with the pick, using a back-and-forth, swiveling motion of your

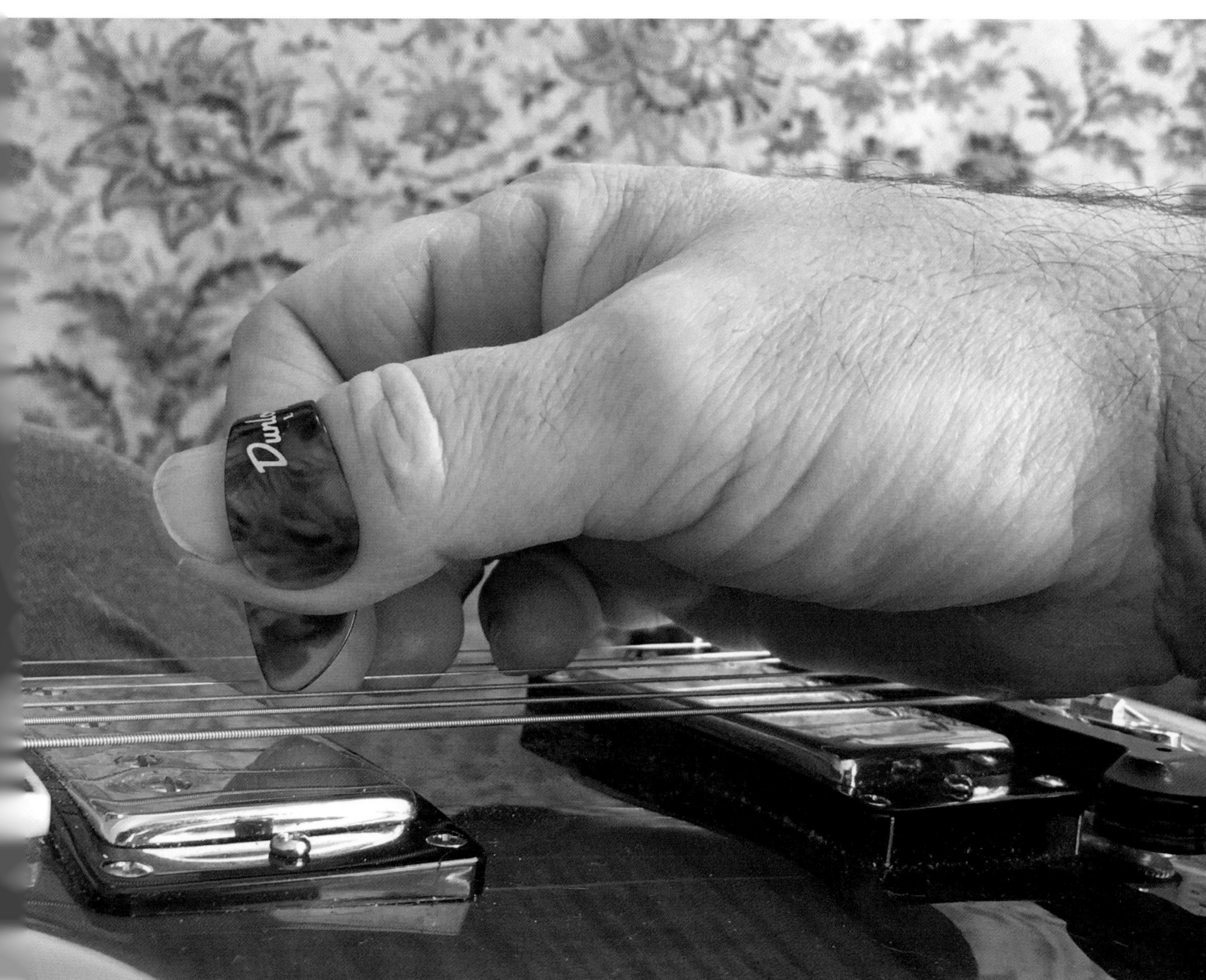

Here's a photo of the underside of my picking hand relative to the guitar. The thumb and index grip the pick or thumb pick, the meat of your palm mutes unwanted strings, and your middle, ring, and pinkie fingers remain relaxed in order to pluck chords when called for.

wrist, and damp the strings with the meat on the outer side of your palm when you need to. Practicing this style isn't that different from normal guitar routines. Try picking repeatedly on a single string, then move to the next string, just to acclimate your hand to the technique, then try alternating strings, then bring your fretting hand into action and try playing scales, and then try playing passages—slowly, you should be mindful of phrasing, and so don't simply play a barrage of uninterrupted 16th notes. Play melodies with some space in them. If it helps, listen to or watch a pedal steel player such as the late, great Buddy Emmons to get a feel for the technique.

YOUR GUITAR AND MIDI

One of the most liberating developments in MIDI guitar history was the abandonment of proprietary guitars and the emerging ability to use your own axe with a divided pickup, but there's a debit side, too. Your guitar may have some properties that make it difficult to use for synths. Body resonance in the wrong places can set your strings vibrating, and your MIDI pickup might translate that as note data. Worn or twisted strings with a bump could cause note misfires and intonation problems, as can worn or poorly finished frets. In general, whatever problems you might perceive on your guitar will be amplified when connected by MIDI to a synthesizer. Give your guitar some love, and keep it well-maintained and in tune. But you knew that already, didn't you?

All the same, many MIDI guitar controllers have ways to curb the data that issue from a problematic guitar. Every MIDI guitar I am aware of lets you tailor its response to your playing

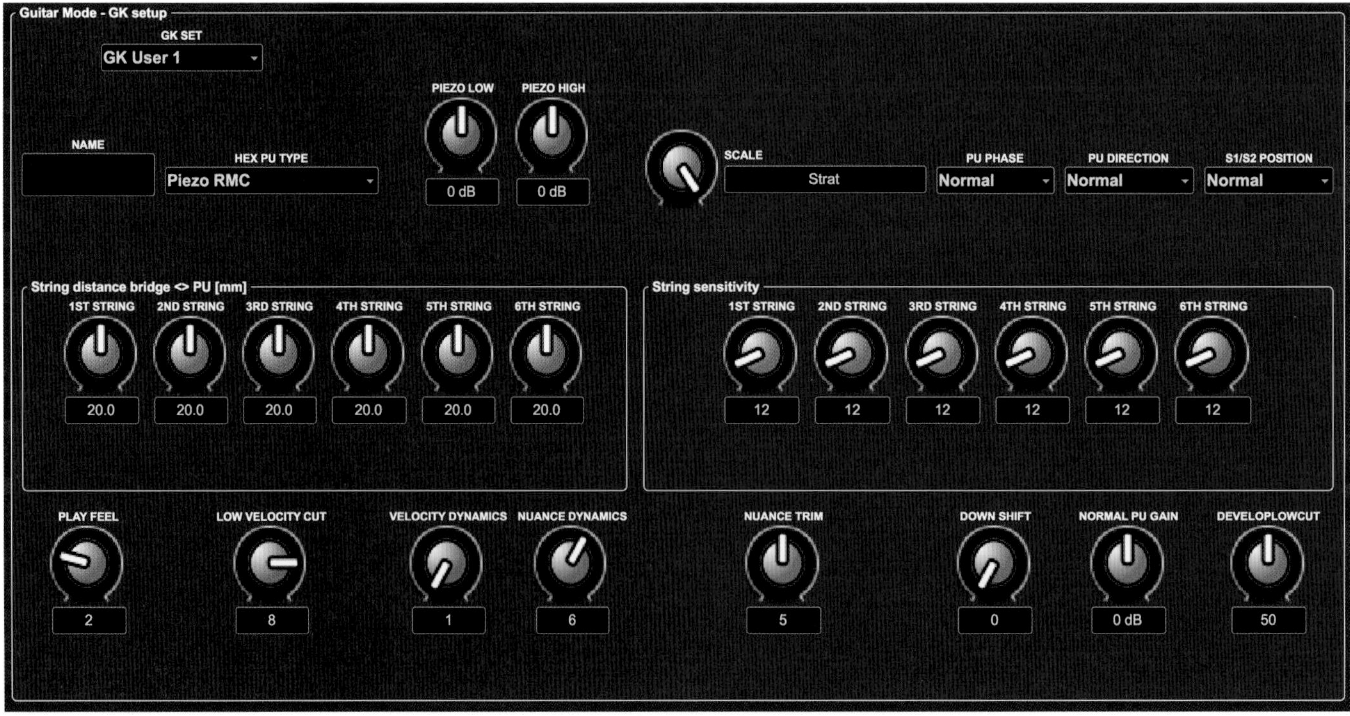

No one's playing technique is exactly the same; consequently, all MIDI guitars let you adjust the instrument's response to your playing. Here's a detail from GR-55 Floorboard, a software editor-librarian.

style, and, by extension, the setup of your guitar. The setup facilities for the Roland GR-55 provide a good example. You can specify the distance of each of the divided pickups from its string, the manufacturer of your pickup, the fingerboard scale, and the sensitivity of each individual string to your touch. If your preferred string action is a bit high, you are more likely to excite strings when you release notes; accordingly, most guitar controller systems offer a low-velocity threshold, which keeps those casual brushes with your strings from triggering unintended notes.

Consider what you play on your guitar as having a conversation with your synthesizer. Depending on the understanding and care you take, your conversation with your synthesizer can be one with an incredibly obtuse and dull listener or an animated conversation with someone you love.

CHAPTER 11

Composing with MIDI Guitar

Techniques for emulating instruments with a guitar. Guitar versus keyboard voicings, instrument ranges, and behavior.

The first time you connect your MIDI guitar to a sequencer, a vast world of sound and music will open up to you. Dive in and enjoy it; you've worked hard and you've earned it. Still, you'll keep on learning, through either your own ears or someone else's. As much as I love making purely electronic music, I am often challenged in my professional life with emulating real-world acoustic and electric instruments.

Disclaimer: This chapter is a collection of clues and tips rather than a chapter on orchestration. There are better places to learn that. What I want to do is lay out how to achieve a reasonable degree of authenticity when MIDI guitar is your vehicle for impressions of trumpet, violin, piano, drums (yes, drums), or even . . . a guitar—believe me, there have been numerous occasions when I have had to record guitar parts with MIDI. It isn't as easy as you think.

Virtually Bluegrass?

Some time ago, I was tasked by a well-known music software company to create MIDI data in the form of bluegrass music for a software program whose virtual guitar fingerboard transcribed how I played the parts. Of course, the solution was to record each string to a separate MIDI channel, but for purposes of intonation in the final product, I was not allowed to use Pitch Bend. Because this product was intended for people who might not know anything about MIDI, it was decided that none of the string channels of the target instrument would use Mono Mode. The target instrument was a Roland Sound Canvas, an early, widely adopted desktop synthesizer that adhered to the General MIDI standard, a specification that called for all instruments under its rubric to have the same sound programs in the same memory locations, transposed consistently, and subject to a standardized set of MIDI commands, among other things. This translated readily to a majority of consumer sound cards and desktop synthesizers.

As much as I have stressed the importance of setting up your guitars and synths to eke out maximum guitaristic performances, there are many good lessons to learn from the limitations imposed by this project. I wanted the performances to be realistic, dynamic, and in the pocket with bluegrass rhythms, so I decided to use my software sequencer in a simplified manner. As pliable as MIDI data may be, I used Digital Performer as if it were a tape recorder, resisting the urge to tweeze tracks that were marginal into some semblance of acceptability, and instead, starting over from the beginning. I accepted a slight degree of imprecision in my performance as well. If you have listened to any bluegrass music in MIDI form, it frequently sounds silly and laughable for good reasons, the major reason being that the MIDI is usually generated by a notation or tablature program, and almost certainly all of the notes match in dynamics, duration, and temporal location. No band could or would play like that. With our MIDI-derived, virtual band, our ear tells us that the notes of each guitar strum happen at the same time, the music doesn't groove, because there is no push and pull, notes from guitar strums all occur at exactly the same time . . . I could go on. Instead, here are things I did to avoid those syndromes.

It should be obvious that MIDI guitar is the best medium for building MIDI performances of guitar tracks, but here's one especially good reason: duration. Bluegrass rhythm guitar is built upon broad, robust strumming with a flatpick, and little damping. If you look at a MIDI editing representation of a raw performance , you will notice that notes are left to ring; in the heat of an

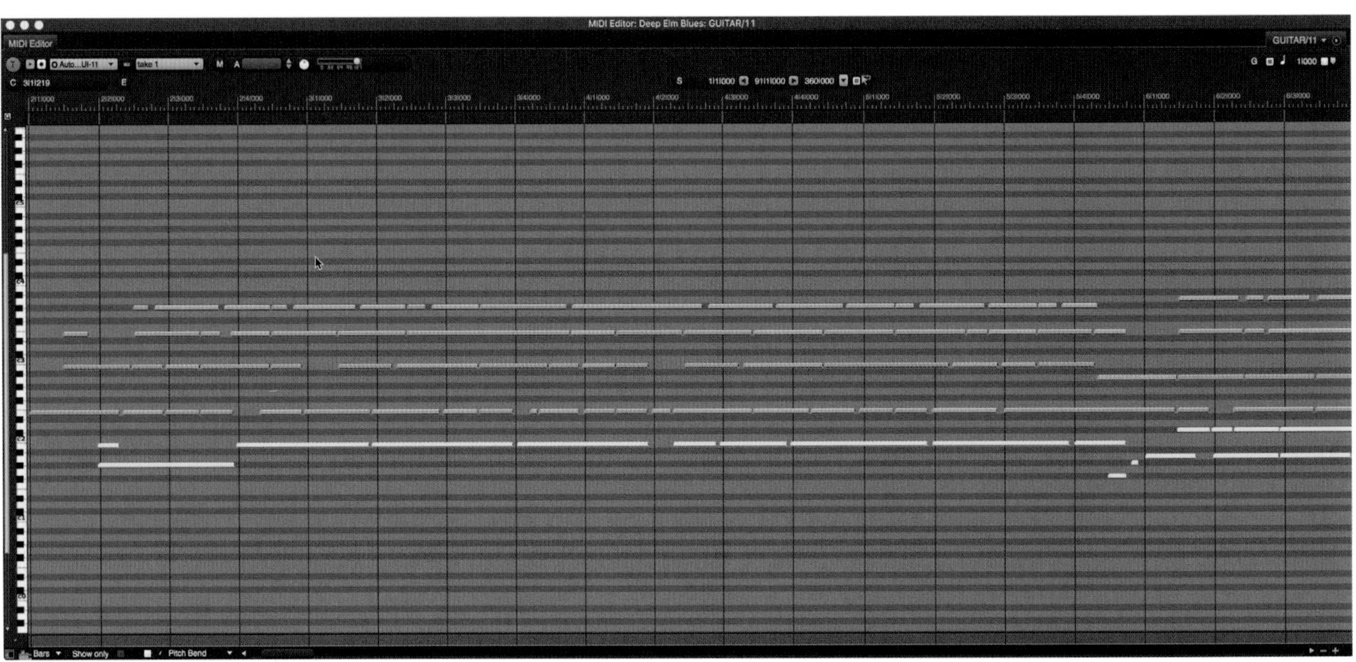

Here's what a bluegrass guitar rhythm part looks like in a MIDI editing window, with pitch running from top to bottom and note duration running from left to right. One of the things that makes it convincing is that the notes are not uniform in duration, and they are left to ring out. Consistently uniform durations, timing, and velocities cause music to sound mechanical.

up-tempo bluegrass number, you have little time to mute strings. Of course, as I've mentioned, you can't have notes from the same string running into each other, so some judicious editing was in order. I didn't want notes to die before their time, but I wanted them to play out realistically.

Because my performances relied on hammering on and pulling off in the lower notes of the guitar, I had to find a trick that prevented the hard sounds of a retriggered note. Remember: I couldn't use Mono or Legato mode to do this. This required more editing and led me to a technique that did an okay, if not perfect, job under the circumstances. If you think about hammer-on and pull-off characteristics, you'll know that the second note is the byproduct of releasing your fingers from an already picked string. In most sequencers, you can see a sort of skinny bar graph that is aligned with each note you play. The taller that line is, the higher its velocity, and in this case, the more likely the reattacking of the note, which can sound overly mechanical. The solution for me was to find those articulations and lower the velocities of the secondary notes to a point where the attack was softened. It was painstaking, to be sure, but the result, absent a true legato performance, was pretty convincing.

Early on, I wrote that guitars can do things that keyboards don't. Guitars have lots of locations to play the same note; keyboards, because of the physical layout of the keys, can issue only a single note from the same key at any given time. Fortunately, doubled notes come naturally to your guitar, and your synthesizer's tone generator is happy to double up on the same note. That works to your advantage in at least one major musical application: reproducing stringed instrument technique. It worked well on guitar, but it created an interesting and useful phenomenon on my virtual fiddle tracks. Because the notes were close but not in exactly the same positions, the onset of the two notes together created a sort of out-of-phase effect, which added a touch of animation to an otherwise uninspiring sound. Solo violins comprising a few short samples are almost invariably lifeless, so the reanimation was welcome.

TIMING IS EVERYTHING

Being mindful of an instrument's articulations is easier when you are not rushed. It's important to remind ourselves when we are recording MIDI tracks that the data is almost infinitely malleable; we have control over every note, and that is an open invitation to record without fear. It's no problem, for example, to record difficult passages of unfamiliar instruments at slower tempos. After all, MIDI is not subject to the issues incurred by stretching audio to fit time. I'm not a big advocate of fixing things in the mix, but MIDI is wonderful for making a few minor tweaks to an otherwise inspired take. The dark side, of course, is getting too lost in the details. A cautionary point or two seems in order here.

Quite often, you may have correct timing, but when you listen to the passage at the proper tempo, the notes sound clipped. As you play, pay attention to the note durations as well as the timing. You can, of course easily extend the duration of the MIDI notes, but the less you are sidetracked by editing, the better. ■

Singular Saxophony

One of the dead giveaways of unconvincing emulative wind-instrument solos occurs when one note lingers into the next note; apart from multiphonic techniques, show me a saxophone player who can play more than one note at a time. Mono synthesizer programs ensure that the release of one note does not run into the next. They often have the option of legato response, so that the sound of the attack doesn't retrigger with every note, making your patch sound like a tuned typewriter.

Although I often play drums from my MIDI keyboard or pads, MIDI guitars work well enough these days to play drums pretty reliably. As a bluegrass banjo player, I am hyper-aware of syncopations and rhythms in general. For that reason, I often abandon my flatpicks in favor of a thumb pick and a pair of finger picks, load my percussion sounds, and finger-pick drum grooves. It's not hard to find and play congas, for example, because most sampled drum and percussion kits group the related kit pieces together. One great aspect of typical sampled drum kits is that they are usually programmed as one-shot sounds; that is, they cycle through their envelopes independently of releasing or damping the note from your controller. As a result, you don't have to be quite as concerned with note durations as you play. In fact, you can reduce drum tracks' MIDI notes after the fact to smaller, uniform durations without any musical consequence. That makes editing a lot cleaner. One aspect of good drum programming to keep in mind: Beware the eight-handed drummer syndrome. Simultaneous snare, hi-hat, tom, and crash cymbals are verboten!

In the previous chapter, using a virtual M1 synthesizer, I discussed how to make synthesizer sounds more playable with your guitar. The M1—and most subtractive instruments—have additional ways to modify the envelope. *Keyboard tracking*, also called *keyboard following* or *key follow,* regulates the influence of the envelope generator with respect to how high or low you are playing on the keyboard. Because sounds have shorter life spans as you play higher notes, keyboard tracking produces a more natural behavior of the sound over time. Generally, the default setting for synthesizer sound programs follows acoustic behaviors, so if notes ring too long at higher pitches or are too short in the lower registers, find your keyboard tracking parameters and set a higher value. Some synthesizers even let you shape this with a curve, so, for example, an instrument's decay might remain consistent over a greater range of pitches.

Chords: Guitar versus Keyboard

If guitars can do things that keyboards can't, it's a sure bet that the reverse is true, too. For starters, the range of an 88-key instrument is far greater than guitar, whose notes, in standard tuning, range over roughly four octaves (depending on the number of frets). Because notes and chords on a piano can be played independently with both hands, polyphony can exceed that of a guitar. Because of the linear, stepwise arrangement of notes on a keyboard, pitches can be voiced in different ways than guitar, producing interesting harmonic textures.

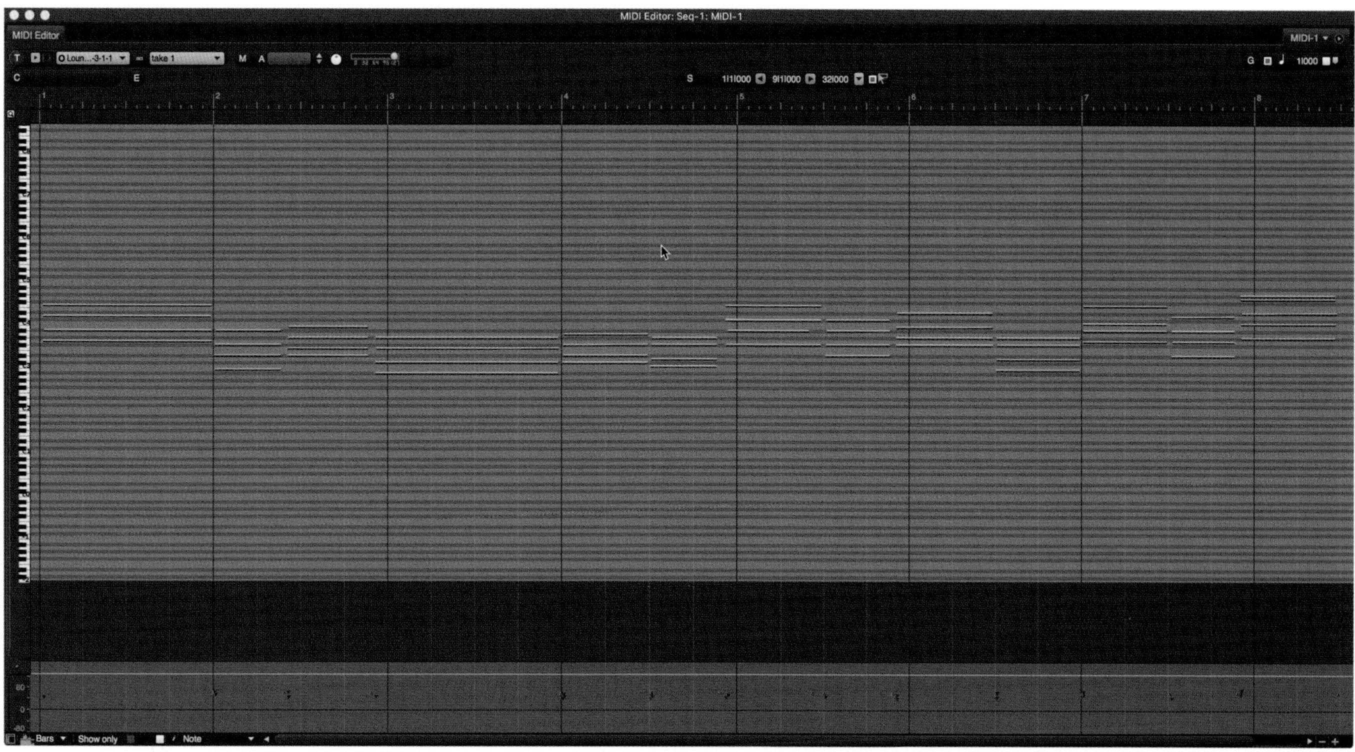

The linear, stepwise arrangement of notes on a keyboard can make emulating a piano or other keyboard difficult to voice from a guitar, and may require editing. Fortunately, in any piano-roll-type MIDI editor, it's easy to add or grab existing notes and move them to new pitches.

There are a few solutions to using a guitar to input keyboard-style voicings. The first and probably most painstaking method is to record a MIDI guitar track and hand-edit the notes. You can get the sound you want, and if you're not in an emulating mood, you can find interesting voicings that go beyond either instrument.

Piano styles are as widely divergent as guitar styles, so listen carefully to what you want to emulate. Some styles can translate readily from guitar; if you are adept at fancy, Travis-style picking, you are likely to have a leg up on stride piano parts.

Another benefit of MIDI sequencing is that you can overdub onto the same track. That, of course, lets you record the independent hands of a keyboard performance separately. Optionally, you can record right- and left-hand parts on separate tracks. Speaking of which, most sequencers let you transpose tracks in real time. If you use a channel and track per string, you can, for instance transpose the bottom two strings down an octave and leave the remainder of the strings intact. For that matter, you can transpose all tracks to different octaves and break out of the closed-position guitar cage. The Roland GR-55, the Boss GP-10, and the Jam Origin software MIDI guitar converter let you create alternate tunings, making it possible to play the voicings directly from your guitar, without benefit of a DAW or computer host program. Some programs and plug-ins will automatically remap notes to chords. Xfer Records Cthulhu maintains a library of keyboard and other types of voicings, which are arrayed chromatically

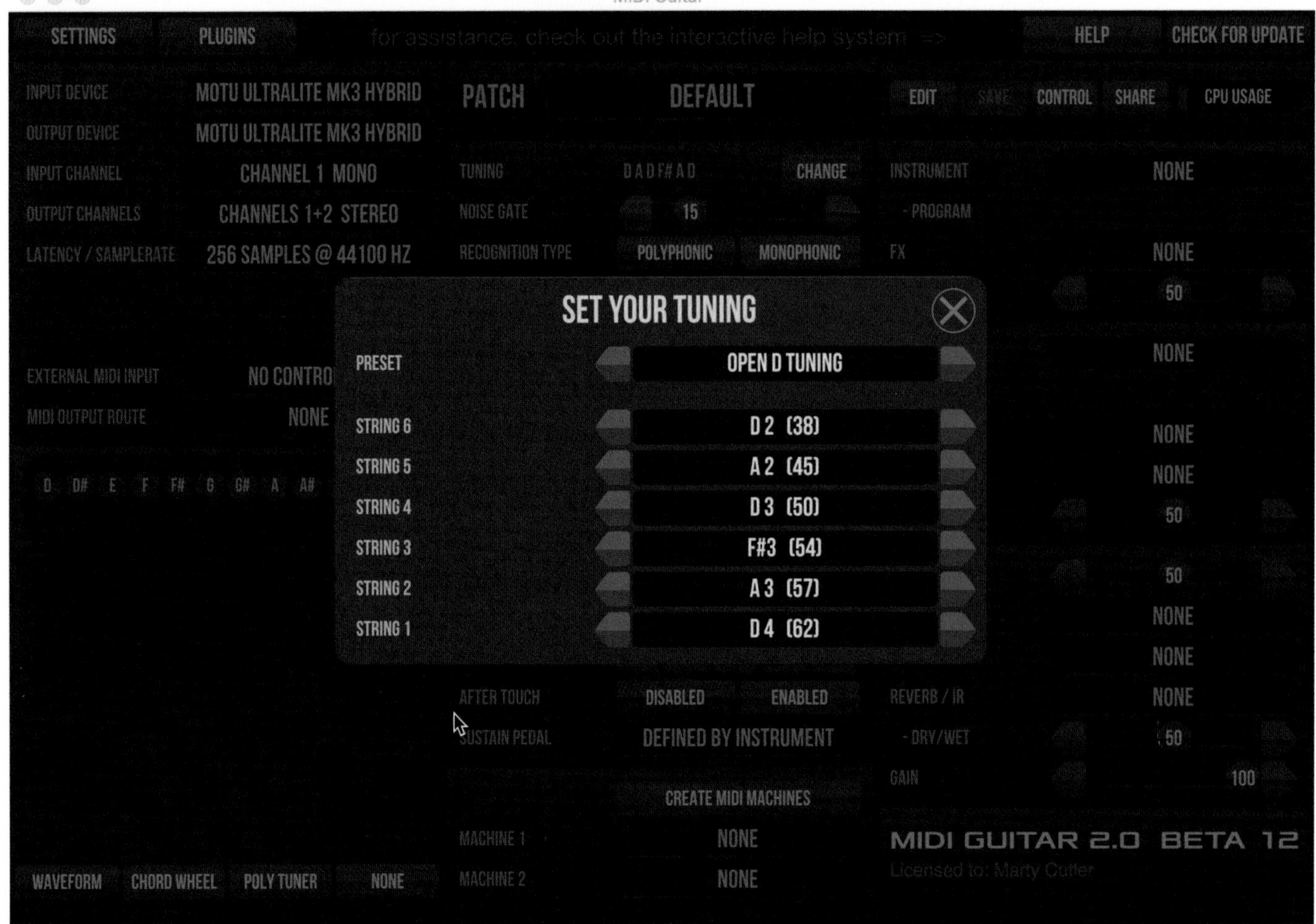

Most MIDI guitars and physically modeled guitars let you program alternate tunings you can play without retuning your guitar. Jam Origin's MIDI guitar can be easily configured to any tuning you like.

across the MIDI note range, and a single note from your guitar can send out sophisticated voicings, including some that are transcribed from Standard MIDI files, so you can add anything to its library from keyboard to string quartet voices.

Early on in this book, I mentioned a few guitar-like instruments, including Starr guitars and the YouRock guitar. I much prefer the feel of a guitar with real strings and frets, but one of their great capabilities is that you can tap with both hands on the fingerboard and play independent parts. Starr instruments are considerably more costly than the YouRock guitar, but they have a deep well of expressiveness and programmability that the entry-level controllers cannot match. Either way, they are both superb solutions to creating two-handed guitar parts, whether in the studio or on stage.

Making the Pitch

For any of this to work convincingly, it's a good idea to familiarize yourself with the pitch ranges of individual instruments. Playing a sampled violin or a trumpet below its intended range can sound very unmusical, partially due to the artifacts created by playing a sample below its capabilities. It's great fun to play brass ensemble patches from your guitar, but if you need to sequence a brass section, nothing beats recording individual components within their proper range. You can find charts all over the internet that illustrate the proper ranges of orchestral and other instruments, but here's an abbreviated selection of orchestral instruments for starters.

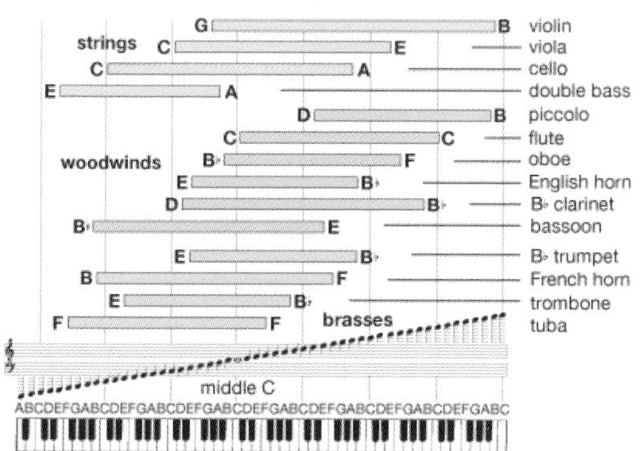

If you are emulating real-world instruments, it's a good idea to familiarize yourself with their capabilities. Here is a short list of orchestral instruments and their effective playing ranges.

There are excellent courses available online for studying realistic orchestration. Gary Garritan offers a free, interactive course based on Nikolay Rimsky-Korsakov's *Principles of Orchestration* <www.garritan.com/principles-of-orchestration/>.

Using a MIDI guitar to emulate other instruments may not be your goal, but undeniably, the practice can enrich your musical and technical skills when you learn what makes those instruments tick, even if your music is purely based on electronic sounds.

CHAPTER 12

Other MIDI Guitar Applications

Teaching and practicing with a MIDI guitar and music software. Collaborating over the internet with MIDI data.

There is no shortage of applications for the practice and dissemination of music, and MIDI guitar plays a significant role in the process. A quick internet search for guitarist Jim Hall yields tons of transcriptions of his solos for download—many of them from his own site. Many sites yield backing tracks in Standard MIDI file format of popular and jazz tunes that you can load into your own host program or MIDI file player app. Because it is merely MIDI data, and not sound, my students can slow the track down to a comfortable speed and speed it up when it's time to push a little harder. At the end of private lessons, I can quickly chart a backing track of the song and provide my student with a MIDI file to take home and practice, as well as a tablature of the lesson. Who can question whether computers and MIDI have revolutionized the way we learn our instruments?

In the mid-'90s, when I hashed out my concept of the Bluegrass Band project with PG Music, the goal was a software package that could not only play back convincing bluegrass music with MIDI and a sound card but would also provide educational value as a multimedia program. In addition to the music, we included biographies of key figures in the music, a trivia game, and most importantly, transcriptions of the exact notes played on all of the instruments: guitar, banjo, fiddle, and mandolin.

I already had a MIDI guitar, so recording guitar and bass presented no obstacles. For bass, I merely had to play on the bottom four strings of the guitar. Banjo, because of its unusual tuning, required a few MIDI contortions that I resolved by having a MIDI banjo built. I had to shelve the idea of a precise fiddle transcription after the only capable MIDI violinist I knew was unable to commit. Mandolin presented a whole other can of worms, as good bluegrass mandolinists who are conversant with MIDI are even scarcer than MIDI banjoists or fiddle players. Fortunately, my old friend and former bandmate Bob Applebaum had a MIDI mandolin, and he was available.

Unfortunately, he lived in Los Angeles, and at the time, I lived in Oakland, California, and a commute was out of the question. Luckily, although the science of telecommunications was still in its pre-adolescent, dial-up-modem days, the internet was still fast enough to send MIDI data through email. I would send Bob rhythm tracks so he could overdub his mandolin parts, and I would edit and add them to the finished product, which I would then email to PG Music, which made its home in Vancouver, British Columbia. I subsequently went on to produce and create many subsequent projects for their Band-in-a-Box software.

It is worth a bit of discussion of the software elements that aided and abetted in this project. First and foremost, I relied heavily on the Standard MIDI file format, due to the fact that MIDI, despite its standards, was not necessarily implemented in a standard fashion by manufacturers. The Standard MIDI file is a way to encode all MIDI data from a sequence so that it could be shared amongst platforms, such as Mac OS and Windows. Nowadays, every piece of music software supports loading and saving of Standard MIDI files in addition to their proprietary formats. The expectation was that the data would be identical when played back on any computer. Playing a MIDI file through a Korg M1 connected to a Mac would sound identical on a PC triggering the same instrument.

So far, so good, but it would undoubtedly sound different when the target instrument was, for example, a Yamaha or Roland synthesizer. For instance, drum-kit layouts varied from one manufacturer to the other. A MIDI note that triggered a kick drum on one company's instrument might play a snare or a bongo on another. There was considerably more. The balance of the average synthesizer from one patch to the other was often inconsistent; certainly that was the case between one manufacturer and the next.

In the early '90s, General MIDI came onto the scene, thanks to the efforts of the MIDI Manufacturers Association (MMA) and the Association of Musical Electronic Industry (AMEI) in Japan, spearheaded by the Roland Corporation. There was considerably more to the specification than was outlined in Chapters 9 or 11. At the top of the list was the requirement that any instrument that bore the GM logo must have a minimum polyphony of 24 notes in order to manage reasonably dense musical passages. MIDI Control Change (CC) messages, such as MIDI Volume and Expression Pedal, must generate consistent results in the target GM instrument. For example, in General MIDI, MIDI Volume (CC7) was used to set an overall volume ceiling, while Expression Pedal (CC11) regulated the volume of individual MIDI channels within the levels set by CC7, essentially relegating Expression Pedal messages to the role of a MIDI limiter. Many musicians unfairly castigated General MIDI, ironically berating it for its uniformity and its standard set of sounds, when in fact more high-ticket instruments soon offered high-quality General MIDI instruments among banks of eminently programmable sounds. General MIDI soon became the lingua franca of multimedia projects that relied on MIDI. To this day, Mac OS retains its DLS Music Device, a built-in synthesizer with a General MIDI sound set, ensuring consistent playback of MIDI files that conform to General MIDI specifications.

Practice, Practice

Apple's built-in synth works acceptably in the Mac version of Band-in-a-Box (hereafter BIAB), but the program now supports plug-ins. When I want to focus on practice, cheesy and low-res as they may be, the built-in Apple instruments are instantly summoned up in the program, and I can type in chord charts or load up an already prepared song file, and I'm ready to go. If you haven't experienced BIAB yet, it's about time you learned a few details about what is, in my opinion, among the best practice tools available on your computer.

Its user interface, studded with buttons often replicated in the menu bar, is cluttered, but that belies a relatively easy-to-use operation. You are presented with a virtual chord chart, and you simply select your song details—time, key signature, and tempo—load up a musical style of your choosing, type in the chords, and press play. If you are not satisfied with the musical style, they are interchangeable, from Hard Bop to Reggae to Polka. You can select the number of repetitions, A and B sections, program rests and shots, expand the length of the song, and much more. When you are satisfied, you can save your work as a Standard MIDI file. If your students don't have BIAB, the file readily imports into any MIDI player or sequencer. There are plenty of MIDI players for all platforms on the internet, ranging from free to very inexpensive, so a student who is learning folk guitar or banjo need not invest in a high-tech, high-ticket audio system that has more features than they will ever need. BIAB can also generate audio tracks or simple lead sheets you can print out for your next rehearsal or lesson.

PG Music's Band in a Box is easily the finest software program available for practicing, with hundreds of instantly interchangeable musical styles to choose from. You can also save complete arrangements to import into other sequencers and customize the tracks to taste.

BIAB aggressively supports its software with updates and new musical style packs that refine and expand to reflect newer music genres and the many variations on jazz styles. You can, for instance load jazz styles that generate piano tracks that are voiced in the manner of the late Bill Evans, or that of Herbie Hancock. (See the section in Chapter 11 on creating convincing piano voicings.) If you are ambitious, you can create your own BIAB styles.

Take Note

Another great set of tools for practice and sharing music are, of course, notation and tablature programs. A couple of my favorites that are tailored for guitar are Arobas Guitar Pro and Notion Music Progression. Both are available for Mac and Windows, as well as for iPad, and both offer easy entry of data; you can enter data with a mouse or your MIDI controller here. Progression scores points for its no-fuss recording setup—the Record button and transport are onscreen and ready when you first launch the program, whereas Guitar Pro has recording functions buried in its sound menu and will not record polyphonically unless your guitar is in Mono Mode; otherwise, it only records the topmost note of your chords. It makes sense that Mono Mode's one-string-per-channel operation will record just as you play them, proper strings and all, but

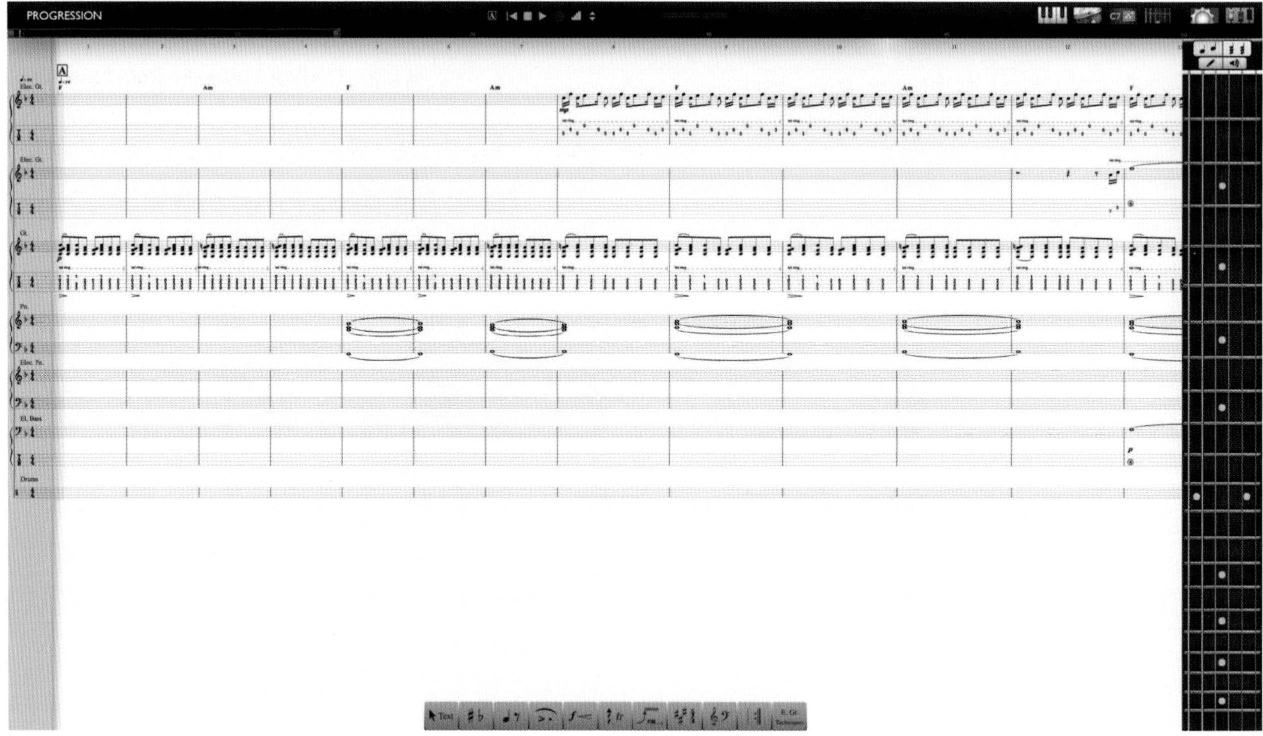

Progression's palette is clean, bright, and easy on the eye, with articulations, note durations, octave markings, and system and chart navigation-mark details tucked away in neat sections. Both Notion and Guitar Pro support simultaneous viewing and editing of tab and standard notation.

Progression can record either way, mapping all of the input notes properly in Mono Mode, or take reasonable guesses that you can later drag to the proper string when recording via a single MIDI channel. Best of all, you can view and print notation and tablature. Tab combined with notation is a boon for guitar students who aren't great readers, because it illustrates the precise fingering needed while relating it to standard notation. Guitar Pro displays articulations and setups from a browser on the left, as opposed to Progression's pop-up palette at the lower portion of the screen. Either arrangement works for me, although Progression's palette is brighter and easier on the eye, with articulations, note durations, octave markings, and system and chart navigation-mark details tucked away in neat sections.

Guitar Pro's accompanying sound library has more instruments and articulations than Progression, and they sound good if a little compressed for my taste, and you can add on more sounds of a number of instruments. All in all, if you are using a guitar notation package to build elaborate arrangements, you are probably better off with a full notation program or a DAW. For educational and transcription purposes, a guitar sound set is valuable for double-checking the accuracy of the notation. More than that can be a distraction.

The Global Studio

The ability to interface your guitar with computers and the internet affords amazing opportunities. These days, I live across the river from New York City, and besides unexpected bridge closings, the commute is pretty expensive. Add to that the increasingly difficult traffic and parking problems, and it is understandable why I am selective about accepting recording sessions there. I don't have a major recording facility in my home, but I pride myself on having a couple of good microphones, great recording software, and enough know-how to record good guitar and banjo tracks. Nowadays, thanks to the internet and file transfer capabilities, I can record sessions for any studio in the world without leaving the comforts of home, and my pajamas. It's simple: The client sends me a stereo mix of his tracks, which I can load into my DAW. I set up my track and record my part, using their music as a tempo reference. I usually record multiple takes, letting the client choose. Email doesn't have the capacity for large files, but there are a few ways to receive tracks and shuttle work back to the client. If you own a website, you can purchase enough online space to receive your client's tracks and upload your files. A provider with a fast connection is a good idea if you don't want to spend your day watching the upload. There are lots of services online that can offer professional musicians to record tracks these days, and a number of clearing houses where you can hire top musicians to record for you; if you have top-flight skills, consider offering your services.

Virtual Virtuosos

Sessionplayers.com grants access to seasoned pros. Some of the names for hire include Robben Ford, Chuck Loeb, and Brent Mason on guitar; David Garibaldi and Tom Brechtlein on drums; and Lee Sklar and Jimmy Johnson on bass. You can even hire engineers and string quartets, if you need them. Hiring requires membership, and you submit a request for a player by clicking a button under their name. You then send a chart and a demo of your work in MP3 format and discuss what you need. High-echelon musicians inevitably incur a higher ticket price, but there is an opportunity to negotiate. Nonetheless, it's a tremendous opportunity to engage top players relatively directly, so if money is no object, go for it!

On an equally professional but smaller scale, you can hire the services of the Visionary Music Group <visionarymusicgroup.com>. Services are distinctly oriented around guitar, including custom guitar tracks, re-amping of previously recorded tracks, expert recording, and a cadre

Tom Gioia's Visionary Music Group maintains a selection of vintage guitars, amps, and processors and offers a number of online recording and collaborative services.

of musicians to record your tracks. Tom Gioia runs Visionary Music Group, which is heavily invested in a large collection of boutique amps, processors, and vintage guitars.

Some music software companies offer collaboration through their own user groups and hubs. Propellerheads, the manufacturers of Reason software, have moved their collaborative hub to its own site, allihoopa.com. There, you can collaborate and share your Reason tracks with other users.

I've hardly scratched the surface of things a guitarist can do on the internet. Most of my research for this book was done by gathering information from user groups and websites of people I know in the field. About the best place I've seen to learn music technology in depth is the subscription site Groove3.com. They not only have comprehensive, graduated tutorials for music software and applications, but you can also study guitar and other instruments from a variety of well-known master musicians courtesy of Groove 3's alliance with Homespun.

The company's roster of hardware and software coverage is deep and up to date, and videos about software comprise multiple chapters, taken at a relaxed but detailed pace. One entire video might be devoted to the modulation section of a plug-in, for instance, and then move on to the next page; nothing gets overlooked. I was surprised at how much I learned. There's some great video on how to clean up MIDI guitar and other tracks in Apple Logic that takes you through setting up the program's MIDI Transform window, step by step.

Between the software in your computer and user groups, session players, and hubs, you have a rich pool of resources to make your music and perfect your craft. Dive in!

CHAPTER 13

Outfitting Your Computer for Guitar

MIDI and audio interfaces. External hard drives.
USB, FireWire, AVB, and Lightning.

A well-known comic once said, "You can't have everything . . . Where would you put it?" Somehow the punch line seems especially relevant here. We could have the best software, the slickest guitars and MIDI converters, and the fastest computers possible, but how do we link our guitars to the computer? Where do we store our work? How do we connect it all? Let's take a step back and look at a few options for connecting a guitar and MIDI studio.

Interfaces

Most of the interfaces you'll find on the market can be broken down into two main types: audio, and MIDI interfaces that conduct audio to your computer and back out, perhaps routed to an external device, such as a mixer, outboard effects, or directly to your monitors. A MIDI interface shunts data from your controller or any other MIDI output to external devices, such as a hardware synthesizer or some other device equipped for MIDI input. Quite often, MIDI and audio interfaces reside in the same unit, which saves space but may make cable organization a bit more involved, depending on how your studio is arranged.

It's not a giant leap of intuition to presume that if you are planning on running a large, professional recording facility, you'll need more input and output (I/O). That is especially true for audio recording. Consider the complexities of recording drums with all of the individual mics dedicated to overheads, cymbals, kick, snare, and toms, and you know that a four-input, two-output interface isn't going to cut it. Then again, we are talking about guitar studios, not Studio A at the record plant.

To begin with, audio interfaces usually offer a selection of recording frequencies and resolutions, with standard frequencies from 44.1kHz up to 192kHz, and resolutions switchable between 16 and 24 bits. Without going too far off topic, let's simply accept that the *frequency* measures how many times per second the interface takes snapshots of the audio, and the *resolution* or *bit depth* is the precision with which the interface measures a change in the audio's amplitude. There are other factors, of course, but I don't want to get too far into the weeds here. For now, just accept that your auditory experience of 192kHz will admit more upper frequencies than at 44.1kHz, and your perception of lower resolutions will be more distorted and include noise. Many of the older digital synthesizers could only offer up 8-bit

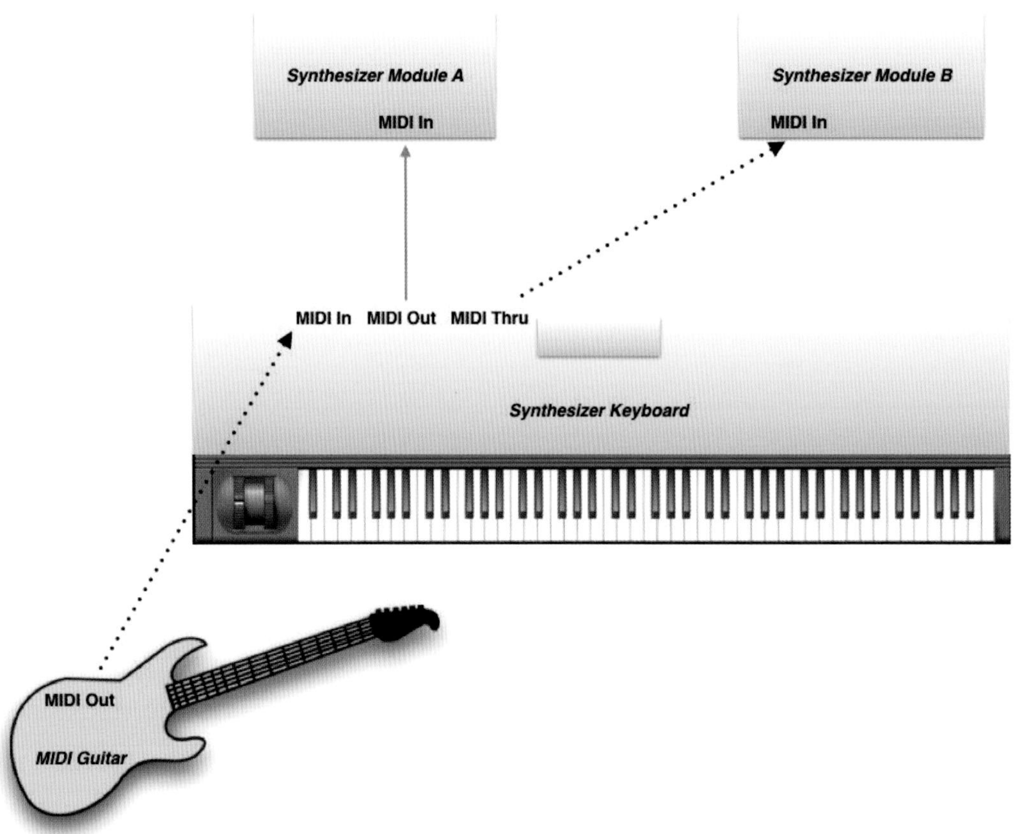

This diagram traces MIDI signal flow. The MIDI guitar's MIDI Out port can trigger the internal sounds of the synthesizer keyboard, whose MIDI Thru Port passes the trigger data along to trigger synth module B. The keyboard can play its internal sounds and generate MIDI data, sending it from its MIDI Out to trigger synth module A. If I added a connection from the MIDI Thru of synth module B to MIDI in of synth module A, the MIDI guitar could control all three synthesizers.

resolution, and they were often fraught with noise created by errors in the device's attempt to measure amplitude.

Oh, all right—one more visual example. Compare a modern-day photo on your mobile gizmo to an old front-page photo from a newspaper. The blur you see is the result of low resolution, whereas your gizmo's high-resolution camera reproduces the image in intimate detail.

As for MIDI interfaces, your options are different. Over a single MIDI cable, you can support up to 16 MIDI channels, but only in one direction; therefore, the MIDI interface will have to at least support MIDI In and MIDI Out. In receives all data, while MIDI Out transmits only data originating from its own source. A good example is a keyboard that can send MIDI to another device, but its input is receiving data from a MIDI guitar. The keyboard cannot pass the MIDI guitar data to the other device from its MIDI out. To do that requires a MIDI Thru jack. Additionally, a single MIDI In and Out port can quickly prove inadequate with so many MIDI devices. Consider MIDI's 16-channel limitation and the fact that a single multitimbral hardware synthesizer might have between 8 and 16 channels available for sequencing. You can rapidly run out of available MIDI channels. The best solution for MIDI systems with lots of hardware devices is a multiple-port MIDI interface, such as the MOTU MIDI Express XT. The unit provides eight separate MIDI inputs and nine separate outputs, with support for a total of 128 channels of MIDI I/O. Each MIDI device in the system can be on its own MIDI data stream, which helps eliminate the possibility of a MIDI logjam and corruption of data that gets transmitted down a single overworked MIDI cable.

The rear panel of MOTU's MIDI Express XT hosts eight discrete MIDI inputs and outputs for a total of 128 MIDI channels (one MIDI input is on the front panel).

If you work in a solitary room with a large array of software instruments and add guitar tracks with a couple of vocal overdubs, then that four-in, two-out interface will do you just fine. You can record gargantuan-sounding guitar tracks with precious little gear these days because of the massive overdub capabilities of a computer-based recording system; you just might not be able to do it all at once. For recording situations that call for small-footprint, high-quality audio, Native Instruments' Komplete Audio 6 (KA6) suits me perfectly. The unit is shaped like a high-tech brick from a heavy-gravity planet: compact and with sufficient mass to prevent it from easily being dislodged or overbalanced. All analog I/O is balanced, including the pair of combination inputs, which accept XLR or 1/4-inch plugs. Each input sports a knob for gain and a button to change inputs from mic to line-level. A monitor section has an on/off button and another that toggles mono or stereo output—handy if you hear phase problems and need to compare. A quarter-inch jack accepts headphones, and you can switch your headphone's source between input pairs one and two, and three and four, which are 1/4-inch jacks situated on the rear panel, above their outputs. Just above the main monitor output jacks are S/PDIF coaxial in and out jacks, which makes the unit eminently expandable with another device, such as a digital mixer or another Komplete Audio 6. Topping off the unit's connections are MIDI In and Out jacks, a switch that engages phantom power, and a Type B USB connector. You'll find no jack for a power supply; the unit draws power from its USB connection. As you might guess from its size, the interface is designed to sit on the desktop, and the top surface offers easy-to-read color LED status and level displays and an oversized master volume knob. The unit supports 16- or 24-bit audio at frequencies up to 96kHz. Most significantly, the audio conveyed by this interface is sweet and detailed, with excellent imaging.

Because of its size, tank-like build, easy setup, and portability I have used it with great success on live gigs. I especially appreciate that it draws its power from my laptop—one less wall wart to worry about. Sometimes the outside traffic or construction noise gets a little heavy, and I have been able to set up a recording system quickly and without fuss in the more remote areas of my home. I even recorded tracks for a national radio spot that way.

If you need more inputs—lots more inputs in a compact space—consider MOTU's Ultralite line of interfaces. The Ultralite MK3 is the senior unit of the three, but is still in production. MOTU recently released MK 4 and the Ultralite AVB. All are viable, great-sounding interfaces, and all support up to 24-bit, 192kHz audio. Each deploys a different connection scheme: MK3 connects to either USB or FireWire ports, and the Ultralite AVB can use USB or AVB connections, a more recent audio protocol that allows extensive daisy-chain expansion and high-speed data rates. MOTU touts the MK4's ridiculously low latency through high-speed USB. Apart from the high-resolution audio all units support, this box is a half-rack unit, really not that much larger than the Native Instruments KA6, but the MK3 starts with two mic/instrument inputs, six line-level analog inputs, 10 channels of analog output, stereo S/PDIF, and a stereo headphone output. The MK4 holds 18 ins and 22 outs, and the AVB I/O offers 18 inputs and outputs. All have incredible I/O, but the MK3 supports FireWire and USB. FireWire, sadly, is going the way of the iPhone headphone jack and has been phased out of current Mac computers, and its support in Windows was never very robust. As for AVB, it is reasonably well-supported on the Mac; less so on Windows machines. There are a number of recent interfaces supporting Thunderbolt connectors, but here again, it isn't clear whether Apple will drop the protocol in favor of USB-C, yet another protocol. Perhaps by the time you read this the issue will have been settled. One thing is clear: USB 2 remains the most universally supported among all of the aforementioned connections, so choose wisely, whether you are in the market for an interface or an external hard drive.

I mentioned previously that the GR-55 and the GP-10 connect to your computer and pass audio and MIDI bidirectionally by way of USB, making them basic MIDI and audio interfaces. Although they are not MIDI converters, Fractal's Axe FX II XL and the Line 6 Helix can pass any incoming MIDI data, as well as any audio input, through their USB connectors. Then again,

Axe FX and Helix are relatively high-ticket items, so forget about the budget. If your needs are modest enough, here is some bare-boned strategizing for getting music into your computer on a budget. If you intend to record MIDI guitar instrumental music, your GR-55 or GP-10 is all you need besides a couple of plug-ins and DAW software. Both send MIDI, and both have built-in modeled guitars, with the GR-55 adding a built-in synth in the bargain. Fishman's TriplePlay system doesn't pass audio, but because it plugs directly into your computer, it is essentially its own MIDI interface. One of the beautiful things about software digital audio workstations is that you can mix and bounce down your tracks without need of an external mixer or recording deck. These aren't optimal solutions, but anything that can get your ideas into concrete form is worth doing.

CHAPTER **14**

Going Live

Preparing your setup for the stage. Amps, stands, laptops, tablets, iPads, and other devices.

A Brief Pep Talk of Sorts

The chapter subtitle says it all—or does it? Let me caution you: There's a huge difference between having a studio full of gear and pressing it into service for the stage. If you want to take your gear onstage, use a separate system from your studio rig, and that includes your computer—especially your computer. You are in great peril if you rely on your studio rig as a source of income. One misplaced, off-balance beer can put you out of business. Fortunately, I never was confronted with that reality, but I have a few hard-won cautionary anecdotes I'd like to pass along. My motto in this case is: "I'm not happy until you're not happy." We'll talk gear soon enough.

I have always enjoyed performing with MIDI gear. My very first time was an abortive solo banjo gig accompanied by a Yamaha QX7 MIDI sequencer and a TX7. The TX was the tone-generating component of a DX7 with no editing capabilities save by computer. The QX7 had very limited memory and required loading new sequence data with a cassette player and (as I recall) a proprietary data cable. To cut to the chase, the cassette interface failed. The moral? Test and rehearse everything. Nevertheless, I pulled off a good if somewhat spartan set of improvised unaccompanied solo banjo jams. Second lesson: stuff happens, so be prepared!

A couple of years later, after I shook off my trepidations, I took a sequencing gadget, the Indus MIDI DJ, to a gig, along with several multitimbral synthesizers and, of course, my banjo. The MIDI DJ resembles a hybrid of a disk drive, a Martian alarm clock, and a tabletop can opener, and had perhaps the most confounding user interface I have ever encountered. The only manual was a foldout sheet that revealed a chthonic menu of three-character symbols for all of the recording and editing functions. Its only benefit was that it could save and load sequences using a 5 ¼-inch floppy disk instead of a cassette. Still, there was no way I was going to record MIDI into this gadget, so instead, I bounced sequences from my computer to the DJ.

After doing my first dry run, there were some timing anomalies and missing data, probably due to its claim of "up to" a 12,000-note capacity per sequence. Your next object lesson? Understand the specs, know your gear, and be wary of any gadget that uses the phrase "up to."

By now you understand that MIDI data is considerably more than just notes, so it follows that something else might be bogging the sequence down. Pitch bend is an awful lot of MIDI data because it incurs new MIDI messages every time it updates. Sensing that that was at least part of the problem, I was able to strip out superfluous Pitch Bend and other unnecessary data, which led to a successful performance. Next lesson: It's 2013, and my bizarre "two guys and a laptop" band (with an occasional satellite member or two), Chef of the Pasture, is playing on a stage at an outdoor festival, and everything is performing like a champion. Then a passerby manages to find the stage's power supply cord with the toe of his shoe and sends my hard drive to slumber land—and the set to a crashing halt. The lesson here can be summed up in two words: duct tape! Seriously, though, whenever possible, be proactive about your stage setup and inspect your working environment.

My preparation routine starts with booking the gig. With bluegrass performances, there isn't much I need to worry about: I make sure I have picks, plenty of spare strings, maybe a couple of capos, and a tuner. Playing Chef of the Pasture gigs is a different mindset. I don't carry my own PA, so I like to know about the club's backline. One venue changed its PA over to a mono system, and the mix made our usually immersive tracks sound like a cheap phonograph that was playing a block away. I am the technical portion of the band, and I own all of the gear. What that means is that I am the one who preps all of the sequences, plug-ins, and the rest, and one of the little tricks I play on myself that helps to keep the music fresh is incessant tweaking of the music. It comes naturally, and so I will draw up a set list, load the tracks into my sequencer, and change a few things: Look for a new patch to assign, change a couple of drum fills, tweak tempo or dynamics by altering some note velocities, whatever works. I practice with the tracks to see if they work in context. If possible, I have a rehearsal with my bandmate so that there are no untoward surprises. It's practically a cliché, but I keep a checklist of everything I need for the gig. Every guitar cord, pick, USB cable, file on my hard drive, and power supply needs to be accounted for. At the end of our set, I break my gear down—often with another band getting ready to take the stage. It's most important that I have everything I need when I play, so packing my gear and missing a pick or a cable is no big deal, but it can ruin your whole evening if it isn't there at the beginning of the set.

When I first started to perform with the computer, I would simply park it on a chair, with the drive on the floor. I switched over to a stand from Roland Corporation built specifically for laptops. The SSPC-1 is built like a tank, with telescoping, adjustable legs and a sturdy platform that is wide enough to accommodate a mouse. Its height is adjustable and can stand far enough above ground that I can thread my hard drive's cable around it a few times and secure it to the stand. It's not as sexy as a new synthesizer, and it's a tad pricey, but it's become an essential part of my onstage gear, and ultimately, you'll be happy to have such a portable and adaptable piece that you can safely adjust to stage logistics and stow away when not in use.

Amplitude Adjustment

What you choose to amplify your instrument depends on whether your gig is MIDI, guitar, or both. Guitar amps can't reproduce the high-frequency detail required by synthesizers and samplers, and one misplaced low-end synth-bass squelch can blow speakers. Synths should use keyboard amps. Lots of amps offer built-in effects, but so many modern synths use onboard effects that it obviates any external processing. Guitars, however, present a different case. In smaller venues, where space becomes cramped, amps with built-in effects could be a boon. If you can handle the expense and the chiropractor fees, consider owning a keyboard and a guitar amp, and possibly another keyboard amp—don't forget that most modern-day synths are stereo.

All of my live-performance MIDI data is generated courtesy of my 2009 Core2 duo Macbook Pro. Admittedly, it's somewhat long in the tooth next to my shiny new quad-core iMac or even my new iPad pro, but it has performed faithfully over the years and remains my accompanist of choice. More and more, though, as iPads gain more processing power, and more music software is ported over to the platform, I am considering retiring the Macbook Pro in favor of the iPad Pro for my live instrument. A burgeoning list of software is developing for the medium. Steinberg already offers Cubasis, a pretty full-featured DAW program with built-in plug-ins and the ability to download additional plug-ins through in-app purchases. Korg Gadget is particularly fun to use due to a battery of unusual and excellent-sounding virtual instruments. I am fairly fluent on Apple GarageBand, but for my part, I am more interested in playing back MIDI files rather than recording and editing them on the iPad. I always prefer the visual benefits of a large-size screen.

Still, software synths on the iPad are wonderful instruments for playing live through my Fishman MIDI guitar, and here is how that is done: Depending on what vintage iPad you have, you will need either the current standard Lightning-to-USB adapter or one that uses the older 30-pin adapter. The Fishman MIDI receiver is a USB stick that handily plugs into the adapter's camera receptacle. As soon as I am certain that the guitar and the receiver are paired, I can begin playing. I have heard reports about latency, but if there is, it was never sluggish enough to make a difference to me, and the feel was hardly any different than when the receiver was plugged into my main computer. It's tempting to buy one of those iPad holders that clip on to a mic stand and just take my wireless MIDI guitar, an iPad, and an audio cable to a gig.

Another remarkably flexible option is iK Multimedia's iRig Duo, which packs two channels of 24-bit, 44.1kHz audio and MIDI I/O. You can connect any MIDI controller's output. The unit supplies a Lightning adapter and breakout cable for MIDI. You'll need the provided pair of AA batteries, but it will operate on USB power if you connect it to your computer. If you have an Android device, iRig Duo is compliant, and iK provides an adapter in the bargain. For recording, the inputs are balanced combo jacks, and iRig duo will supply 48V phantom power.

CHAPTER 15

Tips and Tricks

Application-specific ideas for electronic guitar.
Setting up your DAW for MIDI guitar.

MIDI and computers are quirky. They can surprise you in pleasant ways, or they can ambush you. I claim to be the voice of experience in these matters, and that means that you are benefiting from my mistakes, successes, and failures. What follows is a seemingly random collection of ideas, tweaks, techniques, maxims, and conventional wisdom that I hope you will find useful.

Express Yourself

One of the less familiar areas of MIDI for fledgling electronic guitar acolytes is the idea that eking expression out of synths with a guitar requires only dynamic, clean playing and the right notes. I've stressed that MIDI is rich in expression, and one way of really understanding that is to study the parameters of your synthesizer. That expressiveness goes well beyond pitch bend, too, and it's really easy to achieve with software instruments because their inner workings are almost invariably more visible than hardware instruments. Once you have an idea about what makes a synthesizer sound pop, find a virtual knob and twist it. You won't break a virtual synth, I promise. Once you've found a knob that does something interesting, right-click and hold your mouse on that knob. A small menu will appear with MIDI Learn in the dialog box. Now twist a wheel on your MIDI controller or move your MIDI guitar's expression pedal and notice that the virtual knob follows the moves on your controller. You may notice as you play that you are now remotely animating your synthesizer, sonically as well as visually. Congratulations! You may be doing this in a DAW program through a MIDI track ready to record. Hit Record and play a few bars on that synth. Return to the beginning of your recording and notice that your track plays back your controller maneuvers as well as the notes.

Small Consolation

Quite often, a MIDI controller is not fully implemented. A good example is Aftertouch, an expressive keyboard action based on the use of a sensor strip that responds to pressure. Because a pressure-sensitive strip is expensive to install, cheaper keyboards don't implement it, and guitars don't implement it.

Fortunately, MIDI guitars can be set up to send any MIDI message you need, and there are a couple ways to hurdle this fence. Any MIDI sequencer worth its salt can receive one MIDI message and turn it into another, often in real time. For instance, my Roland GR-55's expression pedal is a good vehicle for sending Aftertouch. In fact, it's a pretty smooth and expressive vehicle for sending almost any Continuous Controller, and I can set it up to send Aftertouch if that's what makes the synth sing. Digital Performer (DP) has had a feature called Consoles for decades. Consoles are control panels you can construct that generate MIDI data, either directly from their sliders or by receiving one MIDI message and sending a proportional

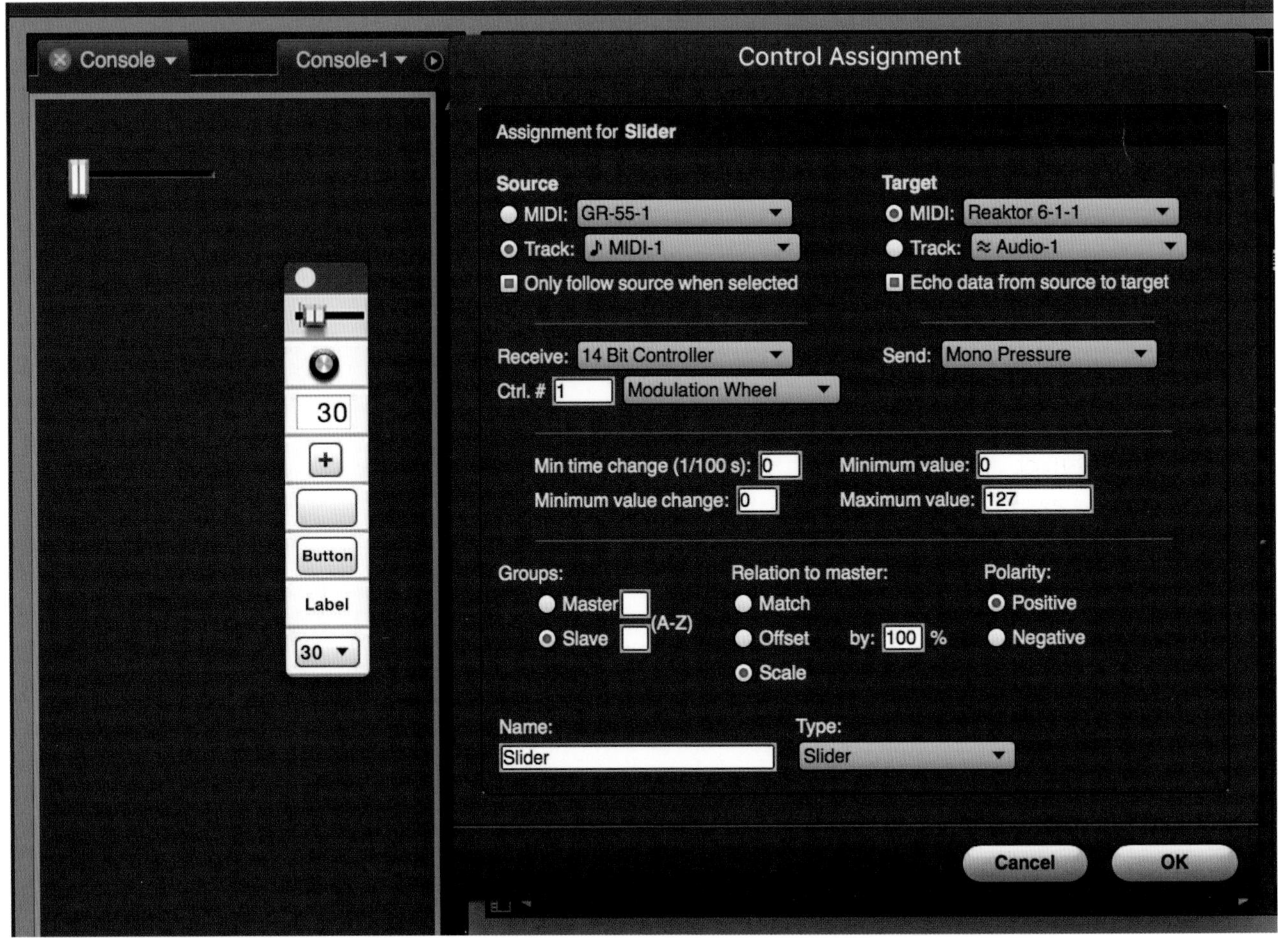

The makings of a MOTU custom console: You drag a knob, slider, button, value box, or other device into the blank console on the left, and edit its functions in the control panel. I dragged a slider into the console, and it will receive Modulation Wheel messages and convert them to Aftertouch in the destination MIDI track.

amount of another message that is what is known as *MIDI mapping*. When you select Create a Console, a palette covered in buttons and sliders pops up, along with a small box. You will, of course want to use a slider, as they are continuous, while buttons are switches. When you drag your slider over to the box, a rectangular menu filled with various radio buttons and other choices appears; that is where you can assign what the slider receives, and from where—in my case, my foot pedal is sending CC number 11, or Expression, and the slider is programmed to send Aftertouch.

Let's stay with DP's Console window. MIDI notes can do more than play pitches. Under the Source section, select your MIDI guitar again. For Receive, set the type of data to Notes. That means your MIDI guitar is sending notes to the virtual console. Select your synth as the target, and below it, choose Pan. Now play. If you have done this correctly, notes are traveling across your soundstage, based on your pitches. You can do the same thing with almost any MIDI command. The late, lamented Axon AX100 MIDI guitar converter mapped vibrato to fretboard position and used a choir patch as the target sound. The vibrato was, to be charitable, overzealous, and wide enough to serve as a landing strip. Still, the idea of a vibrato you could control by fretboard position was a reasonable one, and sure enough, there were parameters to set maximum and minimum values, decreasing the maximum value to a more temperate depth worked quite well.

Set Phasers to Stun

MIDI guitar doesn't always have to mean guitars playing synthesizer. We can just as easily put MIDI to work with our guitar processors. Let's not leave that console window yet. This time, using your MIDI guitar as the source, set the received data to Velocity. As a target, select a MIDI controlled effect, such as a phase shifter on a Line 6 Helix, and while its Phaser Speed parameter is in MIDI Learn mode, send it a Continuous Controller, such as CC#1, or Modulation, through the Console's Send menu. Note: Consult your effects manual for setting up your device's MIDI Learn capabilities, and send it MIDI by playing notes. If you have set this up correctly, playing notes more forcefully will increase the speed of the phaser effect, and a lighter touch will slow it down. This works great with MIDI-controlled flanger and leslie effects as well. Make sure you save your console and anything else you have built; you'll probably want to use it again.

Setting Up a Multitimbral Track in DP

Under the DP Project menu, select Create Instrument with Options and choose Omnisphere as an instrument, with six MIDI tracks. (If you are not using DP, consult your manual.) In Omnisphere, select Multi mode and load a patch of your choice into the first part and then into consecutive parts, using the Clone Part 1 command from the pull-down menu. You are then free to choose different patches for each string, change the pitch for each, set independent Pitch Bend range, and so on. In DP's Track view, set each track's input to your MIDI guitar's consecutive MIDI channel.

SQUEAKY CLEAN OR JUST SQUEAKY?

In Chapter 8, I made the ability to clean up MIDI guitar data efficiently and accurately a feature of the highest importance. I don't want to walk that back, but let me add a thought: Have you listened to your guitar tracks lately? That's not intended to be an insult; what I'm getting at is the nature of imperfection. Granted, unedited MIDI guitar tracks can sound really bad if misfires happen all over the place. Maybe it's time to give your guitar setup a little love and check your frets, your tuning, and your strings. If instead you are hearing your MIDI guitar track as you intended to play it, save for the thump of a string here and there, those extraneous glitches you hear faintly may be a false trigger created when you accidentally brushed a low string or triggered a note from hitting the side of your guitar. If you have a misfire that breaks the solo, by all means, get rid of it, but sometimes a thump or a midrange glitch can actually add a touch of realism to the solo. And trying to hunt a glitch of that kind down can sometimes be a waste of time. Sometimes, the tiniest bit of slop can be a good thing.

CHAPTER **16**

Troubleshooting

MIDI and audio signal flow, latency, compatibility issues, when and when not to update or upgrade.

"If it's not one thing . . . it's two things." —MARTY CUTLER

In MIDI and other electronic guitar systems, things inevitably go wrong, and the problems can be difficult to figure out. There's a good reason why, and it is key to understanding why bad things happen to good musicians. I stated this earlier: MIDI and audio are not the same! Even so, for the modern guitarist, they are unavoidably dependent—some might say codependent—on each other.

It's a Hardware Issue

Why are no sounds coming out of your synthesizer? Reasons could include:

1. Your 13-pin cable connection to your MIDI converter is loose, shorted, or not connected at all.
2. Your divided pickup switch is not set to the synthesizer position.
3. Your MIDI volume pedal is not down.
4. Your MIDI converter's MIDI Out is not connected, or you connected to the synth from the MIDI Thru port.
5. You are passing MIDI through a computer and a sequencer, and MIDI is not armed on the track you're using.
6. The MIDI cable from the MIDI interface to the synth is disconnected or dead.
7. The audio cables from the synth outputs to the amp are disconnected or dead.
8. The synth is powered down.
9. The amp is powered down.
10. Because.

Sometimes, Number 10 is unfortunately responsible, but if we trace the problem from start to finish, along a logical path, as we did here, there's a good chance of finding a solution. In the previous situation, we attempted to trace the problem from the guitarist outward, for the most part being guided by our sense of signal flow and the way these devices interact. Things can get pretty complicated from there, but once we have eliminated signal flow as the issue, we've cleared out many of the usual suspects and red herrings.

Of course, a closer look would reveal that we may have overlooked an element or two in our diagnostic path. Depending on your rig, there could be issues lurking beyond the hardware and circuitry, especially if your setup passes through a computer.

It's a Software Issue

As I write this, my guitar runs through my main recording setup. Its hub is a loaded iMac, running Mac OSX 10.11.6, El Capitan. That OS came pre-installed with my new Mac, and I was aware of numerous complaints lodged by musician friends who had taken the plunge, perhaps incautiously. I could look forward to getting new issues out of the way, hard on the heels of taming my semi-retired, older Mac.

Sure enough, my mail app would suddenly become unresponsive to my mouse clicks, the audio would suddenly vanish, sometimes taking MIDI with it, and my USB hub with hardware keys, authorizing some of my most favored software instruments, was offline. At present, after repairing permissions, updating firmware and drivers, and trashing preference files, my studio is a peaceable kingdom once again. Of course, Apple has been talking about a more frequent OS upgrade cycle. A friend of mine in IT proudly wore a shirt that proclaimed that technology is not for wimps. Amen.

There are things we can learn from this tale of woe. You've probably heard the suggestion not to jump into version 1.0 of the next operating system; I'll fine-tune that for you: Don't jump into any version of the next operating system unless you have determined that your software will still be functioning, and even then not until you have a good reason to make that change.

Latency

If you've ever felt uncomfortable playing a keyboard or MIDI guitar, or even a normal guitar, and you just can't seem to get the notes out on time, you understand latency. The speed with which we process digital audio these days is considerably swifter than it was when musicians first started to record audio into their computers, and companies first ventured into software synthesizers. CPUs were slower, hard drives and data transfer were slower. As fast as our CPUs have become, digital audio still travels through the same conversion process. Most of the time,

I am as happy as can be, with a peppy audio interface, a fast (for now) Mac, and plenty of RAM, and yet things occasionally feel as if I'm wading through a pool of molasses.

As with MIDI, digital audio has to jump through many hoops before we hear the result. The process of analog-to-digital-back-to-analog isn't instantaneous, and it introduces a delay between sound, the conversion, and our ear. Latency is delay. It can be caused by an audio interface that relies on poorly written driver software or firmware. In that case, check with the manufacturer's website for updated software; generally, the release of new driver software remedies performance issues rather than, say, introduces social network messaging. It's rare that updating a driver tosses you from the frying pan into the fire.

Sometimes latency can occur as the result of your stand-alone virtual instrument or your DAW software's audio preferences. If your MIDI guitar performance feels a trifle spongy, check your audio preferences; latency could be a result of unnecessarily high buffer settings. Basically, buffering determines the time it takes for your audio interface to convert and process the audio signal, measured in samples per second. Your computer is in the middle of the digital-audio signal flow, processing the audio, including routing it through tracks and applying (for instance) a flanger plug-in or reverb before it outputs the signal back to the interface for conversion back to an analog signal you can hear. With higher buffer rates, your computer will hold more samples before it outputs the signal to the audio interface. With smaller buffers, it takes less time to process and convert the audio, but if your buffers are set too low, you might hear pops and crackles arising from overloaded computer processors. Spend some time adjusting your music software's buffers. There's an apocryphal quote attributed to the late Ralph Stanley—a famed bluegrass banjo player—regarding adjusting the tension on a banjo head: "Tighten 'er till she breaks, then back 'er off some." Fortunately, you'll only hear crackles and pops; nothing will break.

Other possible solutions to seemingly insoluble computer-based MIDI and audio problems include trashing software preferences. Sometimes your software preference files become corrupt, resulting in software which may misbehave by freezing, getting sluggish, hanging on startup, or even quitting unexpectedly. You can trash preferences by going into your User Library Preference folder, locating the file, and dragging it to the trash. This may sound drastic, but really, all you'll need to do is set up some software preferences again.

Zap your computer's Parameter Ram. Restart your computer and hold down the Command, Option, P, and R keys. You'll need to reset a few Finder operations, but you won't feel a thing, I promise.

Use your software's disk repair tools. On the Mac, it's called Disk Utility; try selecting First Aid with your system disk selected. Download a donationware app by the name of OnyX <http://www.titanium.free.fr>; it's a comprehensive system repair and cleanup utility. There are others, but this one works really well and lets you tweak selected parameters, as opposed to Apple's Disk Utility, whose operations are more opaque.

When in doubt, you can always log out or just restart your computer; you'd be surprised at how often this is a solution.

Through all of these issues, bear in mind that the object is to make music. For the budding electronic guitarist, there is a lot to think about and a lot to learn, but the rewards of new capabilities, a fresh sonic palette, and new modes of music creation are greater than ever. Enjoy your journey!

APPENDIX A. CONTROL CHANGE MESSAGES (DATA BYTES)

The following table lists all currently defined Control Change messages and Channel Mode messages in control number order (adapted from "MIDI by the Numbers" by D. Valenti, *Electronic Musician* 2/88, and updated by the MIDI Manufacturers Association). This table is intended as an overview of MIDI and is by no means complete.

Registered Parameter Numbers (RPNs) are an extension to the Control Change message for setting additional parameters. Appended at the bottom is a table of all currently defined RPNs.

Table 1: Control Changes and Mode Changes (Status Bytes 176–191)					
Control Number (2nd Byte Value)			Control Function	3rd Byte Value	
Decimal	Binary	Hex		Value	Used As
0	00000000	00	Bank Select	0–127	MSB
1	00000001	01	Modulation Wheel or Lever	0–127	MSB
2	00000010	02	Breath Controller	0–127	MSB
3	00000011	03	Undefined	0–127	MSB
4	00000100	04	Foot Controller	0–127	MSB
5	00000101	05	Portamento Time	0–127	MSB
6	00000110	06	Data Entry MSB	0–127	MSB
7	00000111	07	Channel Volume (formerly Main Volume)	0–127	MSB
8	00001000	08	Balance	0–127	MSB
9	00001001	09	Undefined	0–127	MSB
10	00001010	0A	Pan	0–127	MSB
11	00001011	0B	Expression Controller	0–127	MSB

12	00001100	0C	Effect Control 1	0–127	MSB
13	00001101	0D	Effect Control 2	0–127	MSB
14	00001110	0E	Undefined	0–127	MSB
15	00001111	0F	Undefined	0–127	MSB
16	00010000	10	General Purpose Controller 1	0–127	MSB
17	00010001	11	General Purpose Controller 2	0–127	MSB
18	00010010	12	General Purpose Controller 3	0–127	MSB
19	00010011	13	General Purpose Controller 4	0–127	MSB
20	00010100	14	Undefined	0–127	MSB
21	00010101	15	Undefined	0–127	MSB
22	00010110	16	Undefined	0–127	MSB
23	00010111	17	Undefined	0–127	MSB
24	00011000	18	Undefined	0–127	MSB
25	00011001	19	Undefined	0–127	MSB
26	00011010	1A	Undefined	0–127	MSB
27	00011011	1B	Undefined	0–127	MSB
28	00011100	1C	Undefined	0–127	MSB
29	00011101	1D	Undefined	0–127	MSB
30	00011110	1E	Undefined	0–127	MSB
31	00011111	1F	Undefined	0–127	MSB
32	00100000	20	LSB for Control 0 (Bank Select)	0–127	LSB
33	00100001	21	LSB for Control 1 (Modulation Wheel or Lever)	0–127	LSB
34	00100010	22	LSB for Control 2 (Breath Controller)	0–127	LSB

35	00100011	23	LSB for Control 3 (Undefined)	0–127	LSB
36	00100100	24	LSB for Control 4 (Foot Controller)	0–127	LSB
37	00100101	25	LSB for Control 5 (Portamento Time)	0–127	LSB
38	00100110	26	LSB for Control 6 (Data Entry)	0–127	LSB
39	00100111	27	LSB for Control 7 (Channel Volume, formerly Main Volume)	0–127	LSB
40	00101000	28	LSB for Control 8 (Balance)	0–127	LSB
41	00101001	29	LSB for Control 9 (Undefined)	0–127	LSB
42	00101010	2A	LSB for Control 10 (Pan)	0–127	LSB
43	00101011	2B	LSB for Control 11 (Expression Controller)	0–127	LSB
44	00101100	2C	LSB for Control 12 (Effect control 1)	0–127	LSB
45	00101101	2D	LSB for Control 13 (Effect control 2)	0–127	LSB
46	00101110	2E	LSB for Control 14 (Undefined)	0–127	LSB
47	00101111	2F	LSB for Control 15 (Undefined)	0–127	LSB
48	00110000	30	LSB for Control 16 (General Purpose Controller 1)	0–127	LSB
49	00110001	31	LSB for Control 17 (General Purpose Controller 2)	0–127	LSB
50	00110010	32	LSB for Control 18 (General Purpose Controller 3)	0–127	LSB
51	00110011	33	LSB for Control 19 (General Purpose Controller 4)	0–127	LSB
52	00110100	34	LSB for Control 20 (Undefined)	0–127	LSB
53	00110101	35	LSB for Control 21 (Undefined)	0–127	LSB

54	00110110	36	LSB for Control 22 (Undefined)	0–127	LSB
55	00110111	37	LSB for Control 23 (Undefined)	0–127	LSB
56	00111000	38	LSB for Control 24 (Undefined)	0–127	LSB
57	00111001	39	LSB for Control 25 (Undefined)	0–127	LSB
58	00111010	3A	LSB for Control 26 (Undefined)	0–127	LSB
59	00111011	3B	LSB for Control 27 (Undefined)	0–127	LSB
60	00111100	3C	LSB for Control 28 (Undefined)	0–127	LSB
61	00111101	3D	LSB for Control 29 (Undefined)	0–127	LSB
62	00111110	3E	LSB for Control 30 (Undefined)	0–127	LSB
63	00111111	3F	LSB for Control 31 (Undefined)	0–127	LSB
64	01000000	40	Damper Pedal On/Off (Sustain)	≤63 off, ≥64 on	---
65	01000001	41	Portamento On/Off	≤63 off, ≥64 on	---
66	01000010	42	Sostenuto On/Off	≤63 off, ≥64 on	---
67	01000011	43	Soft Pedal On/Off	≤63 off, ≥64 on	---
68	01000100	44	Legato Footswitch	≤63 Normal, ≥64 Legato	---
69	01000101	45	Hold 2	≤63 off, ≥64 on	---
70	01000110	46	Sound Controller 1 (default: Sound Variation)	0–127	LSB
71	01000111	47	Sound Controller 2 (default: Timbre/Harmonic Intens.)	0–127	LSB

72	01001000	48	Sound Controller 3 (default: Release Time)	0–127	LSB
73	01001001	49	Sound Controller 4 (default: Attack Time)	0–127	LSB
74	01001010	4A	Sound Controller 5 (default: Brightness)	0–127	LSB
75	01001011	4B	Sound Controller 6 (default: Decay Time - see MMA RP-021)	0–127	LSB
76	01001100	4C	Sound Controller 7 (default: Vibrato Rate - see MMA RP-021)	0–127	LSB
77	01001101	4D	Sound Controller 8 (default: Vibrato Depth - see MMA RP-021)	0–127	LSB
78	01001110	4E	Sound Controller 9 (default: Vibrato Delay - see MMA RP-021)	0–127	LSB
79	01001111	4F	Sound Controller 10 (default undefined - see MMA RP-021)	0–127	LSB
80	01010000	50	General Purpose Controller 5	0–127	LSB
81	01010001	51	General Purpose Controller 6	0–127	LSB
82	01010010	52	General Purpose Controller 7	0–127	LSB
83	01010011	53	General Purpose Controller 8	0–127	LSB
84	01010100	54	Portamento Control	0–127	LSB
85	01010101	55	Undefined	---	---
86	01010110	56	Undefined	---	---
87	01010111	57	Undefined	---	---
88	01011000	58	High Resolution Velocity Prefix	0–127	LSB
89	01011001	59	Undefined	---	---

90	01011010	5A	Undefined	---	---
91	01011011	5B	Effects 1 Depth		
(default: Reverb Send Level - see MMA RP-023; formerly External Effects Depth)	0–127	---			
92	01011100	5C	Effects 2 Depth (formerly Tremolo Depth)	0–127	---
93	01011101	5D	Effects 3 Depth		
(default: Chorus Send Level - see MMA RP-023; formerly Chorus Depth)	0–127	---			
94	01011110	5E	Effects 4 Depth (formerly Celeste [Detune] Depth)	0–127	---
95	01011111	5F	Effects 5 Depth (formerly Phaser Depth)	0–127	---
96	01100000	60	Data Increment (Data Entry +1) (see MMA RP-018)	N/A	---
97	01100001	61	Data Decrement (Data Entry –1) (see MMA RP-018)	N/A	---
98	01100010	62	Non-Registered Parameter Number (NRPN) - LSB	0–127	LSB
99	01100011	63	Non-Registered Parameter Number (NRPN) - MSB	0–127	MSB
100	01100100	64	Registered Parameter Number (RPN) - LSB*	0–127	LSB
101	01100101	65	Registered Parameter Number (RPN) - MSB*	0–127	MSB
102	01100110	66	Undefined	---	---

103	01100111	67	Undefined	---	---
104	01101000	68	Undefined	---	---
105	01101001	69	Undefined	---	---
106	01101010	6A	Undefined	---	---
107	01101011	6B	Undefined	---	---
108	01101100	6C	Undefined	---	---
109	01101101	6D	Undefined	---	---
110	01101110	6E	Undefined	---	---
111	01101111	6F	Undefined	---	---
112	01110000	70	Undefined	---	---
113	01110001	71	Undefined	---	---
114	01110010	72	Undefined	---	---
115	01110011	73	Undefined	---	---
116	01110100	74	Undefined	---	---
117	01110101	75	Undefined	---	---
118	01110110	76	Undefined	---	---
119	01110111	77	Undefined	---	---

Note:	Controller numbers 120–127 are reserved for Channel Mode messages, which, rather than controlling sound parameters, affect the channel's operating mode.				
120	01111000	78	[Channel Mode Message] All Sound Off	0	---
121	01111001	79	[Channel Mode Message] Reset All Controllers		
(See MMA RP-015)	0	---			
122	01111010	7A	[Channel Mode Message] Local Control On/Off	0 off, 127 on	---
123	01111011	7B	[Channel Mode Message] All Notes Off	0	---
124	01111100	7C	[Channel Mode Message] Omni Mode Off (+ all notes off)	0	---
125	01111101	7D	[Channel Mode Message] Omni Mode On (+ all notes off)	0	---

126	01111110	7E	[Channel Mode Message] Mono Mode On (+ poly off, + all notes off)	Note: This equals the number of channels, or zero if the number of channels equals the number of voices in the receiver.	---
127	01111111	7F	[Channel Mode Message] Poly Mode On (+ mono off, +all notes off)	0	---

Table 1a: Registered Parameter Numbers
To set or change the value of a Registered Parameter:

1. Send two Control Change messages using Control Numbers 101 (65H) and 100 (64H) to select the desired Registered Parameter Number, as per the following table.
2. To set the selected Registered Parameter to a specific value, send a Control Change message to the Data Entry MSB controller (Control Number 6). If the selected Registered Parameter requires the LSB to be set, send another Control Change message to the Data Entry LSB controller (Control Number 38).
3. To make a relative adjustment to the selected Registered Parameter's current value, use the Data Increment or Data Decrement controllers (Control Numbers 96 and 97).

Parameter Number		Parameter Function	Data Entry Value		
MSB: Control 101 (65H) Value	LSB: Control 100 (64H) Value				
00H	00H	Pitch Bend Sensitivity	MSB = +/– semitones		
LSB =+/– cents					
	01H	Channel Fine Tuning			

(formerly Fine Tuning - see MMA RP-022)	Resolution 100/8192 cents				
00H 00H = –100 cents					
40H 00H = A440					
7FH 7FH = +100 cents					
	02H	Channel Coarse Tuning			
(formerly Coarse Tuning - see MMA RP-022)	Only MSB used				
Resolution 100 cents					
00H = –6400 cents					
40H = A440					
7FH = +6300 cents					
	03H	Tuning Program Change	Tuning Program Number		
	04H	Tuning Bank Select	Tuning Bank Number		
	05H	Modulation Depth Range			
(see MMA General MIDI Level 2 Specification)	For GM2, defined in GM2 Specification.				

For other systems, defined by manufacturer					
...	...	All RESERVED for future MMA Definition	...		
3DH (61)	Three-Dimensional Sound Controllers				
	00H	AZIMUTH ANGLE	See RP-049		
	01H	ELEVATION ANGLE	See RP-049		
	02H	GAIN	See RP-049		
	03H	DISTANCE RATIO	See RP-049		
	04H	MAXIMUM DISTANCE	See RP-049		
	05H	GAIN AT MAXIMUM DISTANCE	See RP-049		
	06H	REFERENCE DISTANCE RATIO	See RP-049		
	07H	PAN SPREAD ANGLE	See RP-049		
	08H	ROLL ANGLE	See RP-049		

...	...	All RESERVED for future MMA Definition	...		
7FH	7FH	Null Function Number for RPN/NRPN	Setting RPN to 7FH, 7FH will disable the data entry, data increment, and data decrement controllers until a new RPN or NRPN is selected.		

APPENDIX B. USEFUL WEBSITES FOR THE ELECTRONIC GUITARIST

Ableton Guitarist
abletonguitarist.com
A blog covering recording guitar with Ableton Live. Plenty of information on the subject, focusing on Live software and its interaction with guitar, guitar-oriented software, and hardware. You'll find good information on using Live with your guitar on gigs as well.

A Brief History of the Synthesizer
https://documentation.apple.com/en/logicexpress/instruments/index.html#chapter=A%26section=5%26tasks=true
Apple provides a very concise but informative history of synthesis.

Barry Cleveland
barrycleveland.com
Barry is an exemplar of the new electronic guitarist, an expert at warping guitar into unexplored sonorities, and a prodigious writer and interviewer as well. It would take an entire book for me to document the creative endeavors of Joe Meek; fortunately, Barry has written that already. Barry's site offers links to his recordings with plenty of examples, and he interviews other modern guitar heavyweights, such as David Torn.

Electronic Musician Magazine
emusician.com
Plenty of reviews, recording advice, interviews, creative tips, and DIY projects geared toward the personal and project studio. (Full disclosure: I frequently write product reviews and other articles here, and it's the magazine most responsible for sending me down the road to guitar, sound design, recording, and MIDI.)

Gary Garritan
www.garritan.com/principles-of-orchestration/
Gary Garritan has some great sample libraries, with a focus on orchestras and pianos. He also maintains a course on principles of orchestration. If you are looking to emulate acoustic instruments with MIDI, here's a great place to start.

GR-55 Floorboard Web Page
https://sourceforge.net/projects/grfloorboard/
Download a free, complete editor-librarian for Roland's flagship guitar synth.

Groove 3
Groove3.com
A truly vast resource for all aspects of recording, including guitars, DAWs, synthesizers, MIDI, and effects and audio processing hardware and software, all in detail, and all taught by experts in their fields. You'll also find instrument lessons taught by an expert cadre of professionals. You can subscribe or purchase downloads for any of the videos that interest you. Groove 3 was a great help in lighting up a few dark corners of my research for this book.

Guitar Player Magazine
Guitarplayer.com
There's a good reason I've been reading this magazine since the '70s; *Guitar Player* is packed with technique, gear, interviews, and attitude. You'll also find recording tutorials, creative uses for effects, and much more. If you've been playing guitar for any time at all, I shouldn't have to tell you this.

Ju-X
Ju-x.com
Free to dirt-cheap audio and MIDI software, including *Hosting AU* (Mac only), a terrific host for effects and software instruments with low-CPU drain, and great for loading older software that may otherwise have compatibility issues with your computer. A good choice for when you just want to load up a synth and play.

MIDI Guitar Unofficial Internet Home Page
www.midiguitar.net
Run by Joel Christian, a long-standing eminence in MIDI guitar wisdom, Joel's site hasn't been updated in a few years but contains great information and plenty of good links.

Mike Rivers—Useful Audio Stuff
mikeriversaudio.wordpress.com
Mike Rivers maintains an authoritative and eclectic (as long as the subject is recording) blog.

V-Guitar Forums
www.vguitarforums.com/smf/index.php
Maybe the best resource for electronic guitar. The site covers MIDI guitar as well as modeled guitars, effects, and gadgets of all kinds; patch exchanges; and advice from a very active community.

Wayne Scott Jones Vintage Roland Guitar Synthesizer Resource
www.joness.com/gr300/index.htm
Don't be misled by the title; you'll find plenty of information about other vintage guitar synth and MIDI guitar gear, including schematics, owner's and service manuals you can download, instrument-specific troubleshooting, and repair tips.

APPENDIX C: BONUS AUDIO FILES

If a picture is worth a thousand words, so is a sound. With that in mind, I've recorded a batch of audio clips illustrating a few concepts and possibilities for the modern guitarist. Recording tools used include Apple Logic, MOTU Digital Performer, and Presonus Capture.

Clip 1. These basic synthesizer waveforms pass in review: sine, triangle, and sawtooth.

Clip 2. A phrase played on a neck-pickup modeled Strat. Starting with dry, then with delay; a large-hall reverb; using a bizarre impulse response with Logic X Space Designer reverb; Flanger, Phase Shifter; Logic X Ringshift, which combines delay with ring-modulation; a spectral gate, which causes the guitar to sound as if it's playing over a telephone. The last two feature amp and stomp-box models—first, an overdriven Fender Deluxe Reverb amp, followed by a custom-model pedalboard plug-in with distortion and octave-divider pitch shifting.

Clip 3. The thick, doubled-and-detuned sound of chorusing lends itself to textural playing. Here, my Epiphone Genesis Deluxe Pro guitar uses MOTU's Ensemble Chorus plug-in in Digital Performer. The groove is supplied by Sample Logic Rhythmology.

Clip 4. Sometimes, all you need is a little crunch in your guitar tone. Here, my Epiphone Genesis Deluxe Pro plays through the Logic X Overdrive plug-in. Bass, piano, and drum MIDI tracks were created in less than ten minutes in PG Music's Band-in-a-Box.

Clip 5. This is an assortment of mostly acoustic-instrument models culled from the Roland GR-55. First up is some noodling on an emulation of a Martin D-28. Notice that varying distance between neck and bridge varies the tone, as in a real acoustic guitar (you can also hear some realistic acoustic string buzz at the end). A Martin Triple-O model with the bottom string lowered (virtually) to D follows; the O stood for Orchestra Model, and these typically possess a fuller, deeper tone. Next, a modeled Gibson J-45 in a custom tuning reveals a deep, brassy sound. Next up, an electric sitar, followed by a little fingerpicking on a resonator guitar model.

Clip 6. What guitarist doesn't want to play organ from the guitar? This is my patch for the Roland GR-55, which pairs a Gibson L-4 emulation with a B-3 synth, and uses the control pedal to activate the Leslie. The expression pedal changes the speed of the Leslie's rotation. Again, Band-in-a-Box is responsible for the backing tracks.

Clip 7. I programmed a relatively dry-sounding Telecaster model, running it through a touch-sensitive wah-wah effect and an amp simulator. Because the GR-55 includes a fine sounding sample-based synth, I couldn't resist layering the guitar with Wurlitzer piano samples to maximize the funk. I also set up a drop-D virtual tuning.

Clip 8. In contrast with Clip 7, this patch sounds enormous! I created this sound from the GR-55 modeled sitar and two oscillators of thick pad sounds. By the way, the GR-55 lets you add your own guitar to the mix, too.

Clip 9. Another benefit of the GR-55 is the hold pedal. Here, I am sustaining a synthesizer pad, while soloing with an acoustic guitar model.

Clip 10. The Boss GP-10 has a few different models and features than the GR-55. I wrote about the pleasures of playing a monophonic synth. Monosynths offer intriguing gliding articulations, and this demo features my emulation of a sound that the Late Keith Emerson was known for. The synth, fretless bass, and fingerpicked acoustic guitar are all GP-10 models; no MIDI was harmed in the creation of this brief track.

Clip 11. This is a rendering of a file I created in the mid-90s for PG Music's program, "The Bluegrass Band." It was done entirely with MIDI guitar, MIDI mandolin, and a MIDI guitar tuned like a bluegrass banjo.

Clip 12. This sequence was done entirely with MIDI guitar. Pulsating synth tones appear, courtesy of UVI Falcon; backwards guitar samples come from Heavyocity Scoring Guitars; percussion loops from East West Adventures in Percussion and SampleLogic Rhythmology; and slapped bass, courtesy of Spectrasonics Trilian.

Clip 13. This is a rubato improvisation, played with Omnisphere and using their Keyscape Creative sound library, which fuses a unique and beautifully sampled collection of keyboards with Omnisphere's powerful synthesis engine to create sounds that travel a long way from their sources. The synth is in mono mode, enabling independent pitch-bend, and I take advantage of that with light, microtonal bends.

Clip 14. This is a complex billowing-pad sound, played by AIR Vacuum Pro, an analog-modeling synth, followed by a rhythmic, sweeping MOTU MX4, a wavetable synthesizer. Xfer Serum, another wavetable instrument, follows with an arpeggio pattern, with digital delay enhancing the rhythm of the pattern. A Korg Wavestation uses wave sequencing to add a spectral wash to its percussive character. Next in line is Prism, one of many synth types available in Native Instruments Reaktor, playing a rubbery-sounding tone with a glassy high end. Prism uses modal synthesis, a type of physical modeling, and can produce sounds with familiarly realistic acoustic properties that have no equivalent in the real world. Applied Acoustics Chromaphone lets you couple components of percussion instruments to create anything from realistic chromatic percussion to bizarre soundscapes, including this one, with a bouncing attack. LinPlug Spectral brilliantly uses complex additive synthesis aided by a subtractive-synth engine and whose array of unusual, enormously sophisticated filters range from conventional to the exotic; you can even draw your own. Spectrasonics Omnisphere 2 is another hybrid synthesizer which combines unorthodox sampling with analog modeling, wavetables, granular, FM, and other synthesis techniques; here, the instrument plays a hybrid of acoustic and bowed electric guitar to produce a gorgeous tone, similar to that of a steel guitar. UVI Falcon is another powerful hybrid instrument with an extraordinary range of sound-design tools. Here, it plays a sweeping, constantly evolving pad-like tone, courtesy of Simon Stockhausen's Ether Fields patch library.

Clip 15. The modern guitar synthesis can't live on analog pads alone. Here's a sampler (pun intended) of rhythmic loops and sounds: Native Instruments India, Heavyocity DM-307, Output Analog Strings, East West Stormdrum, Sample Logic Rhythmology, Output Rev, and finally East West Stormdrum 3. A reasonably adept MIDI guitarist can trigger and layer loops from the guitar while soloing over the parts.

Clip 16. This is an example of convolution synthesis. It's hard to believe that the swirling pads and drums came from a single pass with my guitar. BT Spitfire Audio Phobos is called a polyconvolution synthesizer, meaning that every note played interacts with a series of impulse responses—the same techniques used by convolution reverbs and amp models. The process creates textural and timbral shifts—in this case, drum loops and synthesizer sounds take on each other's characteristics.

GLOSSARY

additive synthesis: A technique in which a waveform is created by building it from its individual component frequencies. See also *subtractive synthesis*.

ADSR: An abbreviation for *attack, decay, sustain, and release*; the contours of a sound's changes in amplitude over time. See also *envelope*.

AES/EBU: An abbreviation for the *Audio Engineering Society* and the *European Broadcast Union*, who jointly developed a standard for the exchange of digital audio signals between professional audio devices.

Aftertouch: A channel-specific MIDI message usually generated by varying finger pressure on a MIDI keyboard. Aftertouch is most commonly used to modulate filter cutoff frequencies, but can be used to affect synthesizer sounds in any number of ways. Aftertouch divides into two types: Channel Aftertouch (also called channel pressure), in which increasing or decreasing pressure performs equal modulation of all notes played, and Polyphonic Aftertouch, which provides individual responses to each note played. The difference between the two is the type of sensors in a MIDI keyboard, with Poly rarely used as a result of the individual sensors required for each key. As a guitarist, you can still implement either control by remapping MIDI signals from your guitar. See also *mapping and re-mapping*.

amplitude: The strength of an audio signal measured in sound pressure levels.

channel: A path for audio or MIDI signal, as opposed to tracks, which store audio or MIDI data.

clipping: Distorting a waveform by overdriving the signal. Fuzz-tone and overdrive effects create clipping.

compression and rarefaction: Compression happens when molecules are forced, or pressed, together. Rarefaction is just the opposite; it occurs when molecules are given extra space and allowed to expand. Compression and rarefaction of air molecules produces sound waves; remember that sound is a type of kinetic energy.

Control Change (CC): Any of 128 possible MIDI messages, with values ranging from 0 to 127. Control Change messages include "switch"-type messages, which convey on and off states for devices such as sustain pedals, chorus, and reverb, as well as Continuous Controllers, such as Modulation, MIDI Volume, and Pan, which change the value or amount of the selected parameter.

Control Voltage (CV): An analog method of controlling effects, synthesizers, and other similar equipment.

controller: For our purposes, a device that can process, manipulate, and generate MIDI data. The category includes MIDI guitars and keyboards, MIDI mixers, MIDI drum pads, and other devices.

DAW: An acronym for *digital audio workstation*, which can record, store, process, and play back audio (and usually MIDI).

DCO: See: *oscillator*.

envelope: The shape of a sound's changes over time. Generally applied to amplitude, but equally applicable to frequency content. See *ADSR*.

envelope generator: An analog or digital component creates a contour over time for a synthesizer sound.

fret-switching: A method of triggering synthesizer notes by replacing frets with switch triggers. This method was used in early guitar-organ hybrid instruments and remains in use with controllers, such as Starr guitars and the YouRock guitar. A common feature of fret-switching instruments is the ability to play music simply by tapping the frets. Fret switching typically provides an instantaneous response and avoids the tracking inaccuracies of pitch-to-voltage and pitch-to-MIDI conversion, albeit at the expense of a more natural guitar feel as well as the absence of guitar tones.

gates: Gates allow audio to pass through only when it is above a set threshold. If the signal falls below the threshold, no signal is allowed to pass. This can be used to reduce noise coming from a signal or, as an effect and when synchronized to a clock, to create rhythmic patterns.

interface: Hardware that expands and improves the input and output capabilities of a computer. Audio interfaces connect microphones, instruments, and other audio signals to a computer, and output audio to monitors, mixers, and other devices. MIDI interfaces conduct MIDI data from synthesizers, keyboards, and controllers for routing through the computer for output to MIDI-equipped devices, such as synthesizers.

I/O: An abbreviation for *input/output*. In general, used to categorize a device's connections with other devices.

LFO: An abbreviation for *low-frequency oscillators*, which create a repetitive pulse governed by a waveform's shape. This pulse is often used to modulate synthesizers, delay lines, and other audio equipment in order to create effects used in the production of electronic music. Audio effects such as vibrato, tremolo, and phasing are examples. Usually, LFOs operate at frequencies of 20Hz and lower, but some can be pushed into audio-frequency rates to create radical timbre changes.

mapping and re-mapping: The assignment of MIDI commands to create a specific response in a synthesizer or other device. For instance, MIDI Modulation (CC01) is often used to trigger an LFO to produce a vibrato effect. However, a synthesizer LFO can regulate volume or pan position or can be programmed to cyclically open and close a filter. Optionally, you can program the modulation message to open and close a filter without the cycling, as you might do with a wah-wah pedal. Typically, modulation messages are generated by a synthesizer's modulation wheel, but you can generate modulation messages from Aftertouch or even by MIDI notes. Modifying MIDI sources and destinations is known as re-mapping.

MIDI: An acronym for *Musical Instrument Digital Interface*, a digital language that enables compatible devices to exchange and interact with digital information. MIDI made its public debut in 1983, when one synthesizer was played remotely by another synth.

MIDI Modes: Affect the way a synthesizer responds to MIDI data. Control Change messages 124 through 127 are used to select between Omni Mode On or Off, and to select between the Mono Mode or Poly Mode of operation. Omni On means that synthesizers respond to incoming messages without regard to MIDI channels. Omni Off causes the device to respond only to selected MIDI channels. Mono mode restricts a device to playing only one note at a time; Poly mode allows playback of simultaneous notes.

modulation: In synthesis, the affecting of change in the properties of a waveform with regard to pitch, loudness, or timbre.

Mono: See: *MIDI Modes*.

multitimbral: A synthesizer feature that allows it to play a number of different programs simultaneously, either independently, over different MIDI channels, or in various combinations, such as split and layered sounds.

Omni: See: *MIDI Modes*.

oscillator: In synthesis, the component of the synthesizer that produces the raw waveform. Some synthesizers rely on voltage-controlled oscillators (VCOs), which are capable of producing a standard set of waveforms, such as square, sine, sawtooth, triangle, pulse, and noise waves. Digitally controlled oscillators (DCOs) can create any number of waveform types.

patch: A preset synthesizer sound.

phase: The position of a point in time (an instant) on a waveform's cycle. Casio's CZ-series synthesizers produced sounds by altering the time it took to get from one point of a waveform's phase to the next, thereby distorting the shape of the waveform over time.

plug-in: An add-on software component in a digital audio workstation. Plug-ins can be synthesizers or audio or MIDI processors.

portamento: A smooth, continuous slide from one note to another.

Program Change: A MIDI command that allows random access to the presets stored in a synthesizer's memory. Also called Patch Change.

pulse width: In synthesis, the duration of a rectangular wave's cycle when a pulse wave's width is altered. Changing the duration of a rectangular wave is called pulse-width modulation (PWM), and the audible effect is that the sound varies from nasal (like a clavinet) when the pulse width is fully rectangular to hollow (like a clarinet) when it is square.

RAM: An acronym for *random-access memory*. For our purposes, this means user-accessible memory, which we can use to create and store our own presets.

sampler: A device that digitally records, edits, stores, and plays back audio signal, usually via MIDI command.

SP/DIF: An abbreviation for *Sony/Philips Digital Interconnect Format*. A type of digital audio interconnect used in consumer audio equipment to output audio over reasonably short distances. The signal is transmitted over either a coaxial cable with RCA connectors or a fiber-optic cable.

splits: Arranging sounds so that they can be played simultaneously by assigning them to different pitch ranges of a MIDI guitar, keyboard, or other device. Common splits include a bass on the lower strings and a piano on the higher pitches.

subtractive synthesis: A synthesis technique that deploys filters to remove frequency content from a complex waveform, thereby "sculpting" its timbre. Subtractive synthesis is probably the most commonly used synthesis technique. See also *additive synthesis*.

System Exclusive: An open-ended, system-wide MIDI message containing relevant parameters of a specific device. For example, it is possible to receive, edit, save, and transmit a synthesizer patch, a full bank, or the entire contents of a synthesizer's memory. Most MIDI-equipped devices, including effects, support the transfer of System Exclusive. It is also referred to as SysEx.

System Real Time: Global MIDI messages that deal with synchronization of clock-driven devices, such as DAWs, sequencers, drum machines, and effects, with regard to timing and start, stop, and continue messages.

track: A location for storing audio or MIDI data, which can then be routed through a channel.

tracking: In MIDI guitar, the ability to convey musical nuance and articulation to a synthesizer cleanly and accurately.

VCO: See: *oscillator*.

Velocity: A MIDI command that interprets the force used to strike a key on a keyboard or pluck a string on a MIDI guitar. Velocity typically increases a sound's volume but can perform a number of functions.

voicing: The creation of a synthesizer patch from the raw components into a fully finished, playable sound. With sampler presets, this includes the looping of sustain sounds, such as strings, creating filter settings to vary timbre, balancing individual sample levels for a consistent dynamic response, and much more.

waveform: The shape and form of a signal, such as an audio wave, moving in a physical medium.

waveshaping: A synthesis technique in which complex harmonics are produced from simple tones by altering the shape of the waveform.

wavetable synthesis: A technique that allows an oscillator to "sweep" a waveform, producing animated changes in timbre.

978-1-4803-9745-3	Make Your Own Music	$24.99
978-1-4584-3785-3	Minding Your Business	$19.99
978-1-4803-5515-6	Modern Guitar Rigs, second edition	$29.99
978-1-4234-8445-5	Moses Avalon's 100 Answers to 50 Questions on the Music Business	$19.99
978-1-4803-5514-9	Music 4.0	$24.99
978-1-4950-4521-9	Music 4.1	$24.99
978-1-4234-5458-8	The Music Business Contract Library	$29.99
978-1-4803-6952-8	Music Marketing for the DIY Musician	$29.99
978-1-4950-4522-6	The Music Producer's Handbook, second edition	$34.99
978-1-4234-8444-8	The Musician's Video Handbook	$34.99
978-1-4234-5440-3	1000 Songwriting Ideas	$29.99
978-1-4803-4569-0	The Pensado Papers	$29.99
978-1-4803-5462-3	The Plain and Simple Guide to Music Publishing, third edition	$24.99
978-1-4584-0039-0	Pro Tools Surround Sound Mixing, second edition	$39.99
978-1-4234-8896-5	The Recording Guitarist	$24.99
978-1-4950-1127-6	Recording Unhinged	$29.99
978-1-4234-3483-2	The Reel World, second edition	$29.99
978-1-4234-9278-8	Rockin' Your Stage Sound	$24.99
978-1-4234-8448-6	Secrets of Negotiating a Record Contract	$19.99
978-1-4234-8847-7	Sibelius	$29.99
978-1-4950-6499-9	String Instrument Setups	$19.99
978-1-4234-6341-2	The Studio Musician's Handbook	$34.99
978-1-4234-9236-8	The Touring Musician's Handbook	$34.99
978-1-61780-557-8	The Ultimate Church Sound Operator's Handbook, second edition	$39.99
978-1-61780-559-2	The Ultimate Live Sound Operator's Handbook, second edition	$39.99
978-1-4584-7449-0	Welcome to the Jungle	$24.99

Prices, contents, and availability subject to change without notice.

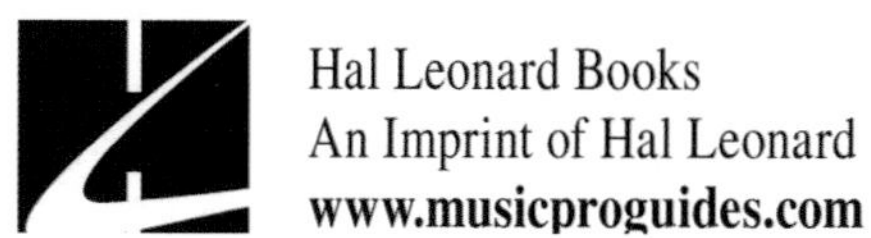

Hal Leonard Books
An Imprint of Hal Leonard
www.musicproguides.com